Writing
Interactive Compilers
and Interpreters

WILEY SERIES IN COMPUTING

Consulting Editor
Professor D. W. Barron
Computer Studies Group, University of Southampton, U.K.

Writing
Interactive Compilers
and Interpreters

P. J. Brown
Computing Laboratory
The University of Kent at Canterbury

A Wiley–Interscience Publication

JOHN WILEY & SONS

Chichester · New York · Brisbane · Toronto

British Library Cataloguing in Publication Data:

Brown, Peter John
    Writing interactive compilers and interpreters.
    —(Wiley series in computing).
    1. Compiling (Electronic computers)
    2. Interpreters (Computer programs)
I. Title
001.6'425   QA76.6   79-40513

ISBN 0 471 27609 X
ISBN 0471 10072 2 pbk.

Typeset by Preface Ltd., Salisbury, Wiltshire
Printed in Great Britain by the Pitman Press, Bath

To
Heather, again

Preface

●

If you wish to implement an interactive language this book is aimed at you. It does not matter whether you are a hobbyist, a student, a professional systems programmer, or even a combination of all three of these. Nor does it matter if your motive is commercial gain, satisfying academic criteria or the sheer enjoyment of making something. The principles and techniques for doing a good job are the same for everybody.

There are many existing books on implementing programming languages, and a lot of them are very good indeed. This book differs from the established literature in three ways. Firstly it deals with interactive languages, which demand different techniques and present different challenges from the traditional non-interactive languages. Secondly it is a practical book—it assumes you actually want to implement something, rather than study theoretical concepts; there is therefore as much material on planning and performing the task of implementing a language as there is on the underlying theoretical principles. Thirdly it aims to be a simple book, assuming no more from the reader than an ability to program and a familiarity with interactive working. If you are more knowledgeable, there are some sections you will be able to skip over.

The language that you wish to implement may be an existing one, like BASIC, or it may be a more specialized language, perhaps of your own design, to cater for a particular application or to exploit a particular device that is connected to a computer.

Firm advice

Since we designed this book to be readable by beginners to compiler writing, we aim to give firm advice. We may, when considering some aspect of compiler design, explore several alternative methods, but we will often end up by plumping for one of them—usually the simplest. The overall effect is that we suggest a fixed framework for the compiler design—just what the beginner wants. If you are not a beginner you may reject some aspects of the framework (and some of the patronizing advice) as not being right for your compiler. If you have ideas of your own this is good; what would be really bad is not to have any. The purpose of the book for you will be to show some of the problems of compiling and present methods to compare yours with. Where the book says 'we assume Method X is used', regard it as a challenge to use your Method Y instead and see how this affects the rest of the compiler.

Acknowledgements

Grateful thanks are due to those who read drafts of this book, and made helpful comments. These include Bob Eager, John Hammond, Gerry Johnson, Graham Martin and Eve Wilson. Especial thanks are due to Ruby Herting, who did the typing.

Above all, Heather Brown deserves appreciation. She has devoted hundreds of hours to reading and checking this book, and has criticized every draft with acid severity.

PETER BROWN
Canterbury, 1979

Contents

Part 3. THE DESIGN OF AN INTERNAL LANGUAGE

Part 4. THE TRANSLATOR

Part 7. TESTING AND ISSUING

Part 1

PLANNING

Chapter 1.1

Why Interactive?

In this introductory chapter we will examine why interactive working is popular. The material presented may be familiar to many readers, but knowledgeable people often miss simple points, so it is worth examining fundamentals.

Some terminology

Explaining terminology is a dull way of starting, but it helps later on. We will therefore now describe a few basic concepts.

A programming language can be implemented by a *compiler*, an *interpreter* or by a hybrid between these two. We shall explain the exact meaning of these terms later. However in the meantime, instead of continually repeating the term 'compiler or interpreter', we will use the single word *compiler* to cover all cases. Thus the task that interests you is to write a compiler.

We will assume, moreover, that the user of your interactive compiler sits at a *terminal* and *types* his input. There are plenty of other possible ways of inputting to the compiler, some of them futuristic: these include dialling, pointing at a screen, speaking and perhaps even thinking. It makes little difference to the compiler what medium is used, and our assumption of typing does not therefore really rule out any of the others.

We should also mention another convention. To avoid the clumsy term 'he or she' we will use the word 'he' throughout. He may be of either sex.

Interactive compilers and their advantages

An interactive compiler is one where the user communicates directly with the computer both when he is typing his program and when he is running it. The communication has all the immediacy of human conversation. When a user makes an obvious error, the computer tells him so there and then. If the computer appears to be doing the wrong thing because of a hidden defect in the user's program, the user can straight-away stop the rot and find its cause; he can then correct his program and restart the run.

Many English words, whether technical or non-technical, have become degraded by advertisers to mean less than they should. Thus 'large size' often really means the smallest size. Similarly 'interactive' is used to describe almost any system where a user sits at a terminal. In this book, we are interested only in the real thing. Non-interactive compilers will be described as *batch* compilers. The word 'batch' describes the traditional form of input using a batch of cards. Nowadays batch compilers are not dependent on cards, but can be used by creating a file at a terminal, and then setting the compiler to work on the file. Sometimes batch compilers allow some degree of interaction when a program is running.

More and more people are using interactive compilers rather than batch ones. The trend towards interactive working started in the sixties with the advent of time-sharing systems. In the seventies, the increased cheapness of hardware has made the movement gather pace. Happiness is communicating interactively with one's own private computer.

The advantages of interactive working go much further than just the possibility of faster response times, and it is valuable to examine what these advantages are. The following are the main ones, and they should all be provided by a truly interactive system.

Advantage 1: interactive editing. The process of developing a program involves alternating runs of the program and edits (i.e. changes) that correct the errors the run has shown up. The traditional batch approach of having the editor separate from the compiler is improved by the interactive compiler that integrates the two activities.

Advantage 2: immediate error detection. If a user types an incorrect line, a good interactive compiler will report it immediately. The user can then correct the error while the purpose of the line is still in his mind. If his error was due to a misconception, for example as to which character to use for a quote, he can avoid repeating the error in subsequent lines. The immediate feed-back is therefore invaluable. Batch compilers only support the detection and subsequent correction of errors after a whole program has been typed in.

Advantage 3: immediate statements. Most interactive compilers provide a facility for *immediate statements,* which are statements that are executed immediately they are typed in. Many BASIC compilers, for example, have the convention that if the line-number is omitted from the start of a statement, that statement is treated as an immediate one. Thus the statement

PRINT SIN(.16)/2

would immediately print back the answer. Such 'desk calculator' facilities are hardly of startling significance, but the real value of immediate statements is in aiding debugging. After an unsuccessful run the user can employ selective immediate statements to help illuminate what has gone wrong. Thus he might print some of his variables or part of an array, and he might even try an immediate GOSUB to test out a subroutine. In addition, interactive compilers often provide special debugging commands and statements that can be used as immediate ones. Batch compilers, on the other hand, can only provide dumps—preferably symbolic ones—and other information of fixed form; this inevitably turns out to be too little information to show some bugs, and too much information to sort out others.

Advantage 4: new applications. The ability of people to interact with running programs has thrown up whole new areas of computer applications. These include programs to aid teaching, play games, and perform interactive simulations.

Consequences of the advantages

These four advantages have not only increased the use of computers, but have also made computer programming possible for a whole new set of people. Most importantly this includes ordinary people, who wish to write programs but are not computer scientists, and for whom the complications and frustrations of a batch system are too much. They also include hobbyists and perhaps you the reader. Sadly they also include computer freaks, hopefully not you.

There is a well-known phenomenon of users appearing out of nowhere if a good interactive compiler is available—'users appearing out of the woodwork' is the rather unkind phrase used.

When you are four goals ahead, there is a danger of relaxing your efforts and letting the opposition hit back. All too often interactive compilers, with the four potential advantages we have stated, toss them away through poor design. Commonly it is the error messages, the user interface or the debugging features that let a compiler down. Don't let this happen to you; gear your compiler design to making all the mileage it can out of the four advantages.

The design of programming languages

There are thousands of programming languages in the world today, but most of them were originally *batch languages,* not designed for interactive working. You can adapt a batch language for interactive working, just as you can fit wheels to a ship so that it can travel on land, but the results are not always satisfactory. Often the adapted batch languages are not fully interactive, and one or more of the four advantages are lost.

The best systems for interactive working are those designed for the task. The most successful have been BASIC and APL (Iverson, 1962; Gilman and Rose, 1970), together with JOSS (Shaw, 1964), which also has imitations under many other names. In this book, we use the BASIC language in nearly all the examples; this is not because we assume the language you are compiling is BASIC, but because BASIC is the language that will be understood by the most readers. (If you have never used BASIC, have a short session with it before you get into this book; you should at least be familiar with the language, even if only to confirm your prejudice that your own favourite language is so much better.)

These successful languages were not only designed for interaction but also for simplicity of use, and this is what has helped to bring in all the ordinary people that batch processing passed by. All too often the designers of programming languages have taken 'easy to learn' to mean 'easy for computer scientists to learn'. Even if you do not like BASIC as a language, you must admit that its designers avoided that mistake. One great gain in ease of use brought in by interactive languages is that most of them have commands built into the language (e.g. LIST, SAVE, RUN, etc. in BASIC). Batch systems tend to have their commands in a 'foreign' language, divorced from the programming language; this is called *job control language*, and most such languages are very foreign indeed.

The end result has been that an interactive language, BASIC, has become the most widely used language in the world, much to the chagrin of all the computer scientists who have been designing elaborate batch languages.

Chapter 1.2

Planning Use of Resources

Once you have decided to write a compiler, you are tempted to start coding straight away. Resist this. It constitutes the *first deadly sin* of compiler writing: to code before you think.

There is a lot of thinking and planning to do before you start coding, and it comes into the following three areas.

(a) The project of writing the compiler. How much will it cost in time and use of resources and how long will it take? Are the resources available? What tools are needed?
(b) Usage. Who is going to use the final product, and how is it to be made available to them?
(c) Further development and maintenance. When the compiler is working and in use, who is going to look after it and are further extensions to be allowed for?

We will take these in turn, but first a word about amateurs and professionals.

Amateurs and professionals

We will use the term *professional* to mean someone who is paid to write a compiler, such as an employee of a software house. Those who give their time for free, such as hobbyists or students undertaking projects, will be called *amateurs*. You, the reader, may be either, or even a hybrid between the two. In common English usage, the word 'professional' is sometimes equated to 'competent', and 'amateur' to 'incompetent'. We certainly do not want this inference attached to the terms. The professional and amateur compiler writers are equally likely to do a good job. As we have said, the principles for good practice contain no references to who or what you are. The main difference between professional and amateur is that the professional is constrained to provide a product that satisfies a well-defined market need, and to make that product as cheaply as he can within a given time. The amateur is less constrained, but nevertheless there remains a requirement to produce something useful in a reasonable time.

7

Costing the project

Everyone underestimates the time spent writing software. The professionals are as bad as the amateurs. Often compilers produced by computer manufacturers are late and half-baked. Indeed it is sometimes unclear who are the amateurs and who are the professionals.

Similarly if a student selects a project that is to be done in, say, a six-month period, the choice is almost always a project that is likely to take twelve months to do properly. Real six-month projects seem a bit trivial to him, and an insult to his intelligence. Nevertheless it is wrong to decry this tendency; attempting something that is right at the limit of our capabilities, or even beyond, can bring great fulfilment. Indeed it is how mankind has advanced. Thus be ambitious, by all means, but let reality have a glimpse.

Manpower needed for software projects is usually measured in units of *man-months*, the amount of work one man would do in one month. Woman-months are assumed to equal man-months. The unit is an unrealistic one because, at the extreme, it assumes that if a project necessitates a total of twelve man-months, then one person could do it in a year, but 365 people working together could finish it in a day. Obviously teams tend to take more man-months than single people. Indeed we all know people who, if they joined a team, would actually slow down overall progress rather than speed it up.

Brooks (1975) in an excellent book *The mythical man-month* discusses this question at length. He mentions some projects where, because they were getting behind schedule, extra people were added. However the problem of a team is inter-communication; when new people join a team the existing people need to spend a lot of time explaining design principles, methods of work, interfaces, and so on. Thus adding people to a team can make a project further behind schedule. This may lead to management adding more people still to the team, thus accelerating the dive towards the final crash.

In spite of this, the conclusion is not that all compilers should be written by one person. In a commercial environment, particularly, this is unfeasible because of the necessity to produce a product as quickly as possible; moreover the project must avoid a total dependence on one person, who might be run over by a bus or get his tie caught in a paper tape reader. Instead the conclusion is to keep a team as small as practicable, and to allow extra man-months for inter-communication. Indeed there are a few factors in favour of teams as against individuals. A good team can help and inspire one another so that the whole is greater than the sum of the parts; in addition a team will avoid most of the ghastly design omissions that an individual may make.

We make no assumptions in this book about how many people are working on the compiler. The term 'you' may mean one person or a team of a dozen.

Further causes of underestimation

Even when the problems of inter-communication are properly allowed for, the estimates of man-months for software projects still usually turn out to be too low. The following are three possible reasons for this:

(a) It is assumed, contrary to all computer experience, that everything will go smoothly.
(b) Time for producing documentation is not properly allowed for. (We will discuss documentation in a subsequent chapter.)
(c) Testing time is not properly costed. *This is a crucial factor*. Brooks says that testing and getting out the 'final' bugs takes half the effort spent between the conception of a software project and the time the first usable product is ready. There is much empirical evidence for this. We have most of us seen software projects where there is, say six months of planning and coding and then for the next six months the software is 'almost working', i.e. still being debugged.

Thus when costing a project, allow time for catastrophes and make adequate provision for testing and documentation. Then, we should perhaps add, double the estimate!

Practical examples of the cost in man-months for compilers are hard to quantify because many factors are involved. However, as a rough estimate, a compiler for a modest subset of BASIC would take at least a man-year to produce a proper product, starting from scratch. If someone claims to have done it in much less time, they are either specially talented, or have not produced a proper product. Both cases exist, but the second is the more frequent.

Costs other than manpower

Compiler writers' time is not, of course, the only factor affecting cost. There are other resources such as computer time, production of documentation, typist's time, and perhaps cost of office space. There is no point in discussing these in detail here as they vary so much according to the nature of the implementor. To some, for example, computer time is 'free', and most other costs are negligible. To others, particularly those in a commercial environment, there is a host of overheads on any project, and it is necessary, before starting a project, to do lengthy and sophisticated estimates of budgets, cash flow, etc.

Even if most of your resources are free, it is well worth making a pre-estimate of the amount of each resource to be used, and then, during the project, keeping exact records to see how well they tally with the estimates. An objective of any project is to learn as much as possible from it, and this is one way of learning.

Tools

One resource which requires examination is the set of tools for writing software. We are not talking here of pencils, but of programs on the computer to aid the compiler writer. The most important tool is a *high-level language*. Your compiler will bring a high-level language to its users; the compiler itself is a program and it needs to be written in a programming language, which is processed by a compiler. You thus need a suitable and friendly compiler for compiling your compiler. We discuss later the selection of a suitable language for writing the compiler in; to pre-empt this discussion, the language should be a high-level language; it should not be low-level *assembly language*, which is made up of individual machine instructions. Most people program exclusively in high-level languages, and have no idea what the underlying machine and its assembly language are like. If you are one of these, do not worry; you do not need to know about machines and assembly languages unless (a) you want to write what we shall call a 'true compiler', or (b) the high-level language you are using is inadequate. The chances are that neither of these applies.

The user

There is a huge difference between a compiler that is used only by its creators and a compiler that can be used by others. Far too many compilers aim to be used by other people but no-one except the creators find them acceptable. This happens when the compiler writers commit the *second deadly sin*: to assume the user has all the knowledge the compiler writer has. In particular they

(a) fail to provide documentation that users can read and understand;
(b) fail to make the compiler *user-friendly*.

We will shortly present a comprehensive discussion of documentation, so we will confine ourselves now to user-friendliness.

Everyone knows the difficulty of using a compiler for the first time. There seems to be so much you need to know; the compiler's rules seem to be numerous and inexplicable; the error responses you get are incomprehensible; sometimes you get into a state where whatever you type the compiler rejects it, and you have no idea what the correct response is.

A new user will have exactly the same problem with your compiler, so it is vital to put yourself in his position. Make his task as simple as possible and ensure that the compiler gives helpful responses when he does something wrong. Make sure everything the compiler prints is meaningful to the user; lots of compilers spew out garbage that is of interest to the compiler writer, such as 'X MODULE LOADING AT 136197', but to the ordinary user it is at best meaningless and at worst downright confusing. Avoid such garbage; take the output from a sample run of your compiler and look at each line; ask yourself if an ordinary user would understand it and find it useful; if not, change it or cut it out.

If you succeed in making your compiler friendly to users, you will find people are soon able to surmount their initial difficulties. Once this has been done the chances are that they are hooked.

When you have written a compiler, it gives you immense pleasure to see other people using it, exactly as if you were a craftsman who had just made a violin and heard it played for the first time. Too often the compiler writer's moment of pleasure is all too brief; the 'idiot user', as he seems to be, types something he was not expected to type, and the compiler gives some crazy response or collapses completely. The second deadly sin has reaped its reward.

Further development and maintenance

The third and last subject for planning mentioned at the start of this chapter was 'further development and maintenance'.

If we planned every aspect of our work for five years ahead life would be dull if we followed the plan, and the planning time would be wasted if we didn't. Nevertheless when planning a compiler it is valuable to think beyond the initial version, even if this seems to be ages into the future. Assume the compiler is successful, and lots of people use it, or even that only one person uses it but it is a vital tool for him. Then the time will come when it is necessary to implement the compiler on a new computer, either because the original one is replaced or because someone else wants it on their machine. Moving a compiler to a new machine is a difficult and dreary task, unless the compiler was originally planned with this in mind. A compiler that is written to be easily implemented on any machine is said to be *portable*—you can carry it about. Portability is discussed at several places in this book.

A second aspect of a successful compiler is that it has to be *maintained*. Maintenance means correcting errors, making changes so that the system becomes more user-friendly, and making small extensions. To the uninitiated this may seem a trivial task, but practice shows that maintenance often costs more than the original writing of the compiler. Thus if this cost can be minimized by writing the compiler for ease of maintenance the savings will be great.

Another aspect of future planning is that the compiler might well be extended, perhaps to cater for a richer language. Indeed the compiler may be planned in several stages: phase I, phase II, etc. Experience shows that, at the outset, it is rarely imagined what the future changes might be. Thus the compiler must be written so that it is relatively easy to make additions and indeed quite significant changes in its design, whatever these changes may be.

In summary, make your compiler as easy as possible to change in the language it compiles, the machine it runs on, the messages it produces, and so on. But don't waste time trying to forecast what the changes will actually be; you will probably get it wrong.

The computer for compiler development

Compilers can be run on very small computers. There exist, for example, numerous versions of '4K BASIC' and '8K BASIC', and it is really impressive what has been crammed into so small a space. However, the compiler itself often requires a bigger machine for its development than the machine on which it is eventually to be used. The compiler is, of course, a program and will amount to hundreds and usually thousands of lines of code. Assuming the compiler is written in a high-level language, a reasonable-sized machine will be needed to compile the compiler.

Thus many compilers for small machines are developed on larger machines. For example, a lot of microprocessor software is developed on large mainframe computers that have been made to simulate the microprocessor environment. In this case there are two machines associated with the compiler: the *development machine*, and the *object machine* on which the compiler is finally to run. There is a further possible complication: this is that some compilers are *cross-compilers*, which carry this double-machine working over to the final user. The user compiles his program on one machine and runs it on another. In this book we will ignore this case, except for a brief discussion in Chapter 8.1.

It may be that you, the compiler writer, are in the happy position of only having one computer available, so there is no problem of choosing which to use. You therefore have no worries except that, if the machine is a very small one, you should remember that compiling the compiler may be the biggest limitation on your project.

If, on the other hand, you have a large and powerful machine you could use for developing a final product for other machines, by all means take advantage of it. However remember that you have both an advantage and a trap. The trap is that you may inadvertently get tied to the development machine, so that your final product does not run on the machine it was designed for. To avoid this, keep checking your work on the object machine at each stage of the project.

The standard of living and expectations of the computer user have risen steadily over the years. Nowadays people may think you could not develop a large program like a compiler unless you have extensive backing-store facilities with a good filing system. If, by any chance, you do not have this advantage open to you, do not be too down-hearted. A lot of the pioneering software of the fifties was written exclusively using media such as paper tape, and yet the average quality of the final product was at least as good as today's.

Bureaucracy

Finally, beware the dangers of over-planning. Some organizations, having finally disciplined themselves to do proper planning, then let the planning get out of hand. The plan, rather than the real project, becomes the focus of attention. Fancy charts are produced—it particularly impresses everyone if these charts are produced by the computer itself—and non-technical people are brought in to 'manage' a project they have no understanding of. Even individuals, working on their own, can get so much involved in their planning that they can never quite face up to doing the real work.

Chapter 1.3

Documentation

Documenting a compiler means writing descriptions of it for all those people who are to work with it. *The third deadly sin* is not to write proper documentation. The sin is omnipresent. It besets amateurs and professionals, professors and students. If one examines in detail the work of some of the great names of computing, it comes as something of a shock to find that they are as guilty as anyone.

People avoid documentation either because they feel they are no good at it or because they find it dull. There is some justification in the former, in that the educational systems of many countries produce scientists who cannot write, and writers who cannot think scientifically. Nevertheless the best way of learning technical writing is to practice it, and to read examples of it. By this means we can remedy any defects there have been in our education, though we may not all succeed (Lang, 1974).

The claim that documenting is dull is wrong. The problems of collecting and ordering material in the best logical order, and of explaining concepts clearly and exactly in the minimum number of words, are at least as challenging and exciting as problems in compiler design. It is only the writing of shoddy documentation that is dull.

Documentation for a compiler should consist of at least the following.

(a) A *user manual*, which explains the facilities the compiler offers. This is to be read by anyone who wants to use your compiler.
(b) An *implementation manual*, which described how the compiler itself works. This is to be read by anyone who wants to work on the compiler, for example to maintain it or modify it, or who wants to find out why your compiler is so good.
(c) An *installation manual*, which tells how to install the compiler on another machine.

Further documentation may be necessary in individual cases. 'Sales literature' is particularly useful; this is not necessarily a glossy brochure, but could be a one-page abstract of what your compiler does and what machines it runs on. This abstract could be published in a newsletter or displayed on notice-boards.

The user manual

The user manual is the hardest item of documentation to write, because users are so diverse. The ideal manual for a beginner to programming is different from one for an experienced programmer. Sometimes this dilemma is solved by writing both a chatty introductory manual and a formal reference manual. If your compiler is for a standard language the problem can be solved by referring beginners to existing books on the language, e.g. for BASIC good books are Alcock (1977) or Kemeny and Kurtz (1971). You could even write your user manual as if it were an Appendix to such a book. Your manual still needs to explain the full user interface and to define exactly which features of the language your compiler provides and which it does not provide.

Whatever form your user manual takes, it is useful to supplement it by a 'quick reference card', summarizing the system. Such documents are issued with many hardware and software systems and must be familiar to most readers. For a programming language they might give a one-line explanation of each statement together with an example. They might also give tables of character sets, names of built-in functions, etc., plus a short but complete example of the use of the language.

If you want to write a single self-contained user manual to satisfy all users, a reasonable compromise is to aim it at the level of the reader who knows something about programming but not much. Provide plenty of examples and, if necessary, explain concepts by example before explaining them more formally. It is often a good plan to put a complete example program (including any 'logging in', etc.) on page one. This can be used to give the reader a feel for the overall form of a program before you plunge into details. Do not make your examples too complicated; do not try to show the cleverest facets of your compiler and do not put too many concepts in one example.

The following are a few further tips for writing user manuals (and books—let us hope this book succeeds in following at least part of its own preaching).

(a) Avoid the second deadly sin of equating the reader's knowledge to your own. If possible, get a really 'unintelligent' reader to check your material before it is issued. If he understands, everyone will.
(b) Use terms consistently. For example, manuals may speak of 'statements', 'program lines', 'commands' and 'instructions', and the reader is not quite sure whether these terms are interchangeable or not.
(c) Provide continuity. Often manuals consist totally of details, with nothing to bind them all together. The introduction to each chapter or section should relate its contents to the rest of the manual.
(d) Get it right. Check facts and examples carefully, and make sure spelling and punctuation are correct and consistent. If a manual does not look well prepared or if it contains errors, the reader soon loses confidence in it, and it becomes useless.

(e) Read. Books on overall style are a matter of personal taste. Our own favourite is Strunk (1959). As examples of good writing on technical matters, we especially like the works of D. E. Knuth and of M. V. Wilkes, and also the book *Software Tools* (Kernighan and Plauger, 1976). Perhaps the most pleasant of all writing on technical matters is in the field of gardening, not computing; read *The Small Garden* by Lucas Phillips (1952) and not only your turnips but also your writing will improve.

The implementation manual

If your compiler is a one-person job, and is never to be touched by anyone else, then you might think that you do not need an implementation manual. You are wrong. It is remarkable that if you look at some of your own code six months after you have written it, you find it appears incredibly difficult to follow. You begin to wonder what twisted mind was behind it. Hence, even if it is only for your own benefit, it is useful to write up a description of the basic principles in the design of the compiler. If the compiler is written in a good high-level language and is, in addition, well commented, then the size of the implementation manual is much reduced. However the need still remains, and it is wrong to assume that the use of a high-level language *per se* removes any further need for documentation. For this reason programs in assembly languages are, paradoxically, sometimes easier to understand than programs in high-level languages, because the writer of the former knows he has got to produce good supporting documentation.

It is possible that the implementation manual be incorporated as a set of comments in the compiler itself. This sounds attractive, but unfortunately does not always seem to work well in practice.

If a compiler is used over a period of more than a year or so, it is almost certain that people other than the original writer(s) will need to work on it. Understanding a large program like a compiler is difficult at the best of times, and new people need all the help they can get. A good implementation manual is the answer.

The installation manual

The purpose of the installation manual is to tell someone how to get your compiler going on his own machine, assuming for example he has just received the compiler in the mail on some kind of tape or disc. The installation manual need not be long. It should just explain clearly what machines the compiler will run on, and provide a step-by-step method of setting it up, with an indication of what to do in the case of errors.

Get some dumb user to check the installation manual out by setting up the compiler using it. Keep away from him while he does it, so that he cannot turn to you for advice, but must rely solely on the manual.

This illustrates a general point. If you hope to have lots of people using your compiler, plan to make them *self-sufficient*, i.e. able to use the compiler without continually coming to you for help. Otherwise the more successful your compiler is, the more your life will become a nightmare.

Points of detail that should go into the installation manual might include: hardware resources needed (e.g. size of store, nature of devices); software resources needed (e.g. operating system, library programs); format in which the compiler is issued; parameters to tailor the compiler to the local environment.

Preparing documentation on the computer

There is a growing trend to produce documentation using the computer. The advantages of this depend on what software tools, such as editors, formatters, cross-reference programs and even type-setters, are available. One possible advantage for the amateur is that the documentation may be issued to outside users on the same magnetic medium as the compiler itself. The user, not you the issuer, has the responsibility of printing out copies of the documentation.

Nevertheless there are still plenty of people who prefer the traditional ways of producing documentation. One computer manufacturer, for example, steadfastly avoids the use of computers for producing documentation, because it once burnt its fingers doing this.

Chapter 1.4

Designing the Source Language and the User Interface

Before coding your compiler you must define exactly what language you are going to compile. This language is called the *source language*. We discuss language design in this chapter, together with other aspects of the user's view of the compiler.

On some professional projects, compiler writers have no say at all in the source language design; the instruction is: 'Here is a language. Compile it'. If you are in this unhappy position you should skip this chapter. Those in chains only become even more unhappy if they look at the world outside.

Source languages come in three grades. The first, the 'regular' grade, is an existing language or a subset of one; here there are chains, but the important point is that the compiler writer chooses them. The second, the 'special' grade, is a completely new language of your own design. The third, the 'plus' grade, is intermediate between the other two; an example would be taking part of an existing language and combining this with your own language for controlling some special peripheral devices that were attached to your computer.

A regular compiler

The great advantage of writing a regular compiler is that your users can exploit the investment that others have put into the source language. They do this by 'importing' programs from other compilers; subsequently they might 'export' the programs they have developed on your compiler. In addition, users who are beginners can read existing books on the source language. Because of these advantages a regular compiler is the most likely kind of compiler to find success in the market place, even though it will have to compete with other similar products.

Just as you can only hold on to valuable goods if you protect yourself from thieves, you can only hold on to valuable advantages if you protect yourself against sins. The sin that can steal away the advantages of a regular language is the *fourth deadly sin*: to ignore language standards.

18

Standards for programming languages

The aim of standards for programming languages is to make all compilers for a language compatible with one another, so that programs are perfectly portable.

In order to progress towards this fine ideal, a huge amount of effort has been devoted to producing national and international standards for programming languages. If you want to understand why this work is necessary try converting a large program, say one of more than a thousand lines, from one non-standard compiler to another. The job will take you months, particularly if you yourself did not write the program in the first place. It would be good to go on to say that if you then tried converting a program from one standard compiler to another the job would be a trivial one. Sadly this is rarely true, because standards are not perfect. There are two important defects of standards: lack of precision, and obsolescence.

Lack of precision in standards is partly accidental—it is hard to describe as large an object as a programming language in a way that is both absolutely exact and comprehensible—and partly intentional. Intentional imprecision often relates to the properties of the computer on which the language is to be run. For example, some standards do not define the number of digits of accuracy for numerical calculations, since machines vary so much in this respect.

Obsolescence in standards is a still more intractable problem. It always seems to take many years of discussion to produce a standard, and, over this time, programming languages change because of new ideas and new fashions. The result is that the standard, when it comes out, has important omissions and embodies ideas that are no longer fashionable. The computing radicals therefore ignore the standard. Most standards bodies try to react to change by producing a new standard every five years or so. This in turn upsets the conservatives, who have just got round to accepting the standard when it changes.

Nevertheless, in spite of all these problems, the advantages of standards outweigh their disadvantages, and standards have brought real gains in portability.

Existing standards

Most of the well-known programming languages now have a standard. (BASIC was one of the last to achieve recognition, and it will take some time before the standard imposes itself on the anarchic world of BASIC dialects.)

Two important bodies which fix standards are ANSI (the American National Standards Institute) and ISO (the International Standards Organization). Standards are widely published in technical journals and books, and it should not be hard for anyone interested to find out about them. Some languages still 'belong' to the individuals who designed them, and in such a case the *de facto* standard may be imposed by the writings of the one designer.

If you are only interested in implementing a subset of a language, standards still have relevance, and indeed some standards prescribe a number of descending levels, each a subset of the higher ones, with a minimal language at the bottom.

Consequences of standards

When you read the description of a standard you would be inhuman if the fourth deadly sin did not tempt you by saying: 'That feature is really stupid; you could do it in a much better way'. Do your best to hold out.

It is a lesser sin to extend a standard than to change it. If you decide to produce extensions, provide an option in the compiler whereby the user who wants a portable program can ask for all his uses of extensions to be flagged with a warning message. Also mark the extensions clearly in your user manual. If you do these things, you can introduce extensions without losing your halo.

Finally, remember that a standard does not impose any chains on the way your compiler works, only on the source language it accepts. The scope for creativity in compiler design remains, and all your efforts can be devoted to it.

A special compiler

Designing and implementing your own programming language is an attractive and rewarding task. The rewards, however, are likely to be solely to yourself rather than to the computing community as a whole. Thousands of programming languages have been designed in the past, and a huge majority have come to nothing. So if you design your own language do not be surprised if no one else uses it.

Superficially, language design is easy: you just collect a lot of nice features together. The problem comes, however, in fitting features together in a clear and consistent manner. Even the best-designed languages have inconsistencies and ambiguities.

There is, in addition, a human problem. Language design is a highly subjective thing, and what looks beautiful to you may look terrible to your friends, though even your best friends may not have the heart to tell you so.

Inevitably, if you design a language you will base it on an existing one, either consciously or subconsciously. Almost any academic computer scientist will tell you that the most widely used languages are terrible languages, and a rotten foundation on which to build. Instead they will suggest you use much more esoteric languages. The same phenomenon happens in any field of creativity. Professional art critics will ridicule the paintings we hang on our walls, and we likewise ridicule their choices. The architect may win a prize for his new house design, but most of us, if offered a chance to live in such a thing, would prefer a tent.

Thus if you design your own language you must choose whether you wish to appeal to high-powered academics or to the public at large. If you are a student whose work is to be marked by a high-powered academic, your choice is, of course, more limited. It is likewise so if you are a professional whose bread and butter depends on selling a product to the public.

The 'plus' grade

The 'plus' grade is a compromise between the regular and special grades. It can be appropriate when you need to design a source language to cover an application for which there is no well-known existing language. Programs for almost all applications need certain basic facilities such as IF statements, looping, arithmetic, subroutines, etc. It is attractive to use an existing programming language to provide these basic facilities, but to design your own extensions for your special application.

What is wrong with BASIC

Before leaving this discussion of language design, we will investigate more closely the criticisms of BASIC as a language, since many readers will doubtless be basing their source language, to some extent at least, on BASIC. We concentrate on down-to-earth complaints, which would find support among existing BASIC users as well as academic computer scientists. Many of the complaints apply to the majority of simple interactive languages, rather than to BASIC alone.

Three objections stand out.

(1) *Meaningful variable names*

BASIC requires that variables have names consisting of a letter optionally followed by a digit (e.g. A, Z3). An extension would be to allow names consisting of a letter optionally followed by any sequence of letters and/or digits (e.g. SUM, PLAYER1, TAXRATE). Such an extension makes programs much easier to read. There are potential problems with variable names corresponding to keywords such as IF and THEN; this is especially so if, as in some BASICs, the LET can be optionally omitted from assignment statements. However, if source language syntax is properly thought out, such problems can be avoided. After all, most other programming languages successfully allow meaningful variable names.

(2) *Subroutine calls*

A similar extension to the first is to allow subroutine calls with meaningful names and with arguments, e.g.

GOSUB HIGHESTCOMMONFACTOR(X,Y)

(3) *Structure*

Most modern programming languages have facilities for grouping statements together, e.g.

IF . . . THEN ⟨*group of statements*⟩ ELSE ⟨*group of statements*⟩

The only hint of such structure in most BASIC implementations is the FOR and NEXT construct.

All these three extensions, and one could add many more, would make BASIC programs easier to read and thus easier to modify. If you are designing your own language modelled on BASIC you would do well to allow for them. If you are designing a standard BASIC compiler you must ignore them, unless you use the device that will be introduced in Chapter 8.1.

Most people, both designers and users, would agree that without extensions such as these, BASIC is not a suitable language for writing large programs. You may argue that you are interested in small programs and that BASIC has amply proved its usefulness in this area.

The user interface

The specification of the compiler, as a user sees it, is not only determined by the source language. Other matters may include the filing system interface, the form of error messages, debugging facilities, editing, and compiler options. We call the sum of all these things, including the source language, the *user interface*.

Ideally the complete user interface should be exactly specified before any work is done on the compiler itself. On a professional project this is mandatory. However the act of writing a compiler will always suggest improvements in the specification. Ambiguities will show up; it will turn out that some extensions are easy to implement whereas other equally useful ones cost a lot; certain features may require modification to fit together better. Such occurrences are particularly common if you have designed your own source language. The amateur will inevitably change details of his user interface as a result of writing the compiler. Nevertheless it is totally wrong to conclude that it is better to let the user interface evolve as a result of building the compiler, and to do no planning of it in advance. The consequence of the latter policy will almost certainly be an unbalanced design, such as a super compiler that produces meaningless run-time error messages, or a source language that is so full of exceptional rules that it is impossible to describe in a reasonable user manual.

Planning the user interface is an area where under-planning is more dangerous than over-planning. Successful generals have a master plan, which they are prepared to change as the campaign develops; a general who tried to avoid changes by having no plan at all would surely lose.

Chapter 1.5

Encoding the Compiler

There are basically three ways of encoding a compiler.

(a) Write it in the assembly language of the machine on which it runs.
(b) Write it in a high-level language.
(c) Write it using some special compiler-building tool.

Advice on the choice of approach can be simple: unless there are good reasons otherwise *use approach* (b). It remains to choose the best available high-level language, and here it is not possible to give definitive advice. Different machines have different languages available; for any given language the quality of its compilers varies hugely from machine to machine. You not only need a good language, but one that is reliably implemented, produces reasonably efficient code, and is properly supported.

A compiler needs to be able to manipulate characters, integers and bits, and, more important, data structures containing mixtures of all these three data types. Hence a compiler should be written in a language which allows all these data types, and preferably provides high-level facilities for supporting data structures.

Hundreds of different languages have been used for writing compilers. Among the most popular are BCPL (Richards, 1969), FORTRAN, C (Kernighan and Ritchie, 1978) and PASCAL (Jensen and Wirth, 1974). The last two are best for data structures.

The advantage of the use of a high-level language is that the workings of your compiler are easier to understand. In consequence the compiler is easier to debug, to maintain and to extend.

Provided you use a good high-level language, this single advantage swamps all the host of disadvantages. We will encounter a number of disadvantages as we proceed through the book, and will quote a big one now. This is that your compiler may be slower than one written in assembly language—typically it will be twice as slow. Do not let this worry you too much: a compiler, like a car, does not depend for its success only on how fast it will go. All that is important is that the speed should be as fast as possible *within the constraints of the overall design*.

Gaps in high-level languages

If you select a high-level language to write your compiler in, you will clearly want a language that covers all the facilities your compiler needs. In a few cases it may be impossible to find such a language; the best language you can find may cover only 95% of your needs. Perhaps it may lack facilities for controlling a particular device or for some other aspect of communicating with the environment in which the compiler runs. If so, you will need to code the missing features in some other suitable language. This may be assembly language, if you know it—or have a friend who knows it.

This approach also requires that your original high-level language makes provision for communicating with routines written in other languages—not all do.

Portability

Use of a high-level language aids portability. To get the greatest portability, use a language that has a standard, as discussed in the previous chapter, and has widely available compilers; make sure the people who wrote the compiler you use did not commit the fourth deadly sin. The language that is probably best for portability is FORTRAN, since standard compilers are available on all but the smallest machines. For some hints on writing portable FORTRAN programs see Sabin (1976), Ryder (1974), and Pyster and Dutta (1978). Unfortunately, FORTRAN is not otherwise the best language for writing a compiler in, though it may be adequate. Certainly academics will tell you that FORTRAN is a terrible language, at least as bad as BASIC.

A refined technique for aiding portability is to 'write a compiler in itself'. Thus, for example, the compiler for the BCPL language is written in BCPL (Richards, 1971). You can only do this if your source language is a suitable one. It would be impractical, for example, to write a compiler for minimal BASIC in minimal BASIC. For more on this topic see Brown (1974), and some of the material in Chapter 8.1.

Assembly language

Maybe you are determined, in spite of advice to the contrary, to write your entire compiler in assembly language. Maybe there really is no other choice. If so, use 'macros' as much as you can; these help make assembly language look more like a high-level language, yet they do not sacrifice any capabilities as a result.

Automation of compiler building

There exist many automatic 'compiler-building tools'. To these you feed a description of your source language together with a description of what you want it translated into; and out comes a ready-made compiler.

Such tools sound superficially attractive, but in general practice are hard to use and produce poor error diagnostics; they also impose a strait-jacket on the design of the compiler, and this may be inappropriate for interactive work. This is not to say that all these tools are bad; if you have a good one available that you know well, by all means use it. However do not expect the task of producing a decent finished product to become trivial as a result. Writing a good compiler is a challenging and difficult task, and no automatic tool will change this.

Some automatic tools have limited aims—they help with one aspect of the compiler. We will mention these at appropriate points in the book.

Coding techniques

More people offer advice on how to program than take it. For what it is worth we have listed some points we consider valuable. If you think they are trivial, wrong, unnecessary, restrictive, etc., then so be it.

(a) Comment your program properly. As we emphasized in Chapter 1.3, do not assume that, because you are using a high-level language, programs can automatically be understood without comments. They cannot. It is especially valuable to place a comment against the declaration of each variable, in order to clarify the purpose of the variable.

(b) Don't be clever. It is undeniably pleasurable to exercise one's ingenuity to save a line or two of code, but your compiler is a worse product if, as a result, it is less understandable.

(c) Lay the code out decently. Use indentation to show the scope of loops, etc. Separate out the logically distinct modules of the compiler clearly. Have some ordering conventions—for example your compiler may contain over a hundred different subroutines; they must be organized into some logical order related to the name or the purpose of each routine. One possible order is alphabetical order; if you use this, choose names so that related routines all have the same prefix to their names, e.g. the names of all routines for printing could begin with PRINT.

Part 2

THE STRUCTURE OF A COMPILER

Chapter 2.1

Filling the Gaps

In this second Part of the book we introduce some of the important data structures that form part of a compiler, and will then outline the overall structure of the compiler.

Before entering the technical discussion we wish to make sure all readers know the basic concepts, so we explain them in this introductory chapter. It may well be that you know it all already, in which case pass on. What we are going to discuss is the nature of the underlying machine codes—if you have ever written an assembly language program you will know this—and the following elementary data structures: stacks; pointers and linked lists; trees; buffers.

Machines, machine code, assembly language

A machine works by executing a sequence of binary instructions that are kept in the machine's store. These binary instructions are called *machine code* Each make of computer tends to have its own unique machine code. In many machines all arithmetic has to be done through a register, as on a pocket calculator. In fact machines usually have several different registers, and sometimes each is geared to a special purpose. Machine instructions tend to be very low-level ones like 'load a value into the register', 'add a value to the register', 'store the register', 'compare the register with a value', 'execute a go to, dependent on the result of the last comparison'. Some computers only have instructions for manipulating integers; values that are not known to be integers need to be manipulated using complicated sequences of integer instructions. Other machines have built-in instructions for dealing with such fractional values; these machines are said to have *floating-point hardware*.

The store of the computer is divided into units of equal size. Often these units are *bytes*, consisting of 8 bits; on some machines, mostly big ones, the storage units are bigger—they are 60 bits on many CDC computers. Storage units are numbered sequentially, and the number associated with each unit of storage is called its *address*. Machine instructions reference storage through these addresses. Thus an instruction may ask to load the byte at the binary address 1011101. Some items of data occupy several bytes; typically an integer occupies two or four bytes. The unit of storage in which integers are stored is called a *word*. Many machine instructions refer to words rather than bytes. Thus an 'add' instruction might add the word starting at the byte whose address was 1011100 to the contents of the register.

Machine code is incredibly hard to write. To make it easier, *assembly languages* were created. Assembly language is just the same as machine code except that it is written symbolically. For example the symbols

ADD   SURCHARGE

might be used to stand for a machine-code 'add' instruction. Elsewhere in the assembly-language program the symbol SURCHARGE would be declared as standing for a word of storage, and the assembly-language translator, called the *assembler*, would translate all occurrences of this symbol into an appropriate binary address.

Assembly language may be easier to understand than machine code, but it is still extremely difficult, tedious and error-prone to write any large program in assembly language. Assembly language is also tied to a particular make of computer, i.e. it is not portable.

Interrupts

Many machines, when they encounter an instruction that contains an error, generate an *interrupt*. This is a means by which the current program is suspended and a call is made of some fixed routine which is associated with the error that occurred. An example of a condition that could cause an interrupt is division by zero. The compiler might contain a statement which said: 'if division by zero occurs, call the following routine'. The routine could perform some action, such as printing a message, and then either resume the original program where it left off or else send control to some other point in the compiler.

In addition to their use in error cases, interrupts are also employed to signal when an input or output device has completed a task.

Unfortunately, although your computer may have good facilities for interrupts, the high-level language in which you write your compiler might not. Thus some of the power and flexibility of the computer may be lost to you, unless you are willing and able to take whatever devious actions are necessary to circumvent the defects of your high-level language.

Data structures

A *data structure* is simply a collection of related items of data. The use of good data structures is a vital key to good program design, and, indeed, data structures have already been mentioned in our introductory material in Part 1. A familiar example of a data structure, found in most programming languages, is the array. We will now introduce some further data structures.

These can be programmed in terms of arrays, just as FOR statements can be programmed in terms of LET and IF statements, but they represent different abstract concepts.

Stacks

A *stack* is one of the most useful data structures in a compiler. It is used for remembering information that needs to be recalled later. We will illustrate it by an example.

The example is a checking program to verify that, within a BASIC program, the variables on FORs and NEXTs match. The reason why this example needs a stack is that FORs may be *nested*, i.e. written one within another, as in

$$\text{FOR K} \dots$$
$$\vdots$$
$$\text{FOR J} \dots$$
$$\vdots$$
$$\text{NEXT J}$$
$$\vdots$$
$$\text{NEXT K}$$

On encountering a new FOR, such as the FOR J, it is necessary to remember the variable used by the previous FOR, i.e. K in the above example. When the inner FOR has been matched up by the NEXT J this information is restored again. Such nesting could go several levels deep.

We encode our checking program in BASIC, since it is assumed that the reader understands BASIC. Our program uses the following variables:

V$ gives the name of the variable on the most recent unmatched FOR. If there is no unmatched FOR, V$ has a null value.

S$ is a string array which is used as a stack. It contains all the previous values of V$ representing the variables on the earlier FOR statements that are still to be matched; the first goes in S$(0), the second in S$(1) and so on. S$ has room for 20 items.

T (for top)   gives the index of the first unused element of S$. Thus initially T is 0 and if, say, S$ contained 5 items, then T would be 5.

Given these variables, the start of the checking program contains the lines

     DIM S$(19)   (declare S$ as an array of 20 strings)
     LET T = 0
     LET V$ = " "

The checking program then inputs lines of the BASIC program to be checked. Every time it comes to a FOR statement it 'stacks' the previous value of V$. This is done as follows:

```
IF T > 19 THEN  . . .     (error: stack full)
LET S$(T) = V$
LET T = T+1
```

V$ is then reset to the name of the variable following the FOR. Note how the above code checks the very unlikely case of T being greater than 19, which would mean that FOR statements were nested more than twenty deep. This, as we shall see, avoids the sixth deadly sin.

When a NEXT is encountered, V$ is tested to see if it is the same as the variable name following the NEXT. If not, an error is reported. If there is a match, the previous value of V$ is restored by 'unstacking' it. This can be done as follows:

```
LET T = T−1
IF T < 0 THEN  . . .     (error in nesting)
LET V$ = S$(T)
```

Note the check for negative T; this error occurs if there are more NEXTs than FORs.

At the end of the program a check is made to make sure T is zero; if not there would still be some items on the stack and hence some FORs must be unmatched by NEXTs.

This example illustrates the most common usage of stacks in a compiler: to deal with nesting in the source language. As well as FOR and NEXT statements, other examples of nesting are the use of parentheses (e.g. (A/(B − C))) and subroutine or function calls.

Pointers

A *pointer* is an index to a data structure, identifying where a given piece of information is. In assembly languages and some high-level languages pointers are absolute machine addresses.

As an example of pointers, assume that a BASIC compiler keeps the source program in some data structure, an array, say, and it is required to know where the first DATA statement is. To accomplish this a pointer is set to give the place in the array where the first DATA statement lies. If there is no such DATA statement, the pointer is given some special internal value meaning 'none'. Often the value '−1' is used in this context, assuming that no genuine pointer can have a negative value.

Pointers are very common *within* data structures, where one item points to another. If you were designing a computer data structure to represent a railway network, say, the entry for each station might contain pointers to the entries for all the other stations to which it was directly connected.

Linked lists

A *linked list* is an example of a simple data structure that includes pointers. A linked list is a sequence of elements within a data structure where each element contains a pointer to its successor.

Consider the following example. An array contains the names of all the girls within an organization. Within that array a linked list contains all your current girlfriends, in order of favour. Thus each element in the data structure consists of a name and a pointer, as follows.

Index	Name	Pointer
1	JOAN	—
2	ANNE	7
3	JILL	—
4	HEATHER	—
→ 5	MANDY	2
6	JEAN	—
7	HELEN	-1 (means end of list)
8	JACKIE	—

The list of girls has an associated pointer which designates its first item. For the above list it points at MANDY. Then MANDY points to ANNE and ANNE to HELEN. The other girls are not on the list.

The advantage of lists is that they can easily be changed. Thus to add JILL to the list between ANNE and HELEN it is only necessary to change ANNE's pointer to 3 and JILL's pointer to 7. Deletions, replacements, etc., are just as easy. There is never any need to shift elements about.

If you were describing a list in a language such as BASIC you would need one array, say N$, for the names, and another, say P, for the pointers. Thus in encoding the above example, N$(5) would be MANDY and P(5) would be 2 (Mandy's pointer). Many languages nowadays have better facilities for describing data structures, and our example could be represented in a single array, whose elements were 'records' consisting of a name together with a pointer.

This example shows a list applied within a pre-defined set of items, the names of all the girls. If you were taking your girlfriends from the whole world, such a pre-defined list would be impractical. In this case you need to use *dynamic storage allocation*. Each time you gain a new girlfriend you take a new piece of storage to store her name and pointer. If a girl is dropped (or drops you when she finds she is just a piece of computer data), her storage is returned. For further discussion of this see Chapter 2.12.

Trees

A last data structure that is useful in compilers is the *tree*. An example of a

34

tree is a family tree such as

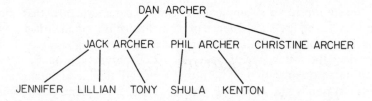

where DAN is the parent of JACK, PHIL and CHRISTINE, and so on. A tree is like a linked list except that each element can have more than one pointer associated with it. These pointers are called *branches* and the elements are called *nodes*, or, at the lowest level, *leaves*. Thus three branches emanate from the node DAN, and KENTON is a leaf.

If exactly two branches emanate from every node, a tree is called a *binary tree*. For example the arithmetic expression $(A-B)+(C+(D/E))$ could be represented as the binary tree

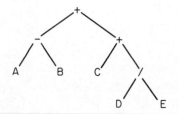

Here a binary operator is at each node in the tree and each operator points to its two operands. Operands may themselves be the result of other binary operations.

Such trees, represented within arrays in a programming language, are often used by compilers. Their advantage is that they reflect the structure of the underlying object.

Buffers

A *buffer* is simply an area for communicating information from one routine to another. Buffers are frequently used in conjunction with input/output routines. For example an output routine may work in units of complete lines whereas the program may produce output in terms of individual characters. The program would then need to build up its output in a buffer until a complete line was ready to be handed to the output routine. Typically a buffer is regarded as an array of single characters, with an associated pointer to show which part remains to be filled (or, for an input buffer, remains to be scanned). Alternatively a buffer may be represented as a single string of characters; if the buffer is an output buffer, each string to be output is added (the technical term is *concatenated*) to the end of the string representing the buffer.

Chapter 2.2

Description of Terminology and Environment

In this brief chapter we define some technical terms that are to be used in the rest of the book. For ease of reference we repeat those few definitions which were given in Part 1.

Source language terminology

The *source language* is, as we have said, the language you wish to compile. The program to be compiled is therefore called the *source program*, and its individual statements are called *source statements*. Each source statement is in turn divided into smaller parts, as shown by the following sample BASIC statement

$$105 \text{ IF } \quad B \uparrow 2 \; <> \; 4 * A * C \text{ THEN } 250$$

The 105 on the front is called the *line-number*. Many interactive languages do not have line-numbers as such, but almost all have some key used for editing; we will take the term 'line-number' to include such keys since the overall purpose is the same. In BASIC the line-number has a secondary use as the potential destination of a GOTO.

At the end of each line, we assume there is a *newline* character. The blank characters at various points in the line, e.g. between 105 and IF, are called *space* characters. (Tabs and the like, if used, also count as space characters.) The fixed symbols that separate out the component parts of a statement are called *delimiters*. Thus the delimiters in the above IF statement are IF, '< >', THEN and the newline character. The symbol B is *not* a delimiter since it is not a fixed part of the syntax of the IF statement—it could equally well be replaced by C3 or SIN(X)/3. Most languages allow alternative delimiters in certain positions. Thus IF might allow delimiters '>', '=', '>=', etc. as alternatives to '<>'; it might also have an optional ELSE delimiter.

An *identifier* is a sequence of letters and/or digits commencing with a letter. Sample identifiers are X, X1, X1A, VERYLONGNAME123. Delimiters that are identifiers, such as IF and THEN above, are called *keywords*. In the text of this book we write identifiers in capital letters; we put

35

other symbols in quotes to distinguish them from punctuation, e.g. ',' is a delimiter of the INPUT statement.

As well as statements which form part of the source program, the source language will contain *commands* to specify some action on the source program (e.g. RUN, LIST, SAVE, DELETE).

Compiler terminology

Terms relevant to the compiler, rather than to the source language, are as follows.

Firstly, remember that *compiler* is used to mean either an 'interpreter' or a 'true compiler'—terms which will be described later for those not already familiar with them.

The *object machine* is the machine on which the user of the compiler runs his programs.

Gries is the book *Compiler construction for digital computers* by David Gries (1971). This is a superbly comprehensive book, and we often refer the reader to it if he is interested in a deeper study of a particular subject. Other good books, well worth looking at, are Halstead (1974), Hopgood (1969), Lee (1974), Rohl (1975) and, for the Algol 60 language, Wichmann (1973). In addition Bauer and Eickel (1974) have edited a large book that brings together contributions by many master craftsmen, while, at the other end of the spectrum, Glass (1969) provides a good simple overview of compiling in 22 pages.

We use the term *vector* for a one-dimensional array of objects used within the compiler. Thus the dictionary may be a vector of dictionary entries.

The *encoding language* is the language in which your compiler is encoded. We assume the encoding language has facilities for *manifest constants*; a manifest constant is a name that is declared at the start of the program to stand for a certain constant, and then used throughout the program in place of that constant. Thus a manifest constant representing the largest legal line-number may be declared thus

$$\text{MAXLINENO} = 9999$$

and then used in a context such as

$$\text{IF LINENO} > \text{MAXLINENO THEN} \ldots$$

Manifest constants make programs easier to change, and can make them easier to read. If your compiler contains the same constant in two or more places, and if the compiler will not work if one constant is changed without the other(s), then that constant should be a manifest constant.

The object machine and time-sharing

Finally a few words about the object machine and the environment in which the compiler runs.

We are not concerned in this book with details of the object machine. A sketchy knowledge of machine code as outlined in the previous chapter is quite adequate. We will use the term *byte* to mean the unit of storage occupied by a single character. Some machines, as we explained in the previous chapter, support bytes in the hardware; others use larger units of storage, and 'pack' characters into these units (e.g. six or eight characters 'packed' into a 48-bit word). The end result is much the same, and we will use the term *byte* in both cases.

Your encoding language may well disguise such details of the object machine from you. If this happens, so much the better, though be warned that the disguise is rarely complete. The nasty machine underneath often peeps through the nice clean high-level language.

An interactive compiler may be designed for a single user or for several simultaneous users under a time-sharing system. In the latter case, the compiler may run under an existing time-sharing operating system, and the compiler itself could be written as if it were for a single user; the operating system would take care of all the swopping between users.

If you want your compiler to allow several simultaneous users, but have no suitable interactive time-sharing operating system, you will have to write your own. This is not a book about time-sharing operating systems, so you will need to refer to a book such as Wilkes (1972).

In this book we assume your compiler is written for a single user (or as if it had a single user).

GOTO statements

There is much fierce and often childish controversy on whether GOTO statements should be allowed. If you are a high-principled stalwart (or, as your opponents would say, a pig-headed bigot) who would never allow a GOTO statement to pass through your compiler, you may tend to react with contempt to our future discussions on problems associated with compiling GOTOs. A little thought, however, will reveal that this attitude is incorrect. Source languages that expel GOTOs do so by providing better constructs that expand, at a lower level, into GOTOs. This lower level expansion is just what your compiler is concerned with. Moreover the GOTO arises in all languages as an integral part of a subroutine call. Hence, irrespective of your source language, you are concerned with the mechanics of GOTOs and the places they jump to (which we call line-numbers). Feel free, however, to delete our word 'GOTO' and replace it by 'expanded form of a construct associated with flow of control'.

Chapter 2.3

Source and Internal Languages

Over the years maple syrup has become increasingly expensive. The result has been that cheaper imitations of maple syrup have been created and these are now so familiar that the term 'maple syrup' now means 'either real maple syrup or an imitation'.

A similar situation holds with compilers. Most 'compilers' for interactive languages are not true compilers at all but are *interpreters*; just a few are *true compilers*.

The average interactive user may be unaware of whether he is communicating with an interpreter or a true compiler. To you, however, the decision as to whether to write an interpreter or a true compiler is the most vital one of all.

The difference between an interpreter and a compiler

The difference between an interpreter and a true compiler can be explained by analogy. Assume you are an English speaker who does not understand French very well, and you are given some instructions in French to do a certain job. Assume further that you are a bit stupid, like a computer, and do not remember anything unless you write it down, and then later read back what you have written. The simplest way of executing the French instructions is to take each one in sequence, figure out what it means—possibly using a French-to-English dictionary as an aid—and then obey the instructions. Thus the performing of an instruction consists of two stages: *decoding* and *action*. The disadvantage of this is that if an instruction is repeated several times you have to repeat the decoding of the French instructions equally many times—do not forget that you are too stupid to remember them automatically. This suggests an alternative approach: first decode all the instructions into English and write them down; then follow these English instructions. This second approach is initially more time consuming, because translating into properly written English is more of an effort than simply figuring out the French instructions in your head; in addition it is more expensive of paper. However it becomes much faster overall if the instructions are to be repeated.

Whether the second approach is worth its overheads depends on the relative time taken for decoding and action. If the action is to swat a fly, minimizing decoding overheads may be paramount; if the action is to dig a canal with a spade, the decoding overhead is negligible.

A similar choice of approach applies to the execution of source-language statements by a computer. The computer needs a program, your compiler, to figure out what the statements mean, and then to perform the required action; this program can either be an *interpreter*, which corresponds to the first of the above approaches, or a *true compiler*, which first translates all the source-language statements into the machine's own language (binary machine code) and then executes these translated instructions.

The spectrum

In practice there are very few 'pure' interpreters which interpret the source program exactly as the user typed it in. To understand why, consider the processing of the simple BASIC statement

$$10 \text{ LET } N=60$$

by a pure interpreter.

To execute this statement the interpreter must take the following sequence of actions.

(1) Skip over the line-number.
(2) Skip intervening spaces after the line-number.
(3) Find the statement name, in this case LET, and look it up in a table of possible BASIC statement names. The interpreter will then jump to its routine to deal with LET statements.
(4) The variable name N will be scanned and it will be related to a position in storage where the value of N is to be kept.
(5) The equals sign is scanned over. If the interpreter had not found an equals sign it would have given an error message.
(6) The right-hand side of the LET is examined to see if it begins with a variable, constant, array reference, function call, parenthesized expression, etc. In this case it is the constant 60.
(7) The constant 60 is translated from its character form, i.e. the character '6' followed by the character '0', to a numeric form.
(8) A check is made for an operator such as $+$, $-$, $*$, etc. In this case there is none, so the number 60 is the value for the right-hand side.
(9) The value 60 is placed into the position in storage associated with N.

Of these, (1)–(8) are all concerned with decoding, and only (9) is concerned with action. Moreover, during the execution of (1)–(8) the interpreter needs to check for a host of possible syntax errors (e.g. LET 60=N, LIT N=60, LET NN=60, LET N=60L, etc., etc.). The end result is that to execute that single simple BASIC statement the interpreter might execute 1000 instructions to decode the statement, but only 2 or 3 to perform its action. If, on the other hand, the statement were translated into machine code by a true compiler, it might take 1500 instructions to perform the translation (i.e. rather more than decoding alone), but only 2 or 3 instructions each time the action was performed. Thus if the statement is executed several times during the execution of the program—and programs almost invariably consist of loops—then the gains are immense.

Because of the huge overheads of interpretation of a source language, almost all compilers translate the source language into an *internal language* which is easier to decode.

Indeed pure interpreters are so rare for (truly) interactive languages that we will assume, throughout the rest of this book, that your compiler uses an internal language. This internal language could take a variety of forms. At one extreme it could be the machine code, as it would be for a true compiler; at the other extreme it could be almost the same as the source language, as it would be for an (almost) pure interpreter. There is a spectrum of possibilities between these two extremes, and real production compilers lie all along the spectrum. As the internal language moves away from the source language towards the machine code, the compiler gets steadily bigger but the user's program runs steadily faster. An increase in the size of the compiler not only has implications in hardware resources, but also in your time, since the compiler will take longer to produce. Thus you are in the position—a position that arises sooner or later in most systems programming tasks—of using your judgement to decide the best trade-off between several competing factors. In particular you trade your time in writing the compiler against the user's time in running programs.

Translating and running

When an internal language is used, the compiler consists of two stages. The first stage is the conversion of source language to internal language. The source program is compiled into an equivalent *internal program*. This conversion, which, as we shall see, is usually done as each line of the source program is fed to the compiler, is performed by the part of the compiler called the *translator*. The term *translate-time* refers to this stage of compilation.

The second stage, which is called *run-time*, is when the internal program is executed (e.g. when the user types a command such as RUN). The part of the compiler concerned with this is called the *run-time system*.

The translator is normally much bigger than the run-time system. We shall be talking mainly about the translator until we return to the run-time system in Part 5 of this book. The design of internal languages is discussed later in this Part of the book, and, in more detail, in Part 3. Before this we shall cover two small matters that may affect the design: the techniques of 'incremental compiling' and 're-creating the source program'.

We shall continue to use the word 'compiler' to cover everything from a 100% interpreter to a true compiler.

Chapter 2.4

Incremental Compiling

Two of the fundamental advantages we cited for interactive compilers were immediate error detection and interactive editing. In particular if a user enters a line that is syntactically wrong, the compiler tells him immediately, and he can correct the error then and there.

A traditional batch compiler is not geared to providing these advantages. Such a compiler takes the entire source program as a unit and scans it from beginning to end, either once, or, for a 'multi-pass' compiler, several times. When an error occurs, the user cannot 'reverse the compiler' back over the error, thus undoing its effects, and then correct the error and set the compiler going again to continue its task.

Interactive languages have led to the development of a new type of compiler, called an *incremental compiler*. An incremental compiler takes the source program one line at a time. It checks each line for errors and translates the line into the internal language. If the line is correct, its translation is then incorporated as an 'increment' to the internal program; otherwise the error is reported to the user and the line is ignored. When a new line is added to the internal program, any previous line having the same line-number is deleted. (If the user simply deletes a source line the result is a deletion of the corresponding internal program line. Thus the overall effect here is actually a 'decrement' rather than an 'increment'.)

For incremental compiling to be practical a line must be a natural unit of the source language. Some source languages allow statements to be spread arbitrarily over lines, e.g. they allow 10 LET A1 = 3 to be written

> 10 LET
> A1
> =3

Such languages are no good for incremental compiling on a line-by-line basis, but interactive languages rarely if ever have this property.

We shall assume here, for simplicity, that a line corresponds to a statement in the source language, since almost all interactive languages meet this requirement. (It only causes minor extra complications if several complete statements can be written on the same line. It is even possible to allow 'long' statements which take more than one line to type, provided the

41

user gives a warning at the end of each line that there is more to come; however such complications are rarely worth their keep.)

Incremental compilers not only offer advantages in error detection and correction; they also compile quicker. In a batch compiler, when the user corrects his program the entire program needs to be re-compiled. With an incremental compiler only the corrected statement is re-compiled.

These advantages are so great that *you should always design your interactive compiler to be incremental*. If you do otherwise you probably sacrifice the full benefits of interaction and this can only be justified when your constraints are really daunting (e.g. a tiny machine or a difficult source language). We assume throughout this book that your compiler is an incremental one.

Problems with incremental compilers

Software people are a cynical lot. They have been caught too often by software vendors to be otherwise. When they hear claims that a new method has great advantages over existing methods, they assume there is also a debit balance. They are always right.

Thus, although incremental compilers have big advantages, they also bring their own new problems with them. The main one is that in most programming languages there are some kinds of statement that cannot be translated independently of all others. Typically these 'problem' statements come in two forms: those that make declarations and those that impose 'block structure'. We shall discuss each in turn, in the context of examples from the BASIC language.

Declarations

In BASIC the user declares functions using the DEF statement, and arrays using the DIM statement. A sample program might read

```
10 DEF FNA(Y) = X*3/Y
20 DEF FNP = 3.1416
30 DIM P(30),Q(4,4)
    ⋮
100 PRINT P(7),Q(3,3),FNP,FNA(10)
```

It is possible for the user to make syntax errors in the usage of declared quantities. Thus he might refer to P(3,3), Q(7), FNP(10) or FNA, all of which are errors. The incorrect references might be typed in before or after the relevant declarations. Moreover declarations may be edited, e.g. DIM X(5,5) may replace DIM X(5), with the result that some previously correct statements may become incorrect and vice-versa.

Another feature of BASIC that acts as a declaration is the line-numbr itself, in its usage as a destination of a GOTO. If the statement GOTO 543 is typed in, there is no way of telling, until the program is run, whether line 543 has been declared.

Block structure

Block structure is concerned with grouping a set of statements as a unit. Constructions that use block structure vary between languages. Examples are FOR ... NEXT (BASIC); BEGIN ... END (ALGOL-based languages); IF ... FI (several recent languages). The value of structure in programming is being increasingly appreciated, and thus these features are becoming common. In many languages, the block structure affects the way statements are compiled. In ALGOL-based languages, for example, declarations do not apply to the whole program, but are local to a block. Thus the meaning of a statement can depend on which block it is in, and it is therefore impossible to compile statements completely independently of each other. The same applies, to a lesser extent, to FOR–NEXT blocks in BASIC. Standard BASIC has a rule (ignored by many compilers) that a GOTO cannot branch into a FOR–NEXT block from outside. Thus in the standard language, the acceptability of a GOTO statement depends on the FOR and NEXT statements encompassing it and its destination.

Implications

In summary, therefore, the meaning of some language features is *context-dependent*, where the context could be determined by declarations or block structure. All practical languages contain some context-dependent features. An incremental compiler, therefore, cannot do all its error checking at the time a statement is typed in, nor can it always fix the meaning of statements.

This has an implication on language design and language usage. Languages designed for interactive usage tend to minimize context-dependence (and are worse languages as a result). To put the same thing another way, interactive users opt for simple languages rather than the better structured ones, because the mechanics of running programs are simpler.

It must be an absolute principle of a compiler that it should detect all syntax errors, including the context-dependent ones. The implication is that, since the translator in an incremental compiler works on a line-by-line basis and therefore can only detect errors that are not context-dependent, it needs to be supplemented by a further checking module that is brought into action when a program is ready to run. This is called the *pre-run module*, and it normally does a single scan through the internal program checking for context-dependent errors and matching up block structure; it will probably change the internal program by filling in extra information. The pre-run module is thus a vestigial batch compiler. The 'pure' incremental compiler is, like the pure interpreter, impractical. Do not, however, be surprised or upset by this lack of purity that seems to pervade everything we are doing. It is almost inevitable in an engineering task, such as compiler writing, where several conflicting factors need to be traded off.

Two approaches to context-dependence

The simplest approach to dealing with context-dependence in an incremental compiler is to ignore the context completely when processing each input line, and to delay all this work until the pre-run module.

We shall, however, briefly explore an alternative strategy. We shall describe this strategy in terms of the simplest type of declaration, the line-number which is the object of a GOTO. It can equally well be adapted to other declarations and to block structure.

Consider again the statement GOTO 543. It is possible, at the time this statement is typed in, for the compiler to check whether line 543 exists. If it does not exist, the line-number 543 can be added to a 'list of lines needed'; if line 543 is subsequently typed in, it is deleted from this list of needs. When the program is finally run, the only task of the pre-run module is to check that the list of needs is empty; if not it prints error messages showing the unfulfilled needs.

Now consider the alternative case, where line 543 already exists. Unfortunately it is not true to say that there are no further problems; the problem is that line 543 could subsequently be deleted from the program. (The same could apply also in the case where 543 was typed in after the reference to it; later still it could be deleted again.) To combat this problem it is necessary to associate with line 543 the information that another statement refers to it. In fact the best way might be to keep, with each line, a list of all the other lines that reference it. If line 543 is subsequently deleted then a check is made of its list of references; if this list is not empty, line 543 is put back onto the list of lines needed.

You can see that this strategy soon generates lots of lists. Worse still the lists themselves are affected by edits. For example, the statement GOTO 543 may itself be deleted or replaced. Then the list of references to line 543 needs to be changed accordingly. Though the strategy becomes very complex, it is used by some compilers, particularly those which process a highly context-dependent source language.

In this book we shall henceforth assume the simpler strategy. Thus when a line is translated into internal language *all context is completely ignored*. This strategy has an implication on the nature of the internal language. For example the line-number that is the object on a GOTO cannot be translated into a pointer to the statement to which the line-number is attached. In particular it cannot be translated into direct machine code. It is however open to the pre-run module to perform some translations on the internal language and to fill in such pointers. We shall discuss this later.

Summary and alternatives

Our scheme for interactive compiling has come up with two principles.

(1) Each source line is translated entirely independently of its context.
(2) Following on from this, interactive languages should minimize context-dependent features. (This should not be taken to extremes, and many would argue that minimal BASIC, for example, goes too far in this respect.)

Possibly your philosophy goes against these principles. You may like languages with a lot of context-dependence, and you may wish to translate each source line in the context in which it is to be run. You wish to forbid your user the pleasure of piecemeal development of programs, since you think it a sinful pleasure. Instead you think the user should prepare his program properly in advance and, before typing any line, should have typed in all the preceding lines that define the context. For example he is required to pre-define all the functions and arrays he uses, and perhaps all other variables too. In short you want to impose the discipline of a batch language on interactive users.

If this is you, you will want to adapt our suggested approach. Since you are taking account of context you will need to re-compile whole sections of the program if the context changes as a result of an edit. Thus your compiler may only be partly incremental. For a discussion of such matters see Barron (1971); Barron's paper, though based on the FORTRAN language, is actually of more general application, and, in particular, presents some ingenious methods for locating the effects of context changes. Other interesting work, related to Algol 60, has been done by Atkinson and McGregor (1978), with a related paper by the same authors plus North (1979). They discuss a spectrum of approaches, and the two papers explore opposite ends of this spectrum. Another approach is to perform incremental compiling in units larger than lines; in some languages it might be appropriate to compile one 'procedure' at a time.

Chapter 2.5

Re-creating the Source Program

A further feature of interactive working that differentiates it from batch working is that a typical user will frequently want to list all or part of his program, especially if he has been doing a lot of editing. To allow this, interactive languages provide a LIST command or the like. There will also be a SAVE command that allows the user to save his program on some kind of backing store. To the compiler, saving a program is much the same as listing

Stage 1: user types a statement

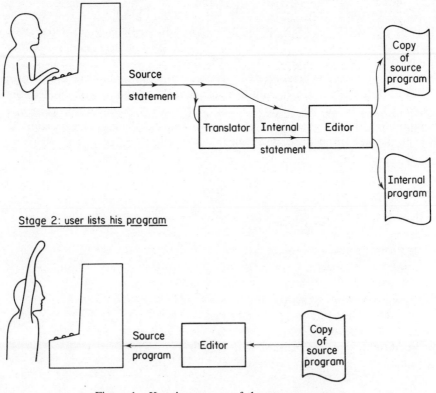

Stage 2: user lists his program

Figure 1   Keeping a copy of the source program

46

it; the only difference is that the text of the program goes to a different device in the two cases. We will thus just consider the case of listing a program.

The parts of the compiler concerned with editing and listing the source program are best kept in a separate module called the *editor*. This editor module will be quite like a simple stand-alone editor except, of course, that it is more closely integrated with the rest of the compiler. In an incremental compiler the editor has the added responsibility of performing the incremental edits to the internal program.

There are two ways the editor can keep the necessary information to provide the capability of listing the source program.

(1) It can maintain two versions of the user's program: one in internal language and one in source language. The latter's sole function is to provide listings.
(2) It can keep the user's program exclusively in internal language form. When a listing is required, it can *re-create* the source language from the internal language. For this technique to work the internal language must be specially designed. The editor will need to use a special extra module called the *re-creator*.

Figures 1 and 2 illustrate the two approaches. In the first case the task of listing is trivially simple—it merely consists of printing back a copy of the

Stage 1: user types a statement

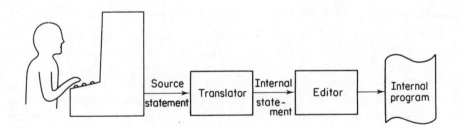

Stage 2: user lists his program

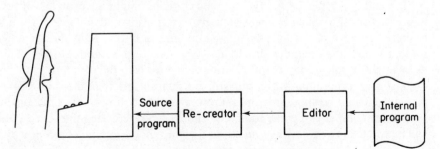

Figure 2   Re-creation of the source program

source program as stored in the computer. However, keeping two versions of the same information, i.e. both the source program and the internal program, is obviously wasteful of storage. Moreover when the program is edited both versions need to be changed, and this is clearly wasteful of time. Approach (2) avoids such waste, but has the overhead of needing the re-creator.

The re-creator

The re-creator need not be a complicated program. For example if the internal language were derived from the source language simply by replacing each keyword by a suitable numeric code (e.g. LET by 36), then the re-creator would not have an onerous task translating these numeric codes back to keywords again. Many compilers do in fact have the internal language that close to the source language.

As the internal language becomes closer and closer to machine code, re-creation of the source becomes increasingly difficult. However you can take one decision that will greatly ease re-creation problems, and thus give yourself much more freedom of choice in your internal language. This is to re-create a source program that has identical meaning to the original but *not* necessarily identical syntax. One case of this would be not to re-create the original spacing; for example the source line

        10LET   A   =   (B+C)

might be re-created as

        10   LET   A   =   (B+C)

Our own experience is that users actually welcome this, provided the re-created spacing is nicely done; thus it is a feature that helps both you and the user.

A second change in the re-created source that should not upset users is to eliminate synonyms for keywords or delimiters. Thus if the 'greater than or equals' operator could be written '>=' or '=>', then the compiler might always use '>=' in re-created source. (It could then translate both '>=' and '=>' into the same internal form, which is a useful simplification.) Similarly if LET could optionally be omitted from assignment statements (e.g. LET A=B could be written as A=B), then the compiler might nevertheless always re-create the LET. Such changes actually have positive advantages for users. If there are several variants of the syntax and only one is in the language standard, then the compiler should always re-create the standard form. Thus users might be allowed to employ various extensions to the standard syntax in their source programs, but could still be guaranteed that their re-created programs would be standard, and therefore could be run on other machines.

Nevertheless if you make too many changes in re-creating the source, you will have a users' revolt. Put yourself in the place of a user and consider which of the following re-creations of the source statement

      10 LET A = (B/C)+23.9

would be acceptable to you.

(1) 0010 LET A = (B/C)+23.9
(2) 10 LET A = B/C+23.9
(3) 10 LET A = (B/C)+.239E2
(4) 10 LET VO = (V1/V2)+23.9

(i.e. where variable names had been changed systematically through-out a program).

There is no doubt what users would say to (4); if the compiler writers coin new names for the users' variables, then the users would coin some well-chosen new names for the compiler writers. Moreover (2) and (3), and even perhaps (1), might cause unhappiness among users, and would confuse beginners.

Having considered the design constraints of the re-creator, we will leave a technical discussion of how it works until Chapter 6.2.

Chapter 2.6

Levels of Internal Language

Having seen some of the uses of the internal language, we can now return to our general discussion of internal language design.

Even if the source is only to be re-created in meaning rather than in exact syntax, there is still a constraint on the internal language. Re-creating the source from machine code is generally impractical; this is because it is a very complicated pattern-recognition task to pick out a sequence of machine instructions and relate them back to a source construction. Try translating the statement

$$\text{LET } X = (X+A(J,K))\uparrow 3$$

into your favourite machine code, if you have one, and then consider the problem of re-creating the original. Tasks such as this are not completely impossible, and for certain languages and machines might just be practical—particularly if some redundant machine-code instructions are added (e.g. an extra LOAD 7 instruction might be a special marker to mean the start of an IF statement); however such an exercise has a feeling of building on quicksands.

Thus for a true compiler, the technique of re-creating the source is not recommended. Instead the approach of keeping the user's program in two forms, source form and internal form, should be taken.

Going towards machine code

We said in an earlier chapter that as the internal language slides towards machine code your compiler gets bigger, but users' programs run faster. We now have a secondary constraint: it becomes increasingly difficult to re-create the source as the slide goes further until, at the ultimate point of machine code, it becomes impractical. A third constraint is the size of the internal program—perhaps you want to be able to run long programs and to store them in as tight a space as possible. The size of the internal program decreases as the internal language slides away from the source language. This is because source languages are for us humans, and we like to communicate with a good deal of redundancy and verbosity. It is true for us all—not just mothers-in-law and professors.

The ultimate in internal program conciseness is not, however, the machine code right at the end of the slide. It is, instead, an *ideal machine code* for running the source language. This ideal machine code has just the operations the source language needs, and these are encoded in the most concise way—the more frequently used needing fewer bits than the less frequently used.

Real machine codes, however, are far from ideal. For a start they are designed to be general-purpose, rather than geared to one particular source language (but see the discussion of 'microprogramming' in Part 8). Hence if the internal language takes the final step towards machine code, the internal form of the program actually gets bigger. The decoding overhead, however, does get smaller.

Summary

We will discuss true compilers in the next chapter. Before that we will pause for breath, and try to summarize these last four chapters. You may well be totally perplexed by the range of choice you have, and all the forces pulling in different directions. To help you to see the wood for the trees, we will now give some firm advice on the design of internal languages.

(1) If your time is limited, make your internal language close to the source language. It is better to have a well-engineered compiler that runs slowly than a hastily stitched-together compiler that runs fast—if it runs.

(2) If your source language involves powerful, time-consuming, operations the overheads of decoding are less important, so point (1) above applies *a fortiori*. For example if the language deals with whole arrays, and thus $A = B*C$ multiplies two arrays together and puts the result in a third, then the run-time for this statement will normally swamp any decoding overheads. Because of this the language APL, which deals with arrays, is normally interpreted at, or close to, the source level. Similar factors apply to languages that manipulate lists, and to languages that manipulate floating-point numbers but run on machines that have no floating-point hardware.

(3) Re-create the source program from the internal language if the two have a simple one-to-one correspondence; otherwise keep the source program separately.

(4) Remember that the real purpose of an internal language is to make the source program easier to run. Thus sketch out the run-time system, and actually code up a few sample parts of it, before fixing the design of the internal language.

(5) Make sure your internal language is suitable for incremental editing.

Chapter 2.7

True Compilers

Writers like to portray the world in black and white, but really it comes in shades of grey.

In a previous chapter we said that most interpreters are not in fact 100% true interpreters because they rarely interpret the pure source language; incremental compilers were likewise found to be less than 100% incremental. In this chapter we look at true compilers, and we will find that these are rarely—probably never—100% true compilers.

Machine code as internal language

We shall define a 100% true compiler as a compiler that produces an internal program made up of a sequence of machine instructions which, when executed, consists entirely of performing actions, with no decoding overhead. Thus the act of running the internal program consists entirely of 'doing' with no 'determining what to do'. (Strictly speaking, we should say there is no decoding overhead *above the hardware level*; the machine itself contains circuits to decode its own instructions, and the time taken to do this is a universal overhead on programs of any nature.)

If the internal language is machine code, it does not necessarily follow that the compiler is a 100% true compiler. To understand why, consider the source statement

$$\text{LET A} = \text{B+C}$$

This can be represented in an internal language as the following sequence of machine instructions:

Stack	B
Stack	C
Call	ADDSUB
Stack	address of A
Call	STORESUB

where ADDSUB and STORESUB are pre-defined subroutines in the run-time system. ADDSUB takes two arguments from the stack, adds them together, and puts the result back on the stack. STORESUB is similar except that it performs a 'Store' operation, and produces no result. (On some machines the code might communicate with ADDSUB and STORESUB through registers rather than a stack.)

Code such as this has the flavour of interpretation. In fact all the instructions are concerned with decoding, i.e. deciding what to do. It is only in the separate subroutines, ADDSUB and STORESUB, that any action takes place. This form of interpretation, where you *execute* the internal language to do its own decoding, is faster than traditional interpreting where a separate program interprets the internal program. However it is still interpreting, and when this technique is used a compiler is not a 100% true one.

In practice, interpretation is used, partially at least, in every 'true compiler'; this is because there are always some operations that are performed by calling subroutines in the run-time system, even though the simpler operations, such as 'Add' and 'Store', may be done within the machine-code internal program. Input and output operations are almost invariably performed by calling subroutines in the run-time system. This is because an apparently simple operation, such as printing a number, often requires hundreds of separate machine instructions, and the internal program would be hopelessly long if these were included 'in-line'. Thus, strictly speaking, no compiler is 100% true.

In the rest of this chapter we discuss the compilers that come nearest to being true ones; these are the compilers that produce machine code as their internal language. Most of our discussion is concerned with identifying works that you would do well to read before designing your own machine-code internal language. We shall use the term *support routines* to describe subroutines in the run-time system, such as our examples of ADDSUB and STORESUB, which are called to perform actions by the machine code. There is a support routine corresponding to each language feature that is not truly compiled.

Minimizing decoding

There are various clever techniques for minimizing the decoding overhead in calling support routines. One that has been used successfully in many compilers is called *threaded code*, which is well described in a paper by Bell (1973). In threaded code all actions are performed by support routines, yet the machine code is extremely concise and the decoding overhead is not large.

Sometimes the hardware itself helps with the decoding by providing specially fast instructions for calling subroutines whose entry points are stored at fixed places. Such instructions may be called 'extracodes' or 'traps'; sometimes there exist 'supervisor call' instructions which the compiler writer can adapt to call his own support routines rather than the supervisor's routines. If you are worried about the overheads of calling support routines, look closely at your machine, and you may have the delight of finding something that the hardware designer provided with just your problem in mind.

Mixed internal language

In some compilers a subset of the language features are translated into machine code whereas the remainder are interpreted at a level close to the source language. One such system, which uses interpretation for features concerned with jumps between statements, is described by Braden and Wulf (1968); this is a useful paper to read as it also covers many other aspects of the design of incremental compilers.

Other compilers only translate to machine code those parts of the user's program that are most heavily used; lightly used parts are interpreted. We shall discuss these compilers in Part 8, when we consider more specialized and advanced topics.

Code generation and optimization

The task of translating into machine code is called *code generation*. Code generation is a difficult and sometimes tedious task. The problem is that machine codes are often full of arbitrary restrictions and anomalies, and it is a mammoth task to match these to a source language that lacks such restrictions and anomalies—or has different ones.

We do not discuss code generation in this book, because it is well covered in the established literature, and generation of interactive code is little different from the generation of batch code. Interested readers are therefore referred to Gries (1971). Hopgood (1969) is also very good. Do not, however, expect too much help, as each machine design presents its own unique problems, so all you can expect to gain from books are some general principles.

Some compilers are fanatical about making user programs run fast. These compilers are not satisfied with simply generating machine code; they aim to get close to the best possible machine code. This is exceedingly difficult to do well, and can make a compiler many times bigger. You can find the subject discussed in some books under the heading of *optimization*. A book specially geared to optimization in compilers is Wulf *et al.* (1975).

Chapter 2.8

Error Checking

Assume you have a smallish program, say of fifty lines, and you type it into the machine. How often will the program contain no syntax errors? Now consider the stage where you have corrected any syntax errors, and run the program. How often will it work the first time? The answer to both questions, for most of us, is that we get it right about 10% of the time. Even if the program is an old and tested one that you are making a few changes to, how often does it run correctly first time? At the extreme case when the program is an old 'tested and reliable' one, and you make no changes to it, does it always work?

If a survey were taken of people's answers to these questions it would lead to an inevitable conclusion: the error case is the normal case, and the case where the program runs perfectly is the abnormal case. Thus comes the *fifth deadly sin*: to treat error diagnosis as an afterthought. Avoid this by making error checking and proper reporting of errors an integral part of your compiler design. If the compiler does not perform well in error situations it will only attract users who do not make mistakes, and there are not many of them about.

As you may know, the definition of a programming language consists of two parts: *syntax* and *semantics*. The syntax is the set of grammatical rules for putting programs together (e.g. there may be a rule that an assignment statement be written in the form LET *variable* = *expression*), and the semantics give the meaning of each syntactic construct in the language.

Errors can be in the syntax or the semantics of a language. Examples of syntax errors in a BASIC program are

(1)   LIT A=3
(2)   LET 3=A
(3)   GOSUB 1000   where there is no line 1000.
(4)   FOR X= . . .   matching   NEXT Y.

(Some writers treat (3) and (4) as semantic errors, but we will not do this.)
    Examples of semantic errors are

(1)   PRINT   1/Z   where Z has the value 0.
(2)   LET X(K) = 0   where the array X only has ten elements, but K has the
                         value eleven.

55

In general, semantic errors cannot be detected until a program is run, whereas syntax errors can all be detected before a program is run.

Syntax errors are the easy ones. They are easy for the user to correct and it is straightforward for the compiler to detect all such errors. Semantic errors are much harder for a user to correct. He should be able to understand the error message easily enough, for example if PRINT 1/Z gives 'division by zero', but in many cases he will have a lot of work unravelling his program to find *why* Z has the value 0, when it was expected to be something else. Your compiler should give him as much help as possible. There are three requirements.

(1) Detect *all* semantic errors, just as you detect all syntax errors. For example, in the statement LET Z=X(K), a check should be made that X(K) exists. There is nothing worse than picking up a random value and putting it in Z. This will cause havoc later and the user will have trouble finding the real error.

(2) Relate all error messages to the user's source program. This applies particularly if the compiler uses an internal language: it is no good saying the program failed in the 117th instruction of the internal program or, worse still, giving a binary dump of core; such information is meaningless to most users. Instead the message must say which line of the source program caused the error.

(3) Provide interactive debugging facilities. To help find a difficult semantic error the user will want to ask the compiler about what has been going on. This is discussed in a subsequent section.

The unlikely and the impossible

Your compiler will inevitably contain limits on the number and size of various quantities. Some limits will be fixed, e.g. it could be required that array bounds are less than 10 000; some will be variable, e.g. there may be a limit on total program size, but the actual limit on the number of program lines might vary according to how long those lines are.

Your compiler must test all such limits and give an error message if one is reached. Even if the limits are unbelievably large, avoid the *sixth deadly sin* of equating the unlikely with the impossible. For example assume your compiler has a limit that FOR statements can only be nested fifty deep. You might argue that no program is ever likely to get near that limit, and therefore it is not worth testing for. But one day someone is working on an automatic system for producing programs (e.g. by translating them from some other form). His system has a bug in it and produces a 'program' that consists of a hundred FOR statements with nothing to terminate them. This 'program' is automatically fed to your compiler. No error message comes out but your compiler lurches into incomprehensible behaviour.

Thus remember that programs are not always written directly by humans, but could be the product of other programs.

Interactive debugging facilities

If a user, when running a program, encounters a difficult bug he needs two kinds of information to help him:

(a) *the current environment*, particularly the values of all the program's variables;

(b) *historical information*, such as a trace of the paths his program has followed.

Of these the first tends to be the more helpful; historical information is often too voluminous to be useful.

At the very start of this book we said that aiding error diagnosis was one of the advantages of interactive compilers, and that immediate statements were an important manifestation of this. If you write your compiler with proper care it should be no overhead to allow any statement to be used as an immediate statement, apart from those statements for which immediate execution is logically meaningless (e.g. FOR or DIM in BASIC). An immediate statement is simply treated as a program of one line (with an imaginary STOP following it), which is executed as soon as it is typed in.

Using ordinary source statements in immediate mode is a great aid to the bug-harassed user, but if you add special extra facilities for debugging he will bless you even more. A particularly useful statement for debugging is one that gives the names and values of all current single variables, and perhaps, on option, further information such as values of arrays and states of files. This is called a *symbolic dump*. A sample symbolic dump is

$$A \quad = 3.96$$
$$B\$ \ = \text{``STRING''}$$
$$Z6 \ = 0$$

Historical information

The most popular tool for providing historical information is the *trace*, whereby the program automatically records its flow of control, e.g. by printing a message at every jump. (Such information is, of course, current rather than historical when the program produces it; it is, however, historical when the user employs it to help unravel a bug.) A trace tends to produce reams of output unless very carefully controlled, and is not much to be recommended. Better is the *program profile*, which gives a listing of the source program together with the number of times each statement has been executed. An example might be

Execution count	Statement
⋮	⋮
253	100 LET A = A+FNC(X)
253	110 IF A > Y THEN 130
2	120 LET Y = O
253	130 . . .
⋮	⋮

58

Selective interactive examination of program profiles can be a great aid in finding bugs. For more on program profiles, and debugging in general, read Satterthwaite (1972).

Further techniques

Another tactic in the user's unending battle against bugs is to illuminate program paths by editing in extra PRINT statements, or even STOP statements, and re-running the program. Some compilers provide a way of doing this which obviates the need to take out all the new debugging statements when the bug is cured and the program appears to be working. (Examples are 'optional print' statements and 'break-points'.) Personally we would, as compiler writers, put effort into providing a profile facility rather than these, but it is a matter of taste.

Conclusion

In summary, when the going gets tough you find who your real friends are. When the user gets a tough semantic error, he finds the true value of his compiler.

Chapter 2.9

Error Messages

Consider the three following possible responses to the same syntactic error.

(a)   10 LET U = X+9.3 − TGN(X)/3
      ERR 203

(b)   10 LET U = X+9.3 − TGN(X)/3
      TABLE LOOK-UP FAILS

(c)   10 LET U = X+9.3 − TGN(X)/3
                       ↑ ↑
      ***ERROR: INCORRECT NAME OF BUILT-IN FUNCTION

The last one is obviously the most helpful; it gives a message that any user should understand; arrows point out where the error occurred; the asterisks make the message stand out.

On the other hand the message 'TABLE LOOK-UP FAILS' illustrates a typical mistake by a compiler writer. He sees the error in terms of the effect on his compiler—the search in the table of function names fails to find a match—rather than in terms of the user. The 'ERR 203' message requires the user to have to hand a separate piece of paper giving the meaning of each error number. Only on the smallest computer is there any excuse for treating the user in such a shoddy manner.

Encoding error messages

The texts of error messages are best grouped together in one place, rather than occurring, say, within PRINT statements scattered all over the compiler. This makes them easy to change. It may even be that your compiler will be used by people who do not speak English, and will need all the messages changed to their native language. If your compiler is a professional product, to be marketed world-wide, this is vital. Non English-speakers may be happy to write programs in English, using a limited vocabulary (LET, IF, RUN, etc.), but they are unhappy with longer English texts.

It may be best to group the error messages together in a separate file—but beware the joker who gets at the file and changes all the messages to obscene ones. There exist useful automatic tools for organizing such files in a concise way. For example words such as 'INCORRECT', 'STATEMENT', 'MISSING' may occur in many different messages, and the automatic tools may avoid the repetition of such words, thus saving space.

Chapter 2.10

Names, Scope and Data Type

The language ALGOL 60, although itself relatively little used, provided the foundations for most modern batch programming languages. One concept popularized by ALGOL 60 is that variables and other objects can have *local scope*. This means that they only exist within part of a program, for example within a certain subroutine. In most interactive languages, however, variables normally have *global scope*, i.e. they apply to the entire source program. This makes the compiler easier to write, as the use of a variable name is independent of its context. This is particularly important in incremental compilers, as we have already discussed in Chapter 2.4. The only kind of local scope that most interactive languages allow is scope that is local to the unit of compilation, i.e. in our case the line. Thus if a function is compiled as a single unit—e.g. a one-line DEF statement in BASIC—then there can be variables local to that function. Such local variables do not introduce any context-dependence outside the line itself.

In this book we assume global scope (plus the above very restricted form of local scope, which is discussed further in Chapter 4.6). If you are interested in exploring the problems associated with a more general scheme of local scope, read Gries (1971).

On the other side of the coin, languages offering extensive facilities for local scope are generally better for the user, particularly if he is writing a large program. Therefore we hope you are writing your compiler in a language which offers such facilities although the interactive language that your compiler processes does not!

A compromise

Our suggestion that your source language have global scope and minimal context-dependence may worry you. If so, the following compromise may help.

Treat the source program as a set of separate subroutines, each with, say, an identifier as its name. One subroutine is called MAIN and is the main program that is entered at the start of a run. Each line-number defines which subroutine the line belongs to. The subroutine name might be a prefix within the line-number, e.g. MAIN30 and MAIN100 are lines within MAIN. For all subroutines except MAIN the variable names are local to that subroutine. However another subroutine can access MAIN's variables by prefixing their name by the word MAIN. Thus a line of the subroutine SUB might be

SUB30 LET B1 = MAINX+3

Here B1 is SUB's local variable but MAINX is MAIN's variable X. Another subroutine, PIG, might contain the line

PIG50 LET B1 = MAINX+3

Here the variable B1 in PIG is treated as completely separate to the B1 in SUB. A subroutine may call any other subroutine when a program is run.

The advantage of this simple scheme is that the translator can treat each subroutine as if it were a self-contained program. Within each subroutine all variables are global to that subroutine. Moreover the use of prefixes ensures that the translator can determine which subroutine each variable name belongs to by looking solely at the statement in which the variable is used; there are therefore no extra problems of dependence on the context supplied by other statements.

Clearly the above is only an outline, and if you are interested you can, within limits, add further facilities or adjust the syntax to suit your needs. Indeed, the 'export and import' of variables between subroutines is an area much studied in programming language design, with special reference to security. You may like to try some of the ideas that have come out of this work. Another source of ideas on how to manage separate subroutines is the language APL. The techniques described in the whole of this book assume the source program is a single unit; you can, however, readily adapt them to deal with the case where the 'program' is a self-contained subroutine used within a larger program.

Mapping names into storage locations

For each variable in the source program, the compiler needs to reserve some storage in which the value of that variable is stored when the program is run. The user refers to variables by means of names, and the compiler has to associate each name with a piece of storage. Assuming global scope, all occurrences of the same name must be associated with the same piece of storage.

Some source languages have a severely restricted set of possible variable names. For example a variable name might be confined to a single letter, giving 26 possibilities, or to a letter optionally followed by a digit (e.g. A0,Z9,X) giving 286 possibilities. When the set of possible names is small, the compiler can use a *fixed mapping of names*, which is built into the compiler and applies to all source programs. In the case where a name is a letter optionally followed by a digit, an array of 286 elements could be reserved to contain the values of the variables. The value of A could be stored in the first element, the value of A0 in the second, and so on, with the value of Z9 in the last. If a particular variable is not used in the current program—and not many programs use more than 50 different numeric variables—then its storage is just wasted. In situations where there are only 26 possible variable names, in particular, this wastage is unimportant.

A tactic which avoids this wastage, at the expense of some complication, is for the compiler to keep a table of those variable names that are actually used in the source program. Before (or even during) the run of the user's program, storage is reserved for each variable that he has used. This method will be called a *dynamic mapping of names*. Clearly if the source language supports a wide choice of possible variable names, a dynamic mapping of names is vital. The table is an example of a 'dictionary', which is discussed in the next chapter.

If the user can choose names for arrays, functions, etc., as well as variables, then the same principles apply to these.

Data type

Most source languages allow the manipulation of several different kinds of object. Some objects, such as arrays, comprise a lot of different values, whereas others, which are called *scalars*, have a single value. The ordinary variables in BASIC, such as A1 or B2$, are examples of scalar variables.

When you analyse a source language you may be surprised at the variety of objects it supports. Even a simple compiler for BASIC may support the following:
(1) scalar numeric objects;
(2) scalar string objects;
(3) user-defined functions (e.g. FNA), with one numeric argument;
(4) user-defined functions with no argument;
(5) several kinds of built-in function (e.g. RND,SIN). Some have arguments, some do not; some deal with strings, some with numbers;
(6) line-numbers (used, e.g., on a GOTO statement);
(7) one-dimensional arrays of numbers (arrays come in various sizes);
(8) one-dimensional arrays of strings;
(9) two-dimensional arrays of numbers.

In addition, there may be further kinds of objects, such as integers, files, etc.

The category into which an object comes is called its *data type*. Thus in the statement

$$\text{IF A\$} = \text{``PIG'' THEN } 100$$

the data types of A$ and "PIG" are scalar strings and the data type of 100 is a line-number.

Languages have differing conventions for specifying the data type of an object. The data type may be fixed by the name (e.g. A$ must be a string variable in BASIC and ". . ." must be a string constant), by the statement in

which the object is used (e.g. since 100 follows the THEN of an IF statement, it must be a line-number) or by a declaration (e.g. DIM and DEF
statements in BASIC). In many languages all variables must have a
declaration. A hybrid method of specifying data type is the *default declaration*
whereby, if an object is not declared, a default data type applies. An example of
this in some BASIC compilers is that arrays, if not declared by DIM statements,
are given default bounds of 10 or 10 × 10, depending on usage. We discuss data
types and declarations further in Chapter 4.5, when we consider the translator.

Chapter 2.11

Dictionaries and Tables

A key task of a compiler is to ascribe a meaning to all the names used in the source language. An important data structure used to achieve this is a *dictionary*. A dictionary consists of a sequence of *dictionary entries,* each consisting of a name and a set of properties associated with that name. A typical dictionary might be a dictionary of all the built-in functions (e.g. SIN, COS, TAN, . . .) that are supported in the source language. The properties of each function might include the data type of the function value, the number of arguments and their data types, and a pointer to the routine within the run-time system that calculates the value of the function.

In addition the compiler might contain dictionaries of statement names (e.g. LET, IF, . . .) and of command names (e.g. RUN, LIST, OLD, . . .). The properties of a statement name might include a pointer to the routine within the translator which analyses the statement.

The dictionaries mentioned so far have been static ones, fixed in the compiler. A compiler will also need *dynamic* dictionaries to contain objects that are introduced by the user, such as the names of his variables, arrays and functions. Such dynamic dictionaries are called *symbol tables* in much of the literature. Some compilers use a large number of different dictionaries, whereas others combine several dictionaries into one, so that they may be left with a single static dictionary and a single dynamic dictionary. If you want to combine two dictionaries, such as statement names with command names, you simply introduce an extra property in the combined dictionary to distinguish the two parts. Weighing the pros and cons of such an exercise is one facet of your skill as a software writer.

Compilers do not always restrict themselves to a dictionary of statement and/or command names. Instead they may encode the entire syntax of the source language into a single table. We shall examine this further when we come to 'grammars' in Part 4.

Pointing into the compiler

Many dictionary entries contain references to routines within the compiler, such as those that translate individual statements or execute individual functions. We call these pointers *actions*. Some encoding languages may allow you to represent these actions directly as pointers to the relevant routines within the compiler. Even if they do, it is better to use an indirect method as described below; this should be appropriate whatever the encoding language.

The indirect method is to encode the action as an index for the equivalent of a BASIC ON statement. The following example illustrates it. The example shows a part of the compiler which uses a dictionary of command names, each with an action field, to decide what action to take for a command just typed by the user.

> Look-up-command-name-in-dictionary-of-command-names
>   (and give an error message if not found)
> Set X = action-for-the-command
> ON X GOTO 50, 100, . . .

Here line 50 is the start of the routine to process the command whose dictionary entry gave action 1, line 100 starts action 2, and so on. Hopefully your encoding language is better than BASIC, and supports a CASE statement or some other improved form of the ON statement.

The need for dynamic dictionaries

Dynamic dictionaries, such as the dictionaries that describe the user's variables, should be considered as an adjunct to the internal program. There is therefore as much freedom of choice in designing these dictionaries as there is in designing the internal language.

There are three purposes that dictionaries may serve.

(a) To relate the name of the object to the place where the value is stored. In this sense the 'value' of a user-defined function may be a pointer to the line of the internal program where the function is defined, and the 'value' of a line-number used on, say, a GOTO statement is a pointer to the line to which the line-number is attached.

(b) To define the data type of the object, or other properties about the way the object is used. In BASIC, the data type information might relate to the bounds of arrays, the existence or otherwise of arguments in the DEF of a function. The 'other properties' may include, say, an indication of whether a numeric variable is the subject of a FOR statement, if such variables are given special treatment by the compiler.

(c) To make the internal program more concise. If an object is in a dictionary, the object is normally replaced in the internal program by an indicator to its dictionary entry. This indicator, as we shall see later, might only occupy one byte, whereas the name of the object itself might be longer.

For each type of object, you must choose whether a dictionary is needed.

There are two pre-requisites:

(1) a dictionary will be needed for arrays, and, almost certainly, for user-defined functions as well;

(2) if there is a dynamic mapping of names, as described in the previous chapter, a dictionary will be needed for all such names.

Finally, it should be emphasized that dictionaries are not just for variables; they can also be used for constants. It is normally useful, for example, to build a dictionary of numeric constants. Each such dictionary entry simply contains the value of the constant (converted from the string of characters supplied in the source program to a corresponding internal form). Every time a constant is encountered in the source program it is looked up in the dictionary. If found, it is replaced by a pointer to the existing dictionary entry. In this way two identical constants share the same storage. This can be quite important, as programs often have many occurrences of the same constant, particularly of the constants 0 and 1.

Encoding dictionaries

Dictionaries may be big. There is thus much merit in designing them to be as concise as possible, consistent with ease of manipulation. We shall now discuss some rather earthy matters about encoding dictionaries; if you have experience of coding such tables you can skip through to the section on dictionaries in incremental compilers.

Dictionaries are easier to manipulate if all entries are of the same size. For some dictionaries this comes out naturally. For example, in BASIC all names of built-in functions consist of three letters, and the format of a dictionary entry might be

Bytes 0–2: name of function

Byte 3: number of arguments, and their data type(s)

Byte 4: data type of function value (this information might alternatively be packed into byte 3)

Bytes 5–6: the action: an indicator of the compiler's routine that performs the function

Thus every entry is seven bytes long. The individual parts of a dictionary entry (or indeed of any other data structure) are called its *fields*. Thus the above entry has four fields.

A dictionary of BASIC statement names, unlike the above dictionary, would not naturally have entries all of the same size. For example the name RANDOMIZE is much longer than the name IF. It would be possible to pad out each name with spaces so that they were all as long as the longest (e.g. to add seven spaces after IF to make it as long as RANDOMIZE), but this might be too wasteful of space. The alternative is to make the entries of variable length. Such entries need to contain an extra field to give the length of the entry. When entries are of variable length, it is usually best to put the fixed-length fields at the start, so that their position is constant, and the variable-length information at the end. Thus a variable-length entry for the name PRINT in a dictionary of statement names might take the form

Byte 0:   8 (total length of entry)
Bytes 1–2:   the action: an indicator to the routine to translate a PRINT statement
Bytes 3–7:   the characters 'PRINT'

Sometimes, when dictionaries contain diverse items, e.g. both arrays and scalar variables, the names may be of fixed length, but the information associated with names may be of variable length. Thus an entry for an array might have ten bytes of information whereas an entry for a scalar might have only two bytes. This in itself is not hard to handle, but try to avoid the case where more than one field of an entry is of variable length, e.g. both the name and the information about the name. In the simple case where only one field is variable, its length can be deduced from the total length of the entry. Thus in the above PRINT example, the length of the entry is 8, and each entry contains three bytes of fixed information. Therefore the length of the variable information, the name PRINT, can be deduced to be five characters.

Changing dictionary formats

In the process of writing a compiler, you will, unless you are luckier or cleverer than most of us, find that your original ideas on dictionary formats need to be modified in the light of experience. You may find that an extra piece of information is needed in each entry, or that the compiler would run better if the whole dictionary structure were re-organized. You must therefore avoid, as much as you can, the *seventh deadly sin*: making the encoding of the compiler dependent on its data formats. Never encode your compiler so that it references the fifth byte of a dictionary entry; one day the dictionary format will change and the fifth byte will become the sixth. Instead, give the required field a name, e.g. MEANING, and use this name in your code. MEANING could be a manifest constant, which is equated to five. The advantage is that this manifest constant could subsequently be changed to six or to any other value without changing any of the lines which used it.

Some high-level languages, such as COBOL and PASCAL and their derivatives, have especially good facilities for describing tables, and these lessen the need for manifest constants as described above. For example a dictionary entry in PASCAL might be described as

```
record
    name:     packed array [1 . . 10] of char;
    meaning:  0 . . 63;
end
```

This means that the record consists of two fields: one is called 'name' and consists of ten characters; the other is called 'meaning' and consists of a number between 0 and 63. (Actually PASCAL allows names to be given to data types, so that a name, analogous to a manifest constant name, might be used in place of the somewhat arbitrary '0. .63'.) If a dictionary called 'functiontable' is declared with entries of the above record type, and you want to examine the 'meaning' field of the Kth entry, you can simply write:

functionable[K] . meaning

If the dictionary format is subsequently changed it is only necessary to change the *record* describing it; the references to each field remain valid, provided the field still exists somewhere in the record.

Making dictionary formats flexible also aids portability; if you move your compiler to another machine it is highly likely that the form of the dictionary inside the new machine will differ from the old.

In most encoding languages, unfortunately, convenient features such as the above are only available to dictionary entries of fixed length. Variable-sized entries need to be built out of much lower-level and cruder building blocks—sometimes it is not even possible to build them at all.

Describing static tables

Static dictionaries, by their very nature, are tables built into the compiler. Sadly, high-level languages are frequently worse than assembly languages for describing the values of static tables of data. Thus you may be in for some tedious work in encoding such tables. There is, moreover, a sin to tempt you. (Unhappily, computing has more than seven deadly sins.) The sin is the *eighth deadly sin*: to use numbers for objects that are not numbers. Thus, for example, do not use numbers such as 0 and 1 to denote your scalar data types; instead use names such as NUMERIC and STRING, which might be manifest constants equated to 0 and 1 internally, but are nice meaningful names for someone (e.g. you) reading the code of your compiler.

Sins are interesting things; they often inspire a puritanic fanaticism to do the extreme opposite of the sin. Thus some compiler writers say that a compiler should contain no numbers at all, except perhaps, as a special treat, the occasional zero or one.

Dictionary look-up

Assume that the statement name has been extracted from a source line and that it is required to find out, by searching a dictionary of statement names, whether it is a legal name and, if so, to translate the rest of the statement. The operation of searching a dictionary is called *dictionary look-up*.

The simplest method of dictionary look-up is the sequential one, i.e. start at the beginning and look at each item in turn until the required item is found or the end of the dictionary is reached. For this method, dictionary entries can be in any order; for static dictionaries it is a good idea to put the most frequently used entries at the start of the dictionary. In some programming languages IF statements and assignment statements account for over 50% of program statements, so if these are the first two entries in a dictionary of statement names the average search time could be quite small. It does not matter if an infrequent statement, such as RANDOMIZE, takes twenty comparisons. For dynamic dictionaries, on the other hand, there is no way of guaranteeing that the most frequently used entries are at the start. Nevertheless the sequential-search method still has advantages; some of the alternative methods require dynamic dictionaries to be sorted into a special order, but sequential search, which has no such requirement, allows the simple approach of adding each new entry at the end of the dictionary.

All software writers should be biased towards simple methods, and thus sequential search should not be rejected unless there is good evidence that its slowness for a particular dictionary significantly affects compiler performance. Clearly this will only happen if dictionaries are large. If sequential search is rejected, there is a host of other methods available. For a good discussion of them see the chapter of Gries (1971) entitled 'Organizing symbol tables'.

Step-by-step search

In some languages, keywords are not separated from adjoining symbols in an obvious way. Thus some implementations of BASIC allow all spaces to be omitted and users can write statements like

```
IFFNA(3)=6THEN 100
REMARKABLE COMMENT
DATASTRING
MATR=A
MATREADA
```

The omission of spaces can lead to ambiguity. For example if ATO were a built-in function, which, like RND, had no argument, then the BASIC line

```
FOR K = ATO–ATO–3
```

could mean

```
FOR K = A TO –ATO–3
```

or

```
FOR K = ATO–A TO –3
```

Complete freedom in omitting spaces is therefore not a recommended philosophy, but compiler writers may have to take the world as it is, rather than as they would like it to be.

When faced with the problem of not knowing in advance where each name ends, you must take the name step-by-step until a complete match is found. If the shortest possible name is two letters, the first two letters of the name are looked up in the dictionary. If this matches the start of a name in the dictionary then more characters of the source name are taken as necessary until either a complete match occurs or there is a mismatch. Special account must be taken of names with a common root, e.g. GOTO and GOSUB or MAT and MATREAD.

Dynamic dictionaries in incremental compilers

In incremental compilers, dictionary organization is quite different from batch compilers. The incremental compiler generally has a source language with global scope (except perhaps for function parameters), thus making things easier; it does however introduce a new problem because, since the user can change his program at any time, information in a dictionary may become obsolete or wrong. In short, dynamic dictionaries are very dynamic indeed.

Consider the simplest kind of dynamic dictionary, a dictionary of the names of all scalar variables used in a program. We shall assume that each time the compiler finds a new variable name it adds it to this dictionary; assume then that the user has just typed the statement

100 LET P = 0

which introduces a new variable P. Thus a dictionary entry is created for P. However the user immediately decides that P is not a good name for his variable and types a new line 100 as

100 LET Q = 0

P is never mentioned again in the program.

The compiler is then left with a dictionary entry for a non-existent variable. To avoid this the following strategy might be adopted:

(a) keep a 'usage count' of the number of references to each dictionary entry;
(b) when a statement is deleted, scan that statement for dictionary references and subtract one from the usage count for each such reference;
(c) delete any dictionary entry whose usage count has become zero.

Following the maxim 'if it is complicated, it is wrong', we shall reject this strategy and look for something better.

Dealing with redundant dictionary entries

One way of avoiding the complication is to delay building the dictionary until the program is ready to run, and the pre-run module has been entered. This, however, has two disadvantages. Firstly it may make response time appear worse; there may be a great pause at the beginning of a run while the dictionary is built—building the dictionary incrementally also takes time, of course, but the tiny times associated with each statement will most likely be swamped by the slowness of input/output devices. Secondly it negates one of the purposes of a dictionary—to make the internal program more concise by replacing variable names by dictionary references. For most compilers one or other of these two disadvantages make it unattractive to delay creating the dictionary until the pre-run module.

Happily there is an alternative method, which still allows creating the dictionary incrementally. This 'method' is to have no method, but instead to adopt the attitude 'I don't care about redundant dictionary entries'. To return to the original example of the redundant variable P, what are the consequences of this? In a typical compiler the consequences are that storage will be reserved for the run-time value of P and this will not be used. Thus the only cost of the dictionary entry for P is that a small amount of storage is wasted (the storage for the value of P plus the dictionary entry itself). This cost is a trivial one compared with the alternatives (such as adding an extra usage count to each dictionary entry). Litter is cheap, although, even when hidden inside a compiler, it is still a mite unsightly.

Given that the 'don't care' method is our preferred one, we shall assume henceforth that it has been adopted. If redundant dictionary entries really upset you, you may be glad to know that when we discuss the pre-run module we shall mention how they can be cleaned out before each run.

Consequences of the 'don't care' method

Those who care about fashion may take great pains to dress in a casual style. Likewise in dictionary design, you can only adopt the 'don't care' style if you take pains to prepare the ground properly. What you must never do is put information into a dictionary which will subsequently cause a wrong action to take place.

We shall discuss this at some length in terms of the BASIC language, which has declarations of functions and array bounds. Other languages will be different in detail, but similar problems, relating to changing information, apply.

Consider first the BASIC program

```
10  DEF FNA = ...
    :
    :
10  LET A = 0
20  PRINT FNA
RUN
```

Here line 10 defines the function FNA, but it is subsequently overwritten by a new line 10. We assume FNA is not defined elsewhere, and thus the use of FNA in line 20 is an error. The original line 10 causes a dictionary entry to be created for FNA. It would have been wrong to place in this dictionary entry the information that FNA is defined at line 10, because, by the time the program is run, this information causes an incorrect action to be performed (i.e. the attempt to print FNA in line 20 would cause a call of the new line 10 which is a LET statement). This contrasts with the earlier example of the unused variable P; in that example a redundant action was performed—reserving space for the value of P—but this action was not incorrect.

Thus the attitude to this example must be: it may be right to create a dictionary entry for FNA when it is first encountered, but it is wrong to supply any information about FNA. This information must be filled in by the pre-run module. We thus have a concept of dictionary entries where certain fields are left undefined when the entry is first created. In fact during translation the dictionary entry for a function such as FNA might consist of its name and nothing else; this is sufficient for the translator, when converting the source program to the internal program, to convert each reference to FNA to a reference to the single dictionary entry for FNA. By the time the internal program is run, the necessary properties of FNA—such as where it has been declared—will have been filled in by the pre-run module.

Similar reasoning applies to all declarative statements. Thus the bounds of arrays, as declared by DIM statements, must not be put into the dictionary at the time the DIM statement is typed in. Instead the translator should simply check each DIM statement for syntax errors and convert it into an internal form. The pre-run module can later copy the appropriate bounds into the dictionary.

Yet another alternative

Possibly an alternative method has occurred to you. (If it has not you can skip this section if you like.) The information that FNA was DEFined in line 10 in our sample program could be placed directly in the dictionary entry when the DEF was encountered. The pre-run module could then check all dictionary entries to make sure that the information in them was still correct. In our particular example it would look at line 10 and find that it was not a DEF of FNA—indeed it was not a DEF at all because line 10 had become a LET statement. It would then delete the information 'defined in line 10' from the dictionary entry for FNA, and replace it by 'not defined'.

We call this the *enter-then-verify* method. It is just about watertight but has some problems, as the following examples show

```
10 DEF FNA = 1
20 DEF FNA = 2
20 LET X = 1
```

A new definition of FNA is added and then deleted, thus resurrecting the earlier one. Some compilers would treat the first line 20 as an error, because it redefines an existing function. However such compilers must be careful to cover the case where the original definition has been deleted, e.g.

```
10 DEF FNA = 1
10 LET X = 1
20 DEF FNA = 2
```

The above must be accepted as a correct program. So must

```
10 DEF FNA = 1
10 DEF FNA = 2
```

where an existing definition is overwritten by a new one with the same line-number. Another sequence that must be accepted is

```
10 DEF FNA = ⟨a wrong expression⟩
20 DEF FNA = 2
```

Here the original DEF gives a syntax error and hence does not count. Therefore line 20 is not an error.

With DIM statements it is possible to create even more contorted examples, because there is an added complication that several arrays can be declared by the same DIM whereas a DEF only defines one function. Consider, for example

```
10 DIM X (3,4), Y(7)
10 DIM X(10,12), RUBBISH
```

Here the second line is incorrect and should be ignored; hence the bounds of X must remain as (3,4) and not be overridden by the newer bounds (10,12).

If you have an enter-then-verify strategy that correctly covers all these examples and more, then by all means use it. Just be warned that experience of compilers based on this strategy shows that they often perform illogical and indeed wrong actions.

Summary of the two approaches

The above discussion of the dynamic nature of dictionaries relates to our earlier discussion in Chapter 2.4 of context-dependence. There we adopted the approach that all context is ignored until the pre-run module. In this chapter we are doing the same thing: the declaration of functions and arrays define a context which is used by other statements that reference the functions and arrays. Again we decide to delay dealing with context until the pre-run module.

Chapter 2.12

Storage Management

When discussing the usage of storage, we will use the term 'data structure' to describe any entity that potentially consists of more than one item of data. Thus all arrays and tables are data structures. One data structure we have already discussed in detail is the dictionary. As with dictionaries, a data structure can be *static*, i.e. of fixed size, or *dynamic*, i.e. of variable size. Any data structure used by the compiler to describe the program being compiled will probably be dynamic, since the user's program grows steadily as he types it in, line by line. It may even shrink at some stages.

If there are several dynamic data structures, there is a problem in fitting them into the available storage of the computer in such a way that all the structures can grow. It would be disastrous, for example, if the growth of one structure caused another to be overwritten. The term *storage management* is used to describe the methods of dealing with such problems.

Some high-level languages automatically take care of storage management, so if you are writing your compiler in one of these you are lucky. Usually, however, you need to do your own storage management.

Storage management in an interactive compiler

Consider the BASIC session

```
10   DIM A(20)
20   LET A(3) = 57
999  END
RUN
PRINT A(3)
```

The last line should print the number 57.

This example, simple as it is, shows why storage management is harder in an interactive compiler than a traditional compiler. The point is that in a traditional compiler, translating the source program to internal language is a separate activity from running the program, and storage management can be treated separately in the two cases. For an interactive compiler the data structures concerned with translating need to be preserved over a run, and the data structures concerned with running need to be preserved over translating.

Our example program illustrates this; it requires the compiler to take the following sequence of actions.

(1) During the initial translation the name A is added to a dictionary of array names.
(2) Before the run, a storage area of 20 (or perhaps 21) elements is reserved for the values of the array A.
(3) During the run, the value 57 is placed in A(3).
(4) After the run, the immediate statement PRINT A(3) is translated. This involves looking up A in the dictionary of array names, and finding the entry that was created in Step (1) above.
(5) When this immediate statement is run, the value 57 is extracted from the storage element that was created in Step (2) and was given a value in Step (3).

Thus the storage area containing the values of the elements of A must not be destroyed while translation takes place, nor must the dictionary of array names be destroyed while running takes place.

In general, as the number of dynamic data structures increases, storage management gets harder. Hence interactive compilers, which require most data structures to exist throughout the entire session, present special problems. A typical interactive compiler might need the following data structures.

(1) Static: the code of the compiler itself; its static tables; values of the variables and constants used in encoding the compiler; a host of smaller data structures.
(2) Dynamic—all these relate to the user's program: internal program; dictionaries of the variables, functions and constants; values of the variables, including the arrays and strings; run-time subroutine links; possibly a stack for arithmetic operands.

As a rule of thumb, if you have two or fewer dynamic areas life is easy; if you have more than two life is hard. Static areas are no problem.

There is therefore often a need to reduce the number of dynamic areas. There are two obvious ways of doing this:

(1) putting a size limit on a dynamic structure, and then treating it as if it were a static area of this size. Thus a dynamic dictionary might be limited to, say, 500 bytes. If the dictionary were smaller than this, the extra space would be unused. If the dictionary were potentially bigger, the compiler would have to give up and refuse to compile the program;
(2) combining several logically separate areas into one physical one. For example several logically separate dictionaries might be combined into one, as we have already mentioned. Moreover the dictionary entry for a scalar variable could also contain the variable's run-time value, thus avoiding the need for a separate area for the latter.

Finally there is the possibility of hardware assistance. Machines with so-called *virtual storage* may give the compiler writer a large number of logically separate segments of storage, all of which can be of effectively boundless size. The catch is that if storage is used as if it were boundless, the time taken to run programs will be equally boundless. Thus, irrespective of whether virtual storage is available, you do well to be miserly with your storage.

Storage management strategies

We assume in this chapter that the dynamic areas all behave like stacks, in that one end is fixed whereas the other grows and shrinks. In practice many of the compiler's dynamic areas, for example dictionaries, will grow but never shrink (except when the user starts a new program from scratch, and all the storage is re-initialized). For a discussion of a more general scheme, where areas of storage are continually being allocated and returned, see Chapter 5.3.

If storage is all in one piece it is said to be *contiguous*. We will assume that there is a single contiguous area of storage available to the compiler throughout the session. This applies in practice to most single-user compilers. It also applies to time-sharing compilers that use fixed partitions of storage. On the other hand some time-sharing operating systems, such as those that provide virtual storage, allow storage to be extended if it ever runs out, and if your compiler runs under one of these you may be able to laugh off some of the problems we are about to introduce.

Of the fixed amount of storage that we shall assume is available, some will be used by static areas. We shall assume these static areas are stored contiguously at the beginning or end of the available storage. Thus the remaining area of storage is still a contiguous area. Our discussion is concerned with fitting a number of dynamic structures into this area. We shall describe three alternative strategies.

Strategy 1: a strategy for two dynamic structures

The simplest method of storage management is illustrated by the following figure.

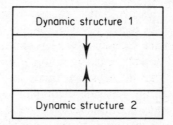

This caters for two dynamic structures. One starts at the bottom and grows upwards while the other does the opposite. The space in the middle is spare, and the two structures can grow until they meet.

The dynamic structures may grow in big chunks, and these chunks may be subjected to their own storage management. For example if a 100 word array is declared, 100 words might be taken as one unit from the spare space and added to the appropriate structure. Within this 100 words the array itself could be stored in any convenient arrangement.

It is vital that every time a dynamic structure grows a check is made to see if the limit has been reached. In the above situation the limit is reached when the two structures meet. Some second-rate compilers allow dynamic structures to overwrite each other unchecked, with the end result that programs are unreliable and users angry. Checking is never too expensive.

Strategy 2: movable structures

When there are more than two dynamic structures, the problems start. One strategy, which retains the property that structures are allocated contiguously, is the *movable-structure* strategy. Storage may be allocated as in the following figure, which shows four structures.

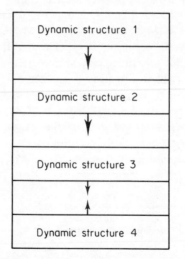

The direction of growth of either of the intermediate structures 2 and 3 can be made upwards rather than downwards, if this is more convenient. An attractive alternative to the above picture is to make structure 2 work upwards, and put it 'back to back' with structure 3.

The initial placement of the structures depends on their expected size. If two structures ever meet, one or other of them is shifted up or down to allow more room, as illustrated by the following figure, which shows the remedial action taken when structure 2 is about to run into structure 3.

Only if all free storage has been used up does the compiler give up. Sometimes it may be necessary to shift several structures if one has become hemmed in from both sides.

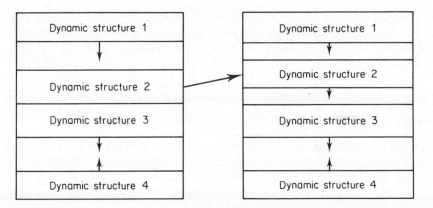

The movable-structures strategy can cater for any number of structures. It does, however, impose the constraint that no item within a structure must be referenced via an absolute pointer, since its position may change. Instead *all pointers must be relative to the start (i.e. the non-growing end) of the structure*. If a structure is moved, the pointer to its start is adjusted accordingly. For example, if structure 3 starts at element 500 within the overall storage area, it is *correct* to specify that a given item of information lies at element 4 relative to the pointer to the start of structure 3, but *incorrect* to say it lies at element 504. If structure 3 moves, the pointer giving its start is changed from 500 to the new position.

Strategy 3: linked lists

The last strategy does not store dynamic structures contiguously. Instead all the structures are interleaved within a single area of storage. When more storage is needed for a structure, a request is made to a master routine. This master routine takes a suitably sized chunk from the common pool. If a dynamic structure shrinks it should return the unused storage to the master routine; alternatively, in some systems, there is an automatic method for such 'garbage collection'. The pieces of storage that make up a dynamic area are joined together in a linked list. If the dynamic area is a dictionary, the dictionary must be searched by following down this list. There is less to be gained from making entries a fixed size, since the resultant advantage of direct searches (e.g. the 'binary chop' method) are lost. On the other hand sorting the dictionary is relatively easy since it can be done simply by changing links, with no necessity to move the entries themselves.

A problem with allocation of storage in linked lists is that storage may become very fragmented, and thus it may be necessary to have a routine to clean it up by moving the unused pieces of storage about so that all the unused pieces become contiguous. A further problem is that lists use up extra storage, because of the need for a pointer field, and this is a relatively heavy overhead if elements are small. For further discussion of lists, see Section 8.10 of Gries (1971), entitled 'Dynamic storage allocation'.

The method to choose

Our prejudice is in favour of contiguously allocated storage and against linked lists. There are three reasons:

(1) the management of linked lists is complicated and prone to nasty errors. A colleague has been trying to debug his garbage collector for the past six months and it still collapses in a heap every other day.
(2) most computers have useful instructions for dealing with contiguous blocks of storage (e.g. indexing, block moves, searching) but not for following down lists.
(3) lists are bad in a virtual storage environment, because they tend to be scattered all over storage, thus requiring a lot of swapping of storage pages.

Doubtless someone with opposite prejudices could produce a contradictory set of reasons.

Using backing storage

When storage runs out, it may be that all is not lost. If backing storage is available certain areas can be swapped out, in order to free some room. Indeed in some compilers the total static size of the compiler itself is actually bigger than the real storage available, so it is inevitable that there will be some swapping to and from backing storage. Such 'quart-into-a-pint-pot' (or, under metrication, 'litre-into-a-50-centilitre-pot') compilers contain elaborate strategies for planning what to swap in and out, as this will be of crucial importance to performance.

We will not go into such strategies in this book, as they depend rather closely on the nature of backing storage. However a reader interested in further details would do well to peruse the description of a classic compiler by Naur (1963).

Chapter 2.13

The Editor

We have already described the basic role of the editor module: to maintain the internal program. Each time the translator has processed a correct line, it gives the translated version to the editor, which then incorporates it into the internal program. If the source program is also being kept, the editor needs to perform a similar operation on each source line. However since the mechanics of editing are similar for any kind of material we shall confine our discussion to the internal program.

Each line supplied to the editor may be an insertion, or, if its line-number corresponds to an existing line, a replacement. In addition there may be special editing commands by which the user can ask the editor to delete single lines of his program or whole blocks (e.g. DELETE 10 TO 100). We assume two simplifying principles.

(1) Editing is in units of complete lines; apart from the line-number, the editor never looks at the individual parts that make up the line. (We discuss this further at the end of the chapter.)
(2) When deleting a line, the editor does not need to know what it is deleting (e.g. it does not have to perform any special operations on a dictionary if it deletes a statement that declares an array).

Representation of the internal program

The way editing is performed depends on the way the internal program is represented. The simplest way—and our maxim is that the simplest is always the best unless proved otherwise—is the following.

The internal form of each line is prefixed by a pair of integers called the *header*: the first is the total length of the line; the second is the line-number. Lines are then put end to end in order of line-number. Thus the representation of the lines

$$10 \text{ LET } X = 33$$
$$20 \text{ PRINT } X$$
$$30 \ldots$$

is

A: length from A to B
  10
  internal form of LET X = 33
B: length from B to C
  20
  internal form of PRINT X
C: . . .

In some languages the line-number would be represented in character rather than number form.

A record is kept of where the program ends.

Insertions

We shall first discuss insertions. Deletions of existing lines will be covered in a later section. If the user types a new line, say line 15, the procedure for inserting it into an internal program is as follows.

(1) Search the internal program, starting from the beginning, until a line-number greater than or equal to 15 is found (or the end of the program is reached). Since we are dealing with an insertion, there will be no existing line 15.
(2) Shift the part of the program beyond this to make room for the new statement.
(3) Place the new statement in the hole just created.

Figure 1 illustrates how this is done in general. Note that if the shifting is done byte by byte, the last byte must be shifted first, then the next to last byte, etc.; this avoids problems of over-writing.

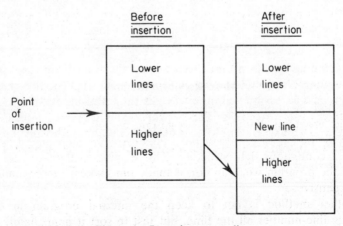

Figure 1   Inserting a new line

The disadvantage of the method is that both the search and the shifting may be slow operations if the internal program is large. For small programs, say up to 100 lines, there is no problem.

This illustrates a general point about designing a compiler. As a designer you are often faced with a choice of methods: a simple method that suits small programs or a complicated method that suits large programs. Thus, right at the start, you should make a fundamental decision. You should either say 'My compiler will be small and will give good performance for small programs. It will accept large programs but do not complain if response is poor.' or 'My compiler caters for large programs. Don't expect the compiler to be small and don't expect specially good performance on small programs.' Once you have made this decision, and it will often be an agonizing one, a lot of other design decisions follow naturally. What you must not do is to commit the *ninth deadly sin*, the sin of the politician: to pretend that you are catering for everyone at the same time. If you do, you will be found out.

Deletions, replacements and lines on the end

Before leaving our simple method, we should mention deletions and replacements. If a line is deleted, the material beyond has to be shifted back to fill the hole. (Shifting should start with the first byte in this case, not the last byte as for an insertion.) A replacement is a deletion together with an insertion. The hole created by the deleted line may be bigger, smaller or the same size as the hole needed for the line to be inserted. Care must be taken in programming these three separate cases.

One final point. Every line typed by the user is essentially an edit. At the very start he is editing a null program. However, in practice, lines are mostly typed in the correct order, and the editor should take advantage of this. A great gain in speed can be achieved by keeping a record of the highest line so far. If the new line is beyond this it can be added on the end of the program without further ado, thus avoiding the searching and shifting (actually a null shift if the new line belongs on the end) outlined above.

More elaborate methods

We shall mention some more elaborate methods, which work better with large programs, but we will not go into details.

One method is to represent the source program as a linked list, rather than as a contiguous data structure. This eliminates the need for shifting parts of the program when an edit is made but makes storage management more expensive.

Another method is not to keep the internal program in order of ascending line-number all the time, but just to sort it immediately prior to a run.

A third method is to keep two separate data structures: one of line-numbers and one of the internal program less line-numbers. In the table of line-numbers, each line-number has a pointer to the encoding of the corresponding line. In this strategy the line-number table may be ordered but the internal program need not be. Thus the amount of shifting is less and sorting is easier. Moreover, assuming that the table of line-numbers has fixed sized entries, it is easier to use fast table look-up techniques.

There is also a host of other methods, each with its own special advantages. Furthermore that is plenty of scope for inventing your own method, with the joy of creativity that this brings.

Editing within a line

If the user types a long and complicated line and gets a single character wrong, he finds it tiresome to re-type the entire line. To remedy this some compilers allow editing within a line. If the input device is a VDU, the cursor is particularly useful in specifying this kind of edit.

If you want to provide such facilities in your compiler, you can do so without abandoning the principle that the internal program is edited in units of complete lines. This is achieved by treating editing within a line as a completely separate activity from the editing of complete lines into the internal program. Editing within a line is done by a *pre-editor* routine on the front of your translator. The pre-editor maintains a buffer, which contains the line to be edited. (By default the line most recently typed—which may be an incorrect line—may be placed in this buffer.) The buffer is displayed to the user in some way, and the user can make any edits he wishes. When the editing has been done the line in the buffer is treated in just the same way as if the user had typed the whole line from scratch.

Chapter 2.14

Input and Output

Input and output devices may be teletypes, VDUs, floppy discs, cassette tapes, LCDs, line-printers and so on. During the life-time of your compiler, which we hope will be many years, new devices will gain favour and old ones wane. We have emphasized in this book that any part of a compiler *may* need changing; the input/output parts *will* need changing.

It is thus vital that changes be facilitated by putting all input/output routines into a separate self-contained module of the compiler. The method of communicating between a module and the rest of the compiler is called its *interface*. The interface typically consists of a set of subroutine calls whereby the outside world can tell the module what is needed. In addition a module may allow communication by means of its data structures, which other modules can read and perhaps write. For instance the input/output module may keep a table of file names and their properties, and this table might be examined by other modules. Designing good interfaces is one of the skills of programming, and this skill is needed in good measure for the interface to the input/output module. The aim must be an interface that is clean and simple, yet general enough to cater for properties of all devices.

The inputs needed by a compiler are likely to include the following:

(a) input of source program and commands;
(b) as (a) but from a file. In this book we shall assume, for the purpose of example, that the command OLD F causes a source program to be taken from the file F, rather than from the terminal;
(c) run-time input;
(d) as (c) but from a file (e.g. INPUT #1:X in some BASICs).

Outputs are likely to include:

(a) error and informatory messages;
(b) program listings;
(c) programs to be saved on a file;
(d) run-time output;
(e) as (d), but to a file;
(f) prompts for input, and re-input after an imput error.

Outside the input/output module the compiler should be *device-independent*, i.e. it should not be concerned with the nature of input/output media. The translator module, for instance, should work in an identical way whether source lines are typed at a terminal or fed from an OLD file. Similarly the editor or the re-creator module should produce lines of a listing to be printed at the terminal in the same way as lines to be saved on a file. Make sure the interface to your input/output module is designed to permit such freedom.

Interactive languages usually contain commands or statements that are concerned with specifying input/output devices. Examples are OLD commands and FILE, MARGIN, RESET and CHAIN statements in BASIC. In processing these the translator or run-time system will need to call the input/output module to tell it what to do. (For simple statements such as MARGIN it may be adequate simply to fill information into a table used by the input/output module.) Thus your interface must allow for such transfers of information, as well as direct requests for input or output.

The unit of communication between the input/output module and the compiler should be the unit most natural for the source language, not a unit tied to a particular device. For most interactive languages this unit will be a line of information, and we shall assume this is the unit used.

If the compiler runs under an operating system, the task of the input/output module will be simply to convert the compiler's input/output requests into the format required by the operating system. If there is no operating system the input/output module must, of course, control the devices directly. In this case it is likely that, when the input/output module communicates with devices such as discs, it will need to repackage information into units different from lines. For example a particular device may require a buffer of, say, 2048 bytes.

If a terminal supports keys such as DELETE, BACKSPACE or RUBOUT, the input routine should deal with the effects of these. The rest of the compiler should have no knowledge of such characters.

If possible the input/output routines should allow for batch working, i.e. where default input comes from a different device from default output, as well as interactive working, i.e. where the two devices are the same. Moreover the rest of the compiler should run independently of whether there is batch use or interactive use. (An exception to this may be error recovery. If, for example, the user supplies an incorrect line of run-time input from an interactive device he should be given another chance; if the device is not interactive, the run should be aborted. Thus the compiler should be able to ask the input/output module questions such as 'Is the current input device an interactive one?')

A few wrinkles

There is no point in going into great detail about the input/output module, because of the huge variety of possible environments and their changing nature. Indeed some of what we have said already may be irrelevant in your particular environment. We shall therefore confine ourselves to some general snippets of advice.

Firstly, remember that input/output devices are not reliable. Therefore make provision for ensuring that each operation is completed successfully, and, if not, for reporting this to the user, giving him all the information he needs about the fault. After an error, make sure the action you take will not cause the error to come up again immediately. As a specific case, do not take the action of closing a file after an error if the error itself arose from failing to close that file. All too often compilers appear to go dead after an input/output error, because they have got themselves in an endless loop.

Secondly, remember to clean up at the end of a run and, even more important, at the end of a session. A run may end with a program error, and there may well be half-finished lines of output. If the input or output is connected to a filing system, do everything you can to prevent this becoming corrupt by making sure it is not left in an unstable state. If it does become corrupt, make sure your actions do not help to spread the corruption.

Thirdly, be very careful with cases where output to different devices is interspersed. Consider the case where the source language allows multi-line functions, and FNA(X) is a function that returns the value of X^3, but, as a side-effect, prints the value of X on file 3; then the statement

PRINT "A";FNA(2);"B"

prints "A" on the default output device, then 2 on file 3, and then the values 8 and "B" on the default output device. If such interspersed output is possible, then there must be a separate buffer (together with its associated pointers) for each output device. Similar reasoning applies to input devices. Moreover the nature of the current device may need to be stacked and restored over a function call. All in all, life is much happier for compiler writers when interspersed input and/or output is *not* possible in the source language.

Finally, if lines of text are output to a file it helps greatly if all spaces can be deleted from the ends of lines. In filing systems which insist that all lines have a fixed length, say 80 characters, over half the backing storage can be wasted with spaces.

Implications on choice of encoding language

The degree of difficulty of the above problems depends on the input/output facilities available in your encoding language. If these are more comprehensive than those needed for your source language, then your task is easy; if they are less comprehensive your task is hard. Unfortunately many high-level languages, which are otherwise quite good for encoding compilers, are weak on interactive input/output (Wasserman, 1978). If the input/output module is written in assembly language—and it may be necessary to resort to this—then everything is, of course, possible but everything is tedious and nasty to encode.

Types of file

A source language may allow communication with files that are treated as binary information, or with files that are 'accessed randomly', i.e. the 300th line of a file can be picked out without the first 299 having to be scanned. If such features are present, they require extra input/output routines. We have only considered the case of files that consist of lines of characters which are accessed sequentially.

All interactive languages need some means of saving files and restoring them later (e.g. SAVE and OLD commands). It is possible to store such files in special internal formats, and indeed if they are stored in the internal language, it makes saving and restoring faster. However, the disadvantage is that the files may become harder to manipulate with other system utilities (e.g. programs to list files, to search files, to copy files). Thus it is generally better to store all files in the standard character form. Indeed our earlier assumption that SAVing a file is similar to LISTing it (and restoring a SAVed program is similar to typing a program at a terminal) depends on files being represented in character form. In all subsequent discussion, we shall keep to files consisting of lines of characters.

Chapter 2.15

Break-ins

This Part of the book has been concerned with the overall structure of the compiler, and we are now nearing the end. However, before entering into more detailed discussions in subsequent Parts of the book, we must introduce a consideration which, although completely absent from the design of a batch compiler, will pervade the design of almost every module of an interactive one. This is the *break-in*.

The need for break-ins

A 'break-in' facility is a vital part of any interactive communication. Thus in communication between humans, if the person who is talking to you is telling you something you know already, or something you think is wrong, you invoke his break-in mechanism and interrupt him. Some humans, unfortunately, do not support any mechanism to stop their flow of talk, but these are the ones you try to avoid. Likewise with compilers. The user of an interactive compiler must have available some key he can type—we call it the *break-in key*—which stops the compiler in its tracks, and lets the user have a say. This key has the special property that it can be typed at any time, even when the computer is outputting. (A few systems use different keys to act as the break-in key according to the state of the compiler, but this added complication is best avoided.)

The *tenth deadly sin* in writing an interactive compiler is to have no strategy for processing break-ins. As we shall see, break-ins provide plenty of thorny problems in compiler design.

Interrupts and polling

There are two possible ways the break-in can be passed to your compiler. One way is as an *interrupt*; this can be treated by your compiler as an unexpected subroutine call—control suddenly goes into a special subroutine you have designated to deal with break-ins. The other way is that a variable external to your compiler—we shall call this variable HAVEBREAK—is set to a special value to indicate a break-in has occurred. In this case your compiler has the responsibility of periodically *polling* (i.e. looking at) HAVEBREAK to see if there has been a break-in. We shall refer to the two possible approaches as the *interrupt approach* and the *polling approach*.

In either case, you may find your encoding language does not have the necessary built-in facilities to cater for break-ins, and thus you may need to do some work to provide the necessary interface.

Whichever approach you use you must guarantee to respond to any break-in within a short time, say a second. In particular *there must be no possible way for your compiler to run for an indefinite time without recognizing a break-in*.

Time of break-in

The user may want to break-in to your compiler at any time. Examples are the following:

(a) while his program is looping;
(b) while his program is printing voluminous output;
(c) while his program is waiting for input;
(d) during a listing or the saving of a file;
(e) while a source program is being read from a file;
(f) while a source line is being entered from a terminal;
(g) while the compiler is printing an error message.

It is vital, when designing your compiler, to make sure that it accepts break-ins at all these times and more, and performs a sensible action in each case. We have enumerated the somewhat tedious list above to help you think about the full impact of break-ins.

Action at a break-in

Some compilers allow the user, having broken-in to the run of his program, to type a few commands or immediate statements, and then resume the original run where it left off. See Heher (1976) for a discussion of a compiler with this property. Such a system is relatively difficult to implement because the state of the original run must be preserved completely over the intervening activities; these activities may include immediate statements, which themselves involve running a 'program' consisting of one statement.

In our discussion here we shall assume a more modest break-in facility, where the break-in is treated like an error that causes the current activity to be aborted. The user's program and its variables must, however, remain intact after the break-in. The action at a break-in might be to output a message such as

```
***BREAK-IN   IN   LINE:
***150   GOTO   150
```

and then to abort the current run, if any, close down any files that are being used (such as a file that was being SAVEd when the break-in occurred), and return control to the user so that he can type a further command or edit his program.

It is important, if a break-in occurs during a run, that the error message identifies the current line, as in the sample message above; this helps the user find endless loops.

In some situations a break-in will require more severe actions by the compiler than for an ordinary error. For example if the compiler is taking a source program from a file and finds a syntax error in a line, then it will report the error but will continue taking further lines of source from the file. With a break-in, the compiler must return to get input from the user's terminal, not from the file.

Unstable states

Both the interrupt approach and the polling approach have their problems. The following example illustrates a problem with interrupts.

Assume that the internal program lines are stored end-to-end, and that when a new line is inserted the lines beyond it are shifted up to make a hole of a suitable size; the inserted line is then copied into the hole. This is exactly what we suggested in Chapter 2.13.

If a break-in occurs during this insertion procedure, the effects could be tragic. In particular, if the break-in occurs during the shifting operation some internal lines will have been shifted up whereas others will not. Alternatively the break-in could occur after the hole has been created but before it has been filled in. In either case if the user lists his program after the break-in he will get garbage.

This is an example of a more general problem. The state of the user's program is described by a set of variables within the compiler, plus data structures like the internal program and its associated dictionaries. This state continually changes as the user edits his program, and as the compiler processes the program. Between changes of state, the program may be in an *unstable state*. This applied in our example above, when the internal program was being shifted about to allow insertion of a new line. Maybe in your compiler, the insertion of a line will not cause instability, but it is very likely that there will be instability somewhere, since it is almost impossible to design a compiler otherwise. For example storage allocation procedures can often get into an unstable state: your run-time system requests some storage for a string, say, and the storage management procedures reserve it, but a break-in occurs before your run-time system has recorded the fact that it has got the storage.

It is in conjunction with unstable states that the difference between a break-in and an error is important. When you write your compiler you fix where in the compiler each error is to be detected, and it is not hard to ensure that no error ever occurs in an unstable state. Break-ins, on the other hand, come at unpredictable times and you have no control over when the user may press the break-in key.

Avoiding some unstable states

Although it is almost inevitable that your compiler will contain some unstable states, there are various methods you can use to minimize them. In particular you can be very careful about the order in which actions are performed in case there is a break-in in between. As an illustration of this, assume that a variable PTR points at the end of a data structure, DS, that describes the user's program and hence needs to be preserved over a break-in. To add a new item, X, to DS your compiler could perform the operations

$$PTR = PTR+1$$
$$DS[PTR] = X$$

or

$$DS[PTR+1] = X$$
$$PTR = PTR+1$$

(plus the appropriate error checking, in each case, for PTR being too large). You may think these two pairs of statements have identical effect, but they do not. If you consider the effect of a break-in between the two statements in each case, you will see the second case is harmless whereas the first is dangerous. This is because, in the first case, PTR is updated to point at an empty position and then X is copied into this empty hole. A break-in could cause this dangerous empty hole to be left around.

However even in the second case you may not be completely safe. The statement PTR=PTR+1 is, we shall assume, compiled into machine code before it is executed (i.e. your encoding language has a true compiler). If PTR occupies 16 bits and your computer can only perform operations on 8 bits, then assigning the new value to PTR needs to be done in two parts. If a break-in occurs during this operation, PTR might be left with a crazy value. If however PTR=PTR+1 compiles into a single instruction, there is no problem, since (almost) no computers allow interrupts within a machine instruction.

Protecting unstable states

If break-ins are to be recognized by interrupts it is necessary to identify all unstable states in the compiler. Thus you must identify all the variables that relate to information that is to be reserved over a break-in, e.g. the internal program, dictionaries, values of the user's variables, records of use of storage, etc. You must then find all places in the compiler where these are changed and decide whether each constitutes an unstable state. Err on the side of caution; if you make a mistake it will be a hard bug to find, as only if break-in is typed at just the wrong instant will the bug be revealed. The sections of code of your compiler that give rise to an unstable state are called *critical regions*. At the start of each critical region you must 'inhibit' break-ins and then 'allow' them again at the end. Some operating systems provide convenient facilities for doing this. Otherwise you need to program it yourself. This can be done by setting a variable NOBREAK to *true* when breaks are to be inhibited. If a break-in occurs while NOBREAK is true, the subroutine that is entered as a result of the break-in interrupt ignores the break-in and carries on with normal processing—we assume this can be done—but records that there has been a break-in. When break-ins are allowed, NOBREAK is set back to *false,* and a check is made to see if there have been any break-ins in the meantime. If so the break-in is taken. The effect of this is to delay any break-in that occurs during a critical region until everything is back in a stable state and break-ins can be allowed again. Outside a critical region a break-in is accepted immediately.

Critical regions should be sufficiently small that it appears to the user as if every break-in is instantaneous. What must not happen under any circumstances is for the compiler to get locked into a critical region.

The polling approach

The above description doubtless makes the interrupt approach to break-ins seem horribly complicated (though in practice it may not be as bad as it appears). You might, therefore, be attracted to the polling approach. However, do not expect this to make all the problems run away.

The difficulty with polling is ensuring that your compiler will always respond to a break-in within a reasonable time, such as the one second we postulated. Your compiler must be so smattered with instructions to do polling that no possible path through the compiler can avoid them for long. Obviously no polling must be done while in a critical region. One possible tactic is always to poll when you come to a new statement, whether it be in the translator, the pre-run module, the run-time system or during a listing. In addition polling should be done after (and ideally during) every input or output operation. Even this might not be enough as an individual statement may take an indefinitely large time to run. In particular, if the source language supported matrix operations, then the execution of a single statement which inverted a large matrix might take ten minutes. It is necessary to do polling *within* statements such as this. The same might apply to built-in functions if these, say, supported highly complicated operations on arbitrarily long strings. In some cases it might even be possible for a single statement to be an endless loop—for example if the source language manipulated linked lists and the user wrote a statement to search a circular list.

The disadvantage of polling, apart from the labour of making sure it is fool-proof, is that it slows the compiler down. This applies particularly to the running of user programs, where an overhead of polling after each statement may take as much time as executing the statement itself. (To combat this, some compilers have a system of counting the statements executed and only polling every time the count reaches a hundred, say. This can save time if polling involves a time-consuming call to an operating system.) A further possible disadvantage occurs when you are debugging the compiler itself; if the compiler gets into an endless loop because of your programming bug, it is quite likely you will not be able to break it.

A new strategy for the interrupt approach

The strategy we have just described for polling can actually also be used for the interrupt approach. Instead of trying to find the unstable states, it might be easier to have break-in interrupts inhibited most of the time but to allow them briefly at odd points in the compiler when it is known that everything is safe. The safe points might be the same as those times we have suggested for polling. This strategy is particularly attractive within those compiler modules, such as the translator, which are likely to contain several instances of unstable states. Safer modules, such as those concerned with listing a program, could still have break-in interrupts allowed all the time.

Further dangerous times for break-ins

There are two particular occasions when a break-in is likely to knock out the compiler, irrespective of the way break-ins are processed. One is during the compiler's initialization; if this is not successfully completed, either because of a break-in or an error (e.g. failure to communicate with input/output devices), then the session must be aborted. To accomplish this, the compiler needs a variable called, say, AMREADY, which has the value *false* when the compiler is loaded and is set to *true* when the compiler has completed its initialization. The session is aborted if an error or break-in occurs when AMREADY is *false*.

The second time where a break-in may be dangerous is while a previous break-in (or error) is being processed. Examine your compiler carefully in this respect; there are dangers, for example, in performing clearing-up actions, such as releasing temporary storage, twice.

Bugs with break-ins

You have finished your compiler and it is seeing successful usage. You are relaxing, happy in thoughts of a job well done, when the telephone rings.

It is a user, and he has not called to congratulate you. Instead he is furious. He had produced a large program, pressing break-in occasionally during the development process, and then SAVEd the program on a file. The next day he tried to use the file and found your compiler had saved complete garbage.

How do you find the bug? You know that there is some position in your compiler where a break-in can occur in an unstable state and therefore leave the internal program or its dictionaries in a corrupt condition. Reproducing what your user did is impossible, even if he can send you a print-out of his entire session.

The answer is that there is no overall solution to this problem. The best you can do is to leave some clues around every time your compiler accepts a break-in. For example the compiler could store, in some fixed place, a record of the instruction that was being executed when the break-in occurred. This does not help with your user at the end of a telephone, but may help with an even more frightening problem: the irate user who has called you to his terminal, which has printed garbage as a result of an earlier break-in, and who is glowering over you expecting you to find out what is wrong. You can examine the fixed location and find out when the break-in occurred so that you can at least correct the bug in the future. Most importantly you are seen to be doing something rather than looking helpless.

Errors akin to break-ins

On many computers, certain errors cause an interrupt. Examples are division by zero, or overflow (i.e. getting an answer that is too big for the machine to hold). These errors can occur when the user's program is run. Fortunately, you have more control over most of these possible interrupts than over break-ins. For instance division by zero can only occur on a divide operation, so provided no dangerous divide operation is executed in an unstable state all is well.

A few errors, however, may be as uncontrollable as a break-in, and hence require similar preventative measures. Some computers, for example, provide an interrupt when a time limit has expired, and this could occur at any time during the compiler's processing.

Summary

In summary, interactive compilers possess, in the break-in facility, a completely new dimension of communication with the user. Providing such extra power is bound to require extra work and thought by the compiler writer. Do not shirk it.

Chapter 2.16

Summary of Design

We are now in a position to summarize all the modules that go to make up the compiler, and see how they interact. The modules are as follows.

The input/output module deals with all input and output to and from the user's terminal, other devices and files. It works in units of complete lines of text.

The translator inputs lines via the input/output module. Lines may come from the user's terminal or from a file. If a line is a command the translator passes it to the 'command module' (see below). If it is a program statement, the translator checks it for errors, and reports any errors back to the user. If there are no errors the line is translated to its internal-language form and handed to the editor. The translator creates dictionaries and other tables relating to the user's program.

The editor maintains the program in its internal form (and perhaps in source form too). It takes lines from the translator, and inserts them into the appropriate place in the internal program. The editor may include an extra 're-creator' module.

The command module interprets command lines (e.g. SAVE, OLD, RUN, LIST), and either performs the necessary actions itself or calls other modules to do them.

The run-time system deals with running the program. It executes the internal program produced by the translator. It also uses the tables, such as dictionaries, produced by the translator.

The pre-run module is called before a run starts. It performs all the error checking and translating that the translator, which looks at each line in isolation, cannot do. The pre-run module works on the internal program and its associated tables.

Finally, it is useful to put the error handling of all modules into a single separate module. This should include treatment of break-ins.

Your compiler need not, of course, follow exactly the above module structure. Some of the modules may be split in several parts, while others may be combined. However, somewhere in your compiler you should have routines which serve each of the above roles.

Use of modules during a session

The relationship between the modules of a compiler is often illustrated by a diagram with a maze of lines and arrows. If you want one of these here you will be disappointed, because we do not believe in them. What we think more useful is to go through a sample session and show where each module plays its part. Such an analysis follows.

(1) *Start of session*. The command module performs the necessary initialization, and enters the translator.

(2) *User types his program*. The translator takes each line in turn (using the input/output module) converts it to the internal form, and feeds it to the editor.

(3) *User types the RUN command*. The translator passes the RUN command back to the command module. (In some compilers the command module is 'in control' in the sense that it, not the translator, inputs each source line; lines that are not commands are then passed to the translator. We assume in this book that the translator is in control. We discuss the matter further when we describe the command module in Chapter 6.3.) After receiving the RUN command, the command module calls the pre-run module and then the run-time system.

(4) *During the run*. The run-time system executes the internal program. Input and output are controlled by statements (e.g.INPUT,PRINT) in the internal program.

(5) *End of run*. Control returns to the command module, which does any necessary clearing up and then hands control to the translator. The situation is now the same as (2) above.

(6) *User types the LIST command*. The translator returns control to the command module which then uses the editor and perhaps the re-creator to produce the listing. At the end control returns to the translator.

(7) *After a fatal error*. If an error causes the current activity to be abandoned (e.g. running or listing a program), the action is similar to that at the end of a run as in (5) above.

(8) *End of session*. The command module closes down.

Part 3

THE DESIGN OF AN INTERNAL LANGUAGE

Chapter 3.1

Reverse Polish Notation

The most substantial parts of your compiler are likely to be the translator and the run-time system. You cannot define either of these, nor can you define the re-creator or the pre-run module, until you have fixed the exact form of your internal language and its associated dictionaries. This is therefore the first detailed task in designing your compiler, and we devote the whole of this Part of the book to it. To start with, we develop a principle to cover the way the nature of the internal program can change.

Filling in context-dependent information

The translator creates the lines of the internal program, but the pre-run module may subsequently fill in some of the context-dependent information in a line.

For example, consider the BASIC source line NEXT K. We shall assume the translator converts this to an internal code meaning 'NEXT' together with a pointer to the dictionary entry for K. The pre-run module will match the NEXT K to a corresponding FOR K. It should also record, in the internal form of the NEXT statement, where the corresponding FOR is. This information will be needed when the program is run. There are two ways this information can be provided. Firstly the translator can leave an extra unused field in the internal form of a NEXT statement and the pre-run module can insert the pointer to the FOR in this field. Secondly the pre-run module can overwrite, within the internal form of the NEXT statement, the dictionary pointer for K with a pointer to the corresponding FOR. The information that K followed the NEXT is no longer needed in the internal program once it has been used to find the matching FOR, and therefore it can safely be overwritten. When the pre-run module makes changes like this to the internal language, it may be considered to convert the original internal language into a *second internal language*.

We shall reject this second approach. If the source needs to be re-created, there is the problem of converting the second internal language back to the original one, before converting the original one back to the source language. Moreover if a program is run, thus causing it to be translated into the second internal language, and then edited, thus introducing new statements in the original internal language, the internal program will be in a mixture of languages—a nasty complication. We thus take the first approach. The unused fields, which are filled in by the pre-run module before each run, are called *context-dependent* fields. When these fields are filled in, the internal program is in *fixed-context* form; otherwise it is in *open-context* form. The overriding principle is that information which the translator creates is sacrosanct and no other module can change it (except that the editor can shift it about, and replace or delete complete lines). However, the translator can provide a few empty fields, such as the context-dependent fields within the internal program, for others to play in. The same principle applies both to the internal program and the associated dictionaries.

Forms of internal language

Five requirements for the design of an internal language are the following:

(a) it should be easy and fast to run;
(b) it should be easy to translate to and from source language;
(c) it should be concise;
(d) it should be easy to edit;
(e) it should reflect the real structure of the user's program.

Some of these requirements conflict with one another. For example, (a) requires closeness to machine code, but (b) requires closeness to the source language. Thus any internal language design involves compromises. You make these compromises when you fix the general level of the internal language, as we have discussed in Part 2, and also when you fix the exact notation. Among the possible notations you can choose from are trees of various kinds, 'triples', 'quadruples', 'Forward Polish' and 'Reverse Polish'. Rather than baffle you with choice we shall select only one of these and describe it in detail. This is the much-used *Reverse Polish* notation (which is also called *postfix* notation). It is a notation that is tolerably close to most source languages, thus falling in with our suggestion in Chapter 2.6, and does as well as most in satisfying the five requirements above.

Principles of Reverse Polish

Polish notation is so called because it was invented by a Pole, Łukasiewicz. It was unlucky for him that he was born with a name which, to us, is so hard to pronounce and spell. Otherwise we might have called his notation 'Łukasiewicz notation', just as we use the term 'Backus–Naur Form' rather than 'American–Danish Form'. There are two types of Polish notation, called *Forward Polish* and *Reverse Polish*. They are logically very similar, but we shall use the latter. The notation was actually invented in

1921, i.e. about thirty years before the first compiler, and is thus an instance of a solution preceding a problem. Indeed it must have been an exciting discovery when the two were matched up.

Before describing the notation, it is necessary to introduce the idea of the *precedence* of arithmetic operators. When we evaluate 4+6/2, we get the answer 7 because we naturally do the division before the addition. (It is not really natural, but it becomes so if you have been trained to do it for many years.) Thus the division operator has higher precedence than the addition operator. As a second example, when we evaluate 7–3–2, we get 2. This is because we 'naturally' evaluate it as (7–3)–2 rather than as 7–(3–2). Similarly 7–3+2 is taken as (7–3)+2, not 7–(3+2). The general rule is that if two adjacent operators are the same, or have equal precedence (like addition and subtraction), then the leftmost takes precedence.

These 'natural' rules for precedence are encompassed in most programming languages. There is always provision for the user to employ parentheses if he wishes to override the precedence rules. Thus he can write (4+6)/2 if that is what he really wants.

The consequence of all these precedence rules is that, given a moderately complicated expression such as

$$A+(B-C/D)-E*F$$

it is quite a task for a compiler to figure out what order it should perform the operations in (e.g. to figure out that C/D is the first operation to be performed). If the internal language represents expressions in the same way as the source language, then programs will run slowly, because the potentially complex task of working out precedence rules needs to be performed by the run-time system each time an expression is evaluated.

The use of Reverse Polish notation as internal language solves this problem. Reverse Polish notation represents expressions in such a way that operators occur in the order in which they are to be done. Parentheses are totally eliminated.

Expressions consist of *operators* and *operands* (e.g. variables or constants). Most operators are *binary* in the sense that they take two operands. In ordinary mathematical notation binary operators are written between their operands (e.g. in A+B the operator '+' comes between its operands A and B). The principle of Reverse Polish notation is that the operator is written after its operands. Thus A+B is written A B +. (In Forward Polish notation operators come before their operands, e.g. + A B.) If an operand is itself the result of an operation, then the same notation is used for this operand. For instance in the expression A*B+C the two operands of '+' are A*B and C. The former is written A B * and the whole expression is written A B * C + . The following are some further examples of Reverse Polish notation.

Source	*Reverse Polish*
A	A
(A)	A
A/B	A B /
A+B*C	A B C * +
A+(B*C)	A B C * +
(A+B)*C	A B + C *
A/B−C/7	A B / C 7 / −
A−B−3	A B − 3 −
A+(B−C/D)−E*F	A B C D / − + E F * −

Reverse Polish is executed by continually taking the leftmost operator and replacing it, together with its operands, by the result. Thus to evaluate 6 5 3 − 7 + * the steps are as follows.

(a) The leftmost operator is the minus sign and its two operands are 5 and 3. Hence 5 3 − is replaced by its result, 2, so that the expression becomes 6 2 7 + *.

(b) The leftmost operator is now the plus sign with operands 2 and 7. This is replaced by its result, 9, giving 6 9 *.

(c) The leftmost operator is now the multiply sign and we get the final result, 54. The original Reverse Polish expression corresponded to the source string 6*(5 − 3 + 7). This also gives the result 54, which is comforting.

Purpose of Reverse Polish

Before going into more details of Reverse Polish notation, we should examine its overall purpose. The main purpose is that, since operators occur in the order in which they are to be used, Reverse Polish programs are quicker and easier to run. This sounds fair, but if you are a sceptic you might reserve judgement until you read the chapter in Part 5 on executing Reverse Polish.

If you accept that this is true, and it is, then Reverse Polish certainly satisfies the first of the five requirements for an internal language, as propounded earlier in this chapter. But does it do this at the expense of any of the other four? The answer is that, on the contrary, it actually helps with two of them: conciseness, and representing the program structure. With a third, ease of editing, it is equivalent to most other internal languages. Only with one requirement does it impose an extra burden, and this is in inter-translating between Reverse Polish and source language. Fortunately, even this is not a major burden and is a price worth paying for the advantage that Reverse Polish is typically *much* faster to execute than any internal language that is close to a source language.

Representing Reverse Polish

While explaining the principles of Reverse Polish notation we shall not worry about exactly how it is represented inside a computer. Instead we shall represent it *symbolically*, as we have done already, as a series of items separated by spaces. Operands will be represented by their source names (e.g. A, B$, 3.6) and operators either by the source symbol (e.g. +) or by italicized identifiers (e.g. *NEWOP*). Thus a sample of symbolic Reverse Polish notation is

$$P \; 6 + Q \; NEWOP$$

The choice of a representation of this inside the computer will be discussed in Chapter 3.3.

Chapter 3.2

Operators

We have introduced Reverse Polish notation in terms of the simple operators familiar in arithmetic. However a programming language uses a lot of other operators besides these and in this chapter we discuss some of them.

Unary, binary and ternary operators

In addition to the binary operators introduced in the previous chapter, many source languages also allow *unary* operators, which have one operand, and *ternary* operators, which have three. Reverse Polish notation works for operators with any number of operands, but any one individual operator must always have the same number of operands.

The most common unary operator is 'negate', which is illustrated in the BASIC statement

$$\text{LET A} = -\text{B}$$

In the source language, the symbol '$-$' may be used both for the unary 'negate' operator (as applied to the variable B in the above example) and the binary 'subtract' operator. In Reverse Polish notation it is necessary to use different operators for the two cases. We shall assume 'negate' is represented by *NEGATE*, to distinguish it from the binary subtraction operator. Given this convention, the expression $-(A*(-B))$ is written in Reverse Polish internal language as A B *NEGATE* $*$ *NEGATE*.

Another example of a unary operator that is present in many programming languages is the logical 'not' operator, which is written '$\neg$'. The logical expression $A \wedge \neg B$ is represented in Reverse Polish as A B$\neg$ $\wedge$.

An example of a ternary operation is a reference to a two-dimensional array element A(I,J). This can be represented by an operator *ARRAYSUB2*, meaning select an element of a two-dimensional array. Its three operands are the array name and the two subscripts. A reference to a one-dimensional array element, B(J), is, on the other hand, a binary operation. This can be represented by an operator *ARRAYSUB1*, which has as its two operands the array name and the single subscript. The following examples illustrate the usage of these two operators.

106

Source	Reverse Polish
A(K,J)	A K J *ARRAYSUB2*
B(K)	B K *ARRAYSUB1*
A(K+N,J*L)	A K N + J L * *ARRAYSUB2*
A(K,J/3)+B(−P)	A K J 3 / *ARRAYSUB2* B P *NEGATE*
	ARRAYSUB1 +

General use of Reverse Polish

The use of Reverse Polish is not confined to representing arithmetic expressions. It can also represent all the other features of a source language, and, indeed, if Reverse Polish is totally to fill its role as an internal language this capability is vital. Each source statement needs to be represented internally as a self-contained piece of Reverse Polish notation. (In a batch compiler, where the internal program is not produced one statement at a time, but as a complete whole, the entire internal program might be one single piece of Reverse Polish notation.) In the interactive case, the internal representation of each line is preceded by a 'header', which is used by the editor. We discussed this in Chapter 2.13. Each header contains a field giving the total length of the internal line. Assuming that internal lines are stored end-to-end, the length field is useful in getting from one line to the next when performing a sequential search of the internal program.

The following examples, taken from the BASIC language—as nearly all our examples are—illustrate possible Reverse Polish representations of complete source-language statements.

(1)	LET A = B+C	A B C + *LET*
(2)	GOTO 100	100 *GOTO*
(3)	IF A > B+C THEN 20	A B C + > 20 *GOIF*
(4)	INPUT A,B,C	A *INPUT* B *INPUT* C *INPUT*
(5)	DIM A(3,2), B(6)	A 3 2 *DIM2* B 6 *DIM1*
(6)	FOR A = B TO C STEP D	A B C D *FOR*
(7)	FOR A=B TO C	A B C *FORSTEP1*
(8)	STOP	*STOP*

It should be emphasized that there is some choice in the form of the Reverse Polish notation. In case (4) above, for example, it might be desirable to have a way of indicating the end of the input list, e.g. an operator *INPUTLAST*. Thus (4) might be written A *INPUT* B *INPUT* C *INPUTLAST*. A similar mechanism might apply to other lists such as those on PRINT, DIM and ON statements.

Later on we shall say more about data types of operands, and will, in fact, refine some of the above examples.

The FOR statement in (6) provides an example of an operator with four operands, a *quaternary* operator. In example (7) there is a variant of

FOR with only three operands. Example (8) shows a case of an operator with no operands, a *nonary* operator.

Ternary operators can, if desired, be represented as a pair of imaginary binary operators, and likewise a pair of related binary operators can be represented as a ternary operator. As an example of the latter, the two operators '>' and *GOIF* used in example (3) can be combined into a single ternary operator *GOGR*. The operands of *GOGR* are the two values to be compared and the line-number to be gone to if the first value is greater than the second. Using *GOGR*, example (3) becomes:

$$A\ B\ C + 20\ GOGR$$

Similarly quaternary operators represent three binary operators. Thus the quaternary operator *FOR* can be represented as three binary operators *FORASSIGN*, *FORTO* and *FORSTEP*, making example (6):

$$A\ B\ FORASSIGN\ C\ FORTO\ D\ FORSTEP$$

Function calls

There is a choice of representation for function calls. One way is to treat each function as a separate operator (e.g. SIN, COS, TAN, etc.). It may be better, however, to avoid this proliferation of operators by introducing special operators that call functions. Thus there may be an operator *CALLBI1ARG*, meaning call a built-in function that has one argument; this would be a binary operator, taking as operands the function to be called and its argument. Thus SIN(X) would be represented SIN X *CALLBI1ARG*. There would be similar operators *CALLBI∅ARG* covering built-in functions, such as RND, which have no argument, and perhaps *CALLBI2ARGS*, etc. In addition there might be operators for calling *U*ser-*D*efined functions, such as FNA in BASIC, e.g. *CALLUD1ARG*. The following are some examples.

Source	*Reverse Polish*
X+RND	X RND *CALLBI∅ARG* +
SIN(FNC(X−1))	SIN FNC X 1 − *CALLUD1ARG CALLBI1ARG*
FNA/FNB(X)	FNA *CALLUD∅ARG* FNB X *CALLUD1ARG* /

Polymorphic operators

A *polymorphic operator* is one that can be applied to operands of more than one possible data type. Polymorphic operators are present in most programming languages that support more than one data type. In BASIC, for example, the relational operators on IF statements are normally polymorphic. You can write

$$IF\ A = B\ THEN\ 100$$

and

       IF A$ = B$ THEN 100

Thus the operator '=' can be applied to strings or to numbers.

Polymorphic operators are a nuisance when it comes to running a program, as it is necessary to look at the operands before you know what to do. When executing the '=' operator, the method for comparing two strings would almost certainly be different from the way of comparing two numbers, so the run-time system would need to find out which to do. Because of this inconvenience, polymorphic operators are normally eliminated from internal languages; instead they are replaced by a set of internal language operators, one for each possible data type. Thus for '=' there would be two different internal operators, *EQNUM* and *EQSTR*, say.

There are actually surprisingly many places where polymorphic operators occur in source languages. Examples in BASIC, in addition to the IF statement, are the LET, INPUT, READ and PRINT statements; all these deal with either string or numeric operands. There are thus many polymorphic operators which need to be eliminated in the Reverse Polish, and this leads to the creation of lots of extra internal operators such as *LETNUM*, *LETSTR*, *INPUTNUM*, *INPUTSTR*, etc. The following are examples of polymorphic operators; some of them are revisions of earlier examples.

Source	Reverse Polish
INPUT A,B$	A *INPUTNUM* B$ *INPUTSTR*
LET A = 3	A 3 *LETNUM*
LET B$ = "PIG"	B$ "PIG" *LETSTR*

Many source languages treat integers as a separate data type from real numbers, because the two are represented in different ways on most current computers. In this case the common arithmetic operators, such as '+', '−', etc., can be applied either to integers or to reals and are therefore polymorphic. Indeed there are even source languages where all operators are polymorphic. Thus polymorphic operators should not be regarded as a nasty special case, but as a central property of high-level languages.

Coercions

Some languages, particularly those which allow both real and integer variables, have 'automatic coercions'. This means that the compiler automatically converts operands to the correct data type. The rules of a source language, reflecting the underlying hardware, may say you can only add two reals together or two integers together; if you try to add an integer to a real, the compiler will automatically convert the integer to real form. This is a *coercion*.

Just as an internal language is better without polymorphic operators, so it is better without automatic coercions. If coercions are needed they should be inserted as explicit internal language operators, e.g. a unary operator *CONVERTTOREAL*. Then a source statement such as

LET R1 = I%

where R1 is real and I% is an integer, would be represented as

R1 I% *CONVERTTOREAL LETREAL*

Note that where we previously had a single operator, *LETNUM*, for assignment of numbers, we now need two operators *LETREAL* and *LETINTEGER*.

For the sake of simplicity we shall not distinguish integers from reals in examples in the rest of this book. We shall thus bring back *LETNUM*, after its brief demise, and use it as the only numeric assignment operator.

Overall rule for data types

The principles outlined in the previous discussion of data types can be encompassed in the following rule: *each internal language operator deals with fixed data types, and it is guaranteed that the operator will be preceded by operands of the correct data type; moreover each operator returns a result of a fixed data type.* In the context of this rule the data type can be taken not only to include numeric, string, etc., but also functions and arrays. Thus the operator *CALLBI1ARG* can be guaranteed to be preceded by one operand which is a built-in function name and a second operand which is numeric; it returns a numeric result. The translator, in its role of detecting syntax errors, eliminates all statements that break the above rule, e.g.

LET A = B$
PRINT COS(B$)

Addresses and values

Most operators work on the values of their operands, but some operators work on the *address* of one or more of their operands. An example of the latter occurs in an assignment statement, such as LET X = Y, which is represented in Reverse Polish as X Y *LETNUM*. Here the value of Y is taken and deposited in the *address* of X. *LETNUM* requires its first operand to be an address, and its value is irrelevant. It may, therefore, be thought necessary to put special markers on all variables in the internal language for which addresses rather than values are required. This is not so. We did not require that every variable have a marker to say whether it was a number or string; instead we associated a data type with each operator and guaranteed that operands would be of the right type. We can regard addresses and values as an extension of the data-type concept, and can extend the definition of an operator such as *LETNUM* to mean that it takes a numeric address as first operand and a numeric value as second operand. The translator must guarantee that the first operand is a reasonable thing to assign to, e.g. it must eliminate LET A+B = 3 or LET 3 = X.

Thus whether a variable is taken as an address or a value depends on the operator that is applied to it. We shall discuss this further when we consider the execution of Reverse Polish by the run-time system.

Chapter 3.3

Encoding Reverse Polish

Up to now we have used a symbolic form of Reverse Polish internal language, which has somewhat disguised the nasty problems of how it is actually represented inside the computer. In this chapter we face up to these problems. Our emphasis in choosing the internal representation will be conciseness in use of storage—packing information in as few bits as practicable. The aim is to enable the compiler to run as large a program as possible within the store of the machine.

There is a large body of theory concerning encoding information concisely, and there is a concept of an 'information theoretical minimum', meaning the smallest number of bits that can be used to encode a given piece of information. In practice it is not sensible to aim for the very minimum size for our Reverse Polish as its encoding would become hugely complicated; the result would be that the compiler would need acres of extra instructions in order to encode and unravel the Reverse Polish, thus cancelling out the savings in the size of the Reverse Polish itself. We shall thus aim for 'reasonable but not excessive' conciseness. These are, of course, subjective terms, and what is reasonable to one person is outrageous to another.

A discussion of packing information into bits is inevitably dirty and nasty. If you are not worried about storing internal programs concisely you can take this chapter with a pinch of salt. If you do read it and are a bit squeamish, you will be glad to know that we warn you when the going gets really bad, so that you can avert your eyes. A lot of the nastiness is because machines (and therefore many high-level languages) tend to work in fixed sized bytes and words. Designers often find they have a field that is naturally, say, 9 bits; but there is a great gain if it can be restricted to fit into an 8 bit byte. If machines had efficient bit addressing—and a few have—many of the problems would go away. If your encoding language has high-level facilities for describing data, the problems may also appear to go away, because the use of bits inside the machine may be disguised from you. However if, as a result, your internal program is stored in a grossly wasteful way, you may wish later that you had seen the problems as you went along. Thus an awareness of how your encoding language represents objects inside the computer may help you.

112

Vectors of run-time values

Before discussing the internal program itself, it is useful to consider how the user's variables and constants will be represented when his program is run. For some data types the size of the run-time value is uniform and fixed. This is usually true for numeric scalars, which are often stored internally in eight bytes. (Four bytes is adequate for integers, but can give poor accuracy for real numbers.) For strings, on the other hand, the size may vary. Objects of the same fixed and uniform size can conveniently be gathered together in a vector. For example there may be a vector containing the values of all the user's numeric variables (assuming that they have global scope). The position of variables within the vector may notionally be reserved by the translator, long before the user's program is actually run. For instance position 3 of the vector might be allocated to a variable X, position 4 to Y, and so on. These vectors may influence the design of an internal language and vice-versa. When we discuss run-time storage in Chapter 5.3 we shall find that even data types of varying size might be addressed indirectly through vectors of pointers, and indeed it may be that all run-time values are directly or indirectly held within vectors.

Encoding individual elements

We shall call the operators and operands that make up a Reverse Polish string its *elements*. In the machine encoding of Reverse Polish it must be possible to separate out the elements from one another and to decide which are operands and which are operators. A good simple rule to start with is to specify that every element will be the same size, one byte, and that the first bit of the byte will say whether the element is an operand or an operator. Assuming a byte consists of eight bits this will then leave room for 128 different operands and 128 different operators. In subsequent examples we shall use the manifest constants OPERATOR and OPERAND to represent the two possible settings of the initial bit.

It is unlikely that an internal language will need more than 128 different operators, even when polymorphic operators are expanded out. Thus the operators can be given internal codes 0, 1, 2, 3, etc., and with luck will not get near 128. Nevertheless it would be wrong to absolutely preclude more than 128, so we shall discuss a way to get round this limit later. The compiler should, of course, be coded with manifest constants for the internal codes, so that the encoding of the compiler can be read and understood without knowing what the individual internal codes are. Moreover this makes the codes easier to change.

With regard to the encoding of an operand, we have already said that its data type is specified by the operator that is applied to it. Thus, if an operand is the object of a '+' operator, this would mean that it is a numeric scalar. All the encoding of the operand needs to specify is which numeric scalar. This can be done in three ways:

(a) by the source form of the operand (e.g. its name if it is a variable), possibly packed in some convenient way;

(b) by an indication of the position of the operand in a dictionary;

(c) by the subscript of the operand within a run-time vector of values. (Clearly this can only apply to operands whose values are stored in a vector.)

It is often possible to hit two of the above birds with the same stone. If there is a static mapping of names into storage locations (e.g. A into position zero, B into position one, C into position two, etc.), then an operand referenced by the number 5 could be deduced to be the variable E and also the variable stored in the fifth position of the vector. Thus the same stone kills birds (a) and (c). Alternatively, as we shall see, the positions of dictionary entries may be directly related to the positions in a vector of run-time values, thus combining (b) and (c).

The most commonly used method of representing operands is (b), the position in a dictionary. We shall assume this is the method used. If this same stone hits (a) or (c) then all the better; otherwise (a) and (c) might be found indirectly by looking at the contents of the dictionary entry—this should give the name of the object and where it is stored.

Encoding dictionaries

We emphasized earlier that the internal program and its associated dictionaries should be regarded as a single entity. Up to now we have been discussing Reverse Polish as an internal language without much thought about the form of the dictionaries. It is time to remedy this defect. A dictionary can be a specially useful aid to making Reverse Polish concise and, in particular, to making it possible to represent operands in a single byte.

When we introduced dictionaries we mentioned two design choices. Firstly dictionary entries could be chosen to have fixed or variable size. Secondly there could be many separate dictionaries (e.g. one for arrays, one for functions, one for scalar variables, one for numeric constants), or alternatively disparate objects could be placd in the same dictionary. When discussing storage management, we introduced a further element of choice: whether to keep data structures such as dictionaries in a contiguous area of storage or as a linked list—we favoured the former. We shall now examine how the desire to represent the internal language concisely affects these choices. Three points can be made.

(1) It does not matter if there are several different dictionaries. In fact it may help. We shall explain this remark in more detail later.

(2) It helps if, within each dictionary, all entries are of the same size and are within a contiguous area. Thus a dictionary can be regarded as a vector of entries and can be referenced using *dictionary subscripts* 0, 1, 2, 3, etc.

Otherwise it may be necessary to reference a dictionary entry by means of a relative pointer giving its distance from the start of the dictionary; this takes more bits than a subscript—for example most dictionaries contain fewer than 128 entries, but many are over 128 bytes in total size.

(3) It helps if there is an exact correspondence between the position of a dictionary entry for a variable and the position of its value. For instance, if a dictionary is a vector of entries all of the same size, and the corresponding run-time values are also stored in a vector, then the Nth dictionary entry can be made to correspond to the Nth run-time value. Alternatively the run-time value could actually lie within the dictionary entry. In either case, if a Reverse Polish element refers to variable N, the same N can be used to find the value of the variable or its name. This is what we meant earlier by killing (c) with the stone that killed (b).

We shall assume in the rest of this discussion that (2) and (3) hold. Thus operands are represented by a subscript that applies both to the dictionary and the run-time vector of values. If (2) and (3) do not hold, as they might not if other factors such as ease of storage management overrode the factors mentioned above, then the encoding of the Reverse Polish will be slightly less concise and/or easy to use.

An example

It is time for an example. Our example shows the encoding of an internal line and its associated dictionary entries. Assume that the very first statement typed during a session is

$$100 \text{ LET } B6 = B6/X - Y$$

Assume further that the dictionary entry for a scalar variable consists of the name of the variable, stored in two bytes, and nothing else. If the name is only a single character, the second byte is filled with the character '.'. When a new variable name is found it is added to the dictionary. Given that the above statement is the first one, the dictionary is null before the statement is translated. Afterwards the dictionary consists of the following six bytes, which represent entries for the three new variable names in the statement:

$$B6X.Y.$$

B6 is entry 0, X is entry 1 and Y is entry 2. The internal form of the statement in our symbolic Reverse Polish is

$$B6 \ B6 \ X \ / \ Y \ - \ \textit{LETNUM}$$

Inside the computer the name B6 is represented as a byte consisting of the OPERAND marker in the first bit, with the dictionary subscript of B6, which is 0, in the remaining bits. We shall write this as OPERAND + 0.

The entire statement, including its header, is represented inside the computer as

$$\text{\textit{header}} \quad \begin{cases} \text{this contains the line-number, 100, and the total length of} \\ \text{the internal line, i.e. 7 + length of header itself in bytes} \end{cases}$$

    OPERAND + 0 (meaning B6)
    OPERAND + 0 (meaning B6)
    OPERAND + 1 (meaning X)
    OPERATOR + internal code for '/' operator
    OPERAND + 2 (meaning Y)
    OPERATOR + internal code for '−' operator
    OPERATOR + *LETNUM*

Within the vector of run-time values, we assume that element 0 gives the value of B6 (since B6 is dictionary entry 0), element 1 is X and element 2 is Y. Thus the run-time system can use these offsets either to address the values of the variables, or, by looking at the dictionary, to find their names. The names might be needed in error messages.

Any further statements that used B6, X or Y would, of course, refer to them using the same dictionary subscripts.

Referencing separate dictionaries

We have represented operands by their dictionary subscripts. The following question arises: if there are several separate dictionaries, is it necessary to specify which dictionary a given operand belongs to? The answer is, perhaps surprisingly, no. This is because the operator that is applied to an operand determines the data type of the operand. Assuming all objects of the same data type lie in the same dictionary, the operator therefore determines which dictionary to use. Hence our earlier claim that multiple dictionaries are no problem. The following example illustrates the point.

Consider the encoding of the function reference SIN(Q), where SIN is entry 3 in a dictionary of built-in function names, and Q also happens to be entry 3 in a separate dictionary containing numeric scalar variables (and perhaps other things besides). Then the Reverse Polish, which in symbolic form is SIN Q *CALLBI1ARG*, is encoded as

    OPERAND + 3 (meaning SIN)
    OPERAND + 3 (meaning Q)
    OPERATOR + *CALLBI1ARG*

When the operator *CALLBI1ARG* is applied to these two operands it resolves the possible ambiguity. The first operand to *CALLBI1ARG* is a built-in function name, and therefore belongs to the dictionary of built-in functions, whereas the second argument is numeric and therefore, if a variable, belongs to the dictionary in which scalar numeric variables appear.

Constants

We have glossed over one point in the above discussion: how to distinguish a constant from a variable, e.g. SIN(X) from SIN(2). An operator gives the data type of its operands, but does not, as we have propounded it, say whether operands are constants or variables. A third possibility is that an operand be the result of another operation, e.g. SIN(X+Y); this, however, can be readily ascertained by looking at the Reverse Polish, e.g. SIN X Y + *CALLBI1ARG*. We could differentiate variables from constants by introducing a set of more specific operators. Thus there could be four operators to do an add, with the following specifications:

ADDCC   add with both operands constants
ADDC1   add with first operand a constant
ADDC2   add with second operand a constant
ADD   add with neither operand a constant.

However, doing this generates a problem familiar to computer scientists, a *combinatorial explosion*. This means that there are so many combinations that a task gets out of hand. It comes up in many forms of artificial intelligence—as a simple example compare a chess program that looks two moves ahead with one that looks four moves ahead.

With our Reverse Polish operators we might be wise to say that, given our expanded polymorphic operators and the like, enough is enough. We do not want any more kinds of operator. We shall thus explore other possibilities. One simple one is to use a bit within each Reverse Polish operand, to say whether it is a variable or a constant.

Another possibility, which appeals because it is both radical and decisive, is to make constants in the internal program look so much like variables that there is no need for the run-time system to know which is which. This works for data types whose values are stored in vectors, and is done by treating a constant as a variable which has an initial value planted in it (i.e. the value of the constant itself) and whose source language name comes from printing its value. Thus the constant 3.1 is a variable with initial value 3.1; if it is ever necessary to print the name of the constant, e.g. in re-creating the source, this is done simply by printing the value as the sequence of characters '3.1'. The implication is that variables and constants go into the same dictionary and their run-time values are intermixed within the same vector. The name field of each dictionary entry corresponding to a constant is set to some special marker to differentiate it from the name of a true variable.

To go back to our previous example, if the source line had been

$$100 \text{ LET } B6 = B6/7 + 8$$

rather than

$$100 \text{ LET } B6 = B6/X - Y$$

then the internal program would have been identical in the two cases. In the new case, however, the dictionary would have been

$$B6 - - - -$$

where '– –' is the special marker to mean a constant, and the value of variable 1 (which is now the constant 7 rather than X) would be initialized to the value 7, and similarly the value of variable 2 would in initialized to 8. If these initial values are to be planted by the translator, it implies that the vector of run-time values is created in advance by the translator, rather than by the pre-run module or the run-time system.

There are, of course, countless other ways of differentiating variables from constants, and we shall cover another in a subsequent section. Indeed you may well find one that suits your circumstances better than either of those described here.

The limitation of 128

Our one-byte-per-element scheme has limits of 128 on the number of different operators and on the number of different operands within any one dictionary. As a general rule, the fewer arbitrary limits that exist within a compiler the better, though it is, of course, inevitable that there will be some limits. Limits that are really bad are those that can only be changed by re-designing the compiler. Hence even if our 128 limit was initially thought to be a reasonable restriction, it would be a serious design flaw if that limit was so enmeshed in the compiler philosophy that it was impractical to lift the limit at a later date. We therefore need an escape mechanism for Reverse Polish elements which, because they break the 128 barrier, will not fit into a single byte. A good way of doing this is to reserve one operator code and one operand code to mean 'escape'. (Codes of 0 or 127 might be good choices.) The escape code is followed by further information in successive bytes. A good rule is always to take the next two bytes, and to use these to supply further operator codes and greater dictionary subscripts. For example the dictionary subscript 268 (which equals $1 \times 256 + 12$) could be represented as the three bytes

OPERAND + *ESCAPE*
1
12

The limit on the number of dictionary entries and on the number of operators then becomes over 64 000, which is unlikely to be a practical limit. (Even so, we should make the number of bytes following the *ESCAPE* a manifest constant with the value 2. We could then subsequently increase it to 3, or even decrease it to 1, if circumstances dictated.) If we had taken only one byte of information after an *ESCAPE*, this would have allowed only 256 further possibilities, which might not be enough to kill completely the problem of reaching the limit.

(It is perhaps worth referring back, at this point, to our earlier claim from Chapter 2.11 that redundant dictionary entries do not matter. There is a small extra cost if a dictionary is pushed over the 128 limit as a result of these, thus making the internal program longer, because references to variables over the limit take extra bytes. However this point does not have sufficient force to destroy our claim.)

Consequences of variable-length elements

Our original standpoint was that each Reverse Polish element be one byte. This wall has now been breached by the three-byte escape element. Given that the wall has broken, do we lose anything by breaching it further and specifying lots of further multi-byte elements? To answer this, it is best to consider the advantages of the original one-byte rule. These are two-fold: (1) the Reverse Polish is compact; (2) it is easy to scan. If it is only a minority of elements that are multi-byte, then the first advantage is not significantly affected. To evaluate the second it is necessary to look at the way Reverse Polish is processed. There are three likely uses:

(a) for running the program.
(b) for the pre-run module (e.g. to match FOR and NEXT statements).
(c) for re-creating the source.

If the Reverse Polish is to be processed sequentially element by element, as it might be in case (a), there is no great disadvantage in having elements of variable size. However, if it is processed selectively, there are disadvantages. For example, consider the task of scanning a Reverse Polish string to see if it contains a *FOR* operator. If each element is one byte this is simple to do; if not, it may be that, say, the second byte of a multi-byte element may chance to be the same as the code for a *FOR* operator. Selective searches such as this, which may well be used in (b) and (c) above, are impossible. Instead an element-by-element search is needed, in order to keep track of the length of elements; if the only multi-byte elements are escape elements, it may just be practical to perform operations such as 'search for *FOR* or *ESCAPE*' rather than an element-by-element search.

Thus, to summarize, the advantage of ease of scanning is lost even if there are only a few multi-byte elements, but the advantage of conciseness is not lost unless the multi-byte elements are frequently used and are inherently wasteful of space.

Opening the floodgates

Once the floodgates of multi-byte elements are open, a host of possibilities is available. Operators can be followed by extra 'information fields'. For instance, to go back to a matter referenced early in Chapter 3.1, a NEXT operator could be followed by a pointer (stored, say, in the next two bytes) to the corresponding FOR. Similarly the FOR could point at the NEXT.

In addition it becomes practical to represent operands in source form rather than through a dictionary subscript. For example, if there was no dictionary of variable names, the name X1 could be stored as the character 'X' followed by the character '1', or some other suitable encoding of the source name. Given that this would not fit into a single byte, it would trigger the escape mechanism. If names could be longer, a more elaborate escape mechanism would be needed. The very complication of such mechanisms is, of course, one of the reasons why compilers use dictionaries covering every kind of variable. It is quite common, however, for compilers to represent constants in source form, particularly when our device for representing constants as variables is inappropriate. This applies particularly to string constants, which are discussed at the end of this chapter, and which introduce a further possible exception to the one-byte rule.

Combining operands into operators

The discussion has been pretty dirty so far and is about to become worse—'obscene' or 'pornographic' would perhaps describe it. It is time, therefore, for the squeamish, if there are any that remain, to depart. Come back in the next section or, if you cannot face that, skip the whole of the rest of this chapter.

We shall now discuss how to gain a few extra bits in the internal representation. The method can be applied to any operator whose operand(s) are guaranteed never to be the result of another operator. This is true, for example, in many BASICs of operators that take line-numbers as operands. Typically a GOTO operator must be supplied a constant line-number as its operand—statements such as GOTO X+3 being forbidden. If so, the strict Reverse Polish notation can be abandoned with a resultant gain in conciseness. One possibility is to place the operand of GOTO as an 'information field' immediately following the GOTO. This field might occupy, say, two bytes. The GOTO plus its extra bytes is regarded as a single operator. Thus 'GOTO 500' is treated as one operator, not the operator *GOTO* applied to the operand 500. The advantage is that you get a few extra bits for encoding the line-number. A line-number can straddle a complete two bytes—there need be no bit at the start to say 'this is an operand', etc. Such a nasty trick can be particularly useful if line-numbers are respresented in source form rather than via a dictionary.

Re-creation and text

If the Reverse Polish is to be designed to allow re-creation of the source, this implies that comments must be kept in the Reverse Polish. Thus in BASIC a REM statement needs to be encoded in a suitable way. Perhaps the best way is to introduce a Reverse Polish operator, called *REM*, and *follow* it with the text of the comment, which itself is followed by some terminator character. The advantage of this is that when the Reverse Polish is run, the operator

REM will be encountered at the very start of the statement and the rest of the statement can immediately be ignored. (The length field in the header can be used to find where the next statement lies.) Only the re-creator module would look at the text following the *REM*.

Even if re-creation is not needed there may be a need to include pieces of text within the Reverse Polish. One likely example is the DATA statement in the BASIC language.

Consider the BASIC program

```
10 DATA 33
20 READ X
30 RESTORE
40 READ X$
```

The data item 33 is first read as a number and then as a string. Thus the data type of the item 33 actually varies at run-time. If you are compiling a language with this property, the translator does best to leave the relevant items in source form. It cannot take any decision on the internal form the item should take (e.g. a numeric form or a string form). Moreover, since the translator cannot process individual items within the DATA statement, it seems sensible to leave the entire DATA statement in source form. Thus it can be encoded, in a similar way to REM above, by an operator called *DATA* followed by the text of the DATA statement itself.

A third likely use of text within the internal language is for string constants. Since these have variable length, it may not be convenient to place them within a dictionary, nor within a vector of run-time values. Thus they are commonly left in source form. However, unlike the text in REM and DATA statements, which can conveniently be placed at the end of the internal line, string constants occur as operands within expressions, and must precede the operator to which they are applied. To ease scanning, it is convenient to precede the text of each string constant by a byte giving its length. This 'length byte' is itself preceded by a special marker, which we shall call *STRCONST*. Given this convention the sample BASIC statement

LET A$ = "PIG"

would be represented internally as

OPERAND + dictionary subscript for A$
OPERAND + *STRCONST*
3 (i.e. length of "PIG")
"P"
"I"
"G"
OPERATOR + *LETSTR*

The length field helps the run-time system in looking beyond the string constant to find what operator is to be applied to it.

Chapter 3.4

A Brief Summary

We have selected an internal language based on Reverse Polish notation. We have not specified an exact design, because this depends greatly on your source language, but we have highlighted likely problems and made suggestions. It is up to you whether you wish to stick to pure Reverse Polish or to include dirty *ad hoc* additions for dealing with such things as variable-length strings of text or for achieving extra conciseness. Even if you maintain purity you can keep Reverse Polish reasonably—though not optimally—concise; a particular aid to conciseness is good dictionary design. Typically a program in Reverse Polish plus its associated dictionaries is only a quarter to a half the size of the original source program. Moreover it might be an order of magnitude faster to run a Reverse Polish program than the original source form. Thus Reverse Polish certainly earns its keep.

We shall conclude by discussing two specialized points, one concerned with error checking and the other with 'puns'.

Error checking

The translator should eliminate all possible errors before the internal language is produced. Statements containing errors do not make it to the internal program. The result is that other modules which use the internal program can rely on the property that, within each line, the internal program is syntactically correct; these other modules are therefore relieved of a good deal of error-checking work. They know, for example, that the operator '+' must be preceded by two numeric operands. (There is still a place for the occasional redundant check to make sure everything is as it should be; we shall discuss this under 'System errors' in Part 7.) The checking of context-dependent relationships between lines, such as functions being declared, cannot be performed by the translator, but must be delayed until later modules. This does not, however, destroy the principle of correctness within each line.

Line-numbers and other puns

In many interactive languages, including BASIC, the line-numbers serve two purposes. Firstly, they are used for editing the user's program, and secondly they are used as 'labels' that are the destinations of GOTOs and similar statements. Most languages contain examples of such 'puns', where the same symbol has more than one possible meaning; do not let them deceive you when you design the internal language and its dictionaries.

For example when dealing with the line-number pun, first consider whether you want a dictionary of *all* line-numbers to help editing. If you reject such a dictionary, then consider the second use of line-numbers, and evaluate whether you need a 'label dictionary' of those line-numbers used on GOTOs and similar statements. You may well decide that such a dictionary is valuable, in the same way as a dictionary of the variable names used in a program is valuable. (If you decided to have a label dictionary, an entry might consist of the name of the label followed by a pointer to the internal line to which the label was attached; this pointer would be filled in by the pre-run module.)

Further reading

For further reading on internal language design see Witty (1977), who describes a slightly impure Reverse Polish notation geared to fast execution; he also gives some algorithms for converting to Reverse Polish. Another technique worth reading about is *indirect threaded code* (Dewar, 1975; Dewar and McCann, 1977); this is a variant of the threaded-code method referenced earlier, and is a good way of achieving fast execution of Reverse Polish; it is particularly useful if the source language is one of those unusual ones that allow the meaning of objects such as operators to change during a run.

For a description of a source language that is close to Reverse Polish notation see papers on FORTH (Moore and Rather, 1973). FORTH is a simple, neat and powerful system which, partly as a result of the use of Reverse Polish notation, can be implemented in a small amount of store (James, 1978).

Finally, good sources of ideas on internal languages are the descriptions of compilers found in popular computing magazines. But beware: though some of these compilers are excellent, many are awful.

Part 4

THE TRANSLATOR

Chapter 4.1

Overall Translator Organization

The tasks of the translator, as we stated when we summarized the compiler in Chapter 2.16, are to perform the following actions for each source line.

(a) *Syntactic actions*. The scanning of the source line, as received from the input/output module, to check its syntax and report any errors back to the user.

(b) *Semantic actions*. The translating of the source line into its internal language equivalent. These actions are called 'semantic' because they define the meaning of the source line in terms of the internal language. As a source line is translated, its internal language equivalent is built up in a temporary buffer called the *internal line*. When the internal line has been successfully completed, it is passed to the editor for incorporation into the internal program.

There are two important principles affecting the translator's actions. Firstly, each source line is translated as an entity in itself, independent of all the other source lines; secondly, no line which has been found to contain a syntax error makes it to the internal program.

Internal languages close to the source language

We are assuming that the internal language is the Reverse Polish notation outlined in the previous Part. If your internal language is closer to the source language than Reverse Polish, your translation task is much simpler; in this case you may be thinking how wise you are, because you can now skip a good deal of this Part of the book. Unfortunately the position is not simple. Your compiler still needs to figure out what each source statement means; all you have done is shift this task from your translator to your run-time system. Thus most of this Part is still relevant to you, though you can, if you like, get some scissors and cut out some of the pages and then paste them back into Part 5.

One-pass translators and multi-pass translators

The part of the translator which performs the syntactic actions is called the *parser*. Most source languages are designed to be scanned from left to right, and

127

we shall assume this to be so (though there are exceptions, such as APL). It is possible to intersperse semantic actions with syntactic actions; in this case the internal line is gradually built up as the scan proceeds along the source line. A translator that does this is called a *one-pass* translator.

An alternative is a *two-pass* translator, which first peforms the syntactic actions and then re-scans the source line to perform the semantic actions. In practice the first pass of such a translator usually converts the source language to an intermediate form, such as a tree, and the second pass scans this intermediate form. The reason for producing an intermediate form is that the second pass does not need to repeat analysis that has already been performed in the first pass. Thus if the intermediate form is a tree, this can reflect information about the structure of the source line, as gleaned by the first pass.

Many translators take even more than two passes, and some take as many as a hundred passes! The worst translators in this respect are those with complicated source languages and those which have machine code as the internal language. Multi-pass translators gradually convert the source program nearer and nearer to the internal form, passing through several intermediate forms on the way. Not only the program but also its associated tables may pass through intermediate forms, and some passes of the compiler may be solely concerned with manipulating tables.

There are certain circumstances which cause designers to favour multi-pass translators, and we shall examine these to see their relevance to incremental compilers.

One special reason for a multi-pass translator is that the machine on which the translator runs is relatively small. If a one-pass translator would occupy 10 000 instructions and the machine can hold only 2000 instructions, then clearly some splitting up is necessary. Splitting up tends to make the translator bigger, and moreover it is never possible to split into exactly equal natural divisions. Although our 10 000 instruction translator could theoretically be split up into five separate passes of exactly 2000 instructions each, in practice it would need to be split up into ten or more. This kind of splitting, where the code for each pass is swopped in from backing store, is impractical for an incremental compiler since it would be hopelessly slow. This is because an incremental compiler would need to go through every pass for each line that was typed in, whereas a batch compiler can process the entire source program as one unit.

A second reason why a translator may be split into separate passes is to make it perform better in a virtual storage environment. In such an environment, it is better to have small sections of code which are heavily used and then discarded, as each pass of a multi-pass translator might be, rather than a larger section of code, such as a one-pass translator, where each instruction is used comparatively less frequently. (See Denning (1970) for a discussion of 'working sets'.) Again, however, this kind of splitting is really a strategy for batch compilers rather than incremental ones.

Finally a translator may be split into passes because it is so complicated that no-one can understand it properly until it is packaged into smaller tasks. We are assuming in this book that your internal language is Reverse Polish, and that your source language is relatively simple. Thus again there is no case for splitting.

The conclusion is, therefore, that none of the reasons for making the translator multi-pass holds, and we shall hence assume that your translator is one-pass, and that semantic actions are interspersed with syntactic ones. If the translator were producing machine-code there would be a stronger case for making it multi-pass, but even in this case there are plenty of successful one-pass translators; for example most PASCAL translators work in one pass.

A good way of looking at a one-pass translator is to think of it as a parser with the semantic actions hung on in the appropriate places.

The art of modularization

A danger with a one-pass translator is that it can become a large hunk of code, incomprehensible to everyone except its author, and eventually incomprehensible even to him. It is therefore important to divide the translator into logically separate modular units. Some of these units may be analogous to the various passes of a multi-pass translator, though, given a one-pass translator, the interactions between modules are stronger as they all work together to process each source line.

Modularization is, indeed, one of the arts of programming. Any fool can chop a program into bits, but choosing the bits to be logically coherent and self-contained requires ability. It is a valuable ability. The difficulty of understanding a program probably goes up in proportion to the square of its size. Thus if you split a 1000 line program into two self-contained parts—say one of 500 lines and the other of 550 lines, since there is bound to be a small increase in size as a result of the division—then the whole thing should be nearly twice as easy to understand. However if the two parts have all kinds of curious interactions between them, so that neither can really be treated in isolation, then the whole thing will be just as hard to understand as the original.

Modularization can be carried out at several levels. Thus the entire compiler can be split up into modules, as we discussed in Chapter 2.16, according to the functions the compiler must perform. Some of these modules, such as the translator, can themselves be split up into lower-level modules, until the entire compiler is broken down into units of manageable size.

The effort required in finding a good modularization highlights a general point. Big programs are nothing like small programs. Anyone can write small programs, but you can only write a big program successfully if your practices are good and your standards are high.

Criteria for division into modules

Modularization would not be an art if it could be achieved by applying a few simple criteria. In practice there is always a host of criteria, some mutually conflicting. There is, however, no dearth of advice. There is an army of 'programming methodology' experts who go round giving lucid and convincing reasons why their own criteria for choosing sub-divisions are the best ones. One of our favourites is Parnas (1972), whose criterion is 'information hiding'. In his scheme all the subroutines that deal with one particular data structure are grouped together in one module. Outside this module, nothing need be known about that data structure. The information about the data structure is thus hidden from the world outside, and any change in the data structure only necessitates changing one module. This achieves ease of maintenance.

One's approach to these programming philosophies is much the same as to those philosophies which propound how we go about our daily lives. Most philosophies have some good in them; some people choose to pursue one philosophy with religious fervour whereas others adopt a somewhat *ad hoc* mixture. A few people take perverse pleasure in doing the opposite of what the preachers say.

Policy on examples

Our policy for examples of source-language constructs is to use the BASIC language, since this is likely to be a common denominator of most readers. We should re-emphasize that it is *not* an assumption that your source language is necessarily BASIC or anything like it.

Later on in this Part of the book, and in subsequent Parts, we introduce sample snippets of code taken from the compiler. These pieces of code would, of course, be written in your encoding language. Here our examples do not use one particular encoding language, but are written in a 'typical' notation common to most modern block-structured languages. The idea is that the notation should be readily understandable, and easy to translate into your encoding language—which we hope contains some concepts of block structure. The following are some examples of our notation:

```
/* a comment   */
COUNT : = 0                    /* assignment statement */
OPSTACK[PTR] : = 0             /* reference to element of array OPSTACK*/
SCANEXPRESSION                 /* call a subroutine with no arguments */
UNSTACKVALUE (X)               /* call a subroutine with the argument X */

WHILE  ...  DO                      /* looping construct */
BEGIN
   :
   :
END
IF  ...  THEN  ...                  /* conditional statement */
IF  ...  THEN  ...  ELSE  ...   /* ELSE clause */
RETURN (X)                          /* return from function, giving
                                       X as its value */
```

Chapter 4.2

Lexical Analysis

Turning from philosophies to practical fact, one module which is frequently separated out within a translator is the *lexical analysis* module. Lexical analysis is the scanning of the source line to divide it into its constituent symbols.

As an example of lexical analysis consider the BASIC statement

$$100 \text{ IF B1} > = 23.6 \text{ THEN } 500$$

The constituents of this line are 100, IF, B1, '>=', 23.6, THEN, 500 and 'newline'. Such units, the fundamental building blocks of programs, are called *tokens*. A lexical analyser takes a source line and divides it up into tokens. In the textbook model, the lexical analyser is painted as a logically separate 'front-end' to the translator. It acts as a subroutine to the parser and has a name such as GETTOKEN. Every time the parser wants to advance its scan it calls GETTOKEN, which duly provides a token in a suitably coded form.

There is no hard and fast rule as to what a token is. For instance in the BASIC statement

$$\text{PRINT USING A1\$: ``STRING'',23.6E9}$$

it would be possible to treat PRINT USING as a single token (particularly if USING must always be preceded by PRINT so that the two form a natural unit) or as two separate ones. Similarly 23.6E9 could be regarded as one token or as 23.6 followed by E9. Furthermore the string constant 'STRING' might be treated as one token or as several. The exact choice of tokens depends on the mutual convenience of the lexical analyser and the parser; making a good choice is part of the art of interface design.

Comments and spaces

In batch compilers one task of the lexical analyser is to delete those parts of the source program that are exclusively concerned with its readability rather than its meaning. Such readability aids include comments and *non-significant* spaces (i.e. spaces that do not come within string constants or other texts).

In interactive compilers, comments and non-significant spaces can only be deleted if the editor keeps the user's program in source form. If the source program is re-created from the internal program, the lexical analyser must not delete comments, but it can delete non-significant spaces provided that the source is not being recreated with the exact original spacing. We shall assume in the rest of this book that non-significant spaces are deleted. The lexical analyser therefore relieves the rest of the translator of the tiresome task of skipping non-significant spaces—it is particularly tiresome if the source language allows keywords to be spaced out, e.g. BEGIN to be spelt as 'B E G I N' or GOTO as 'GO TO'.

Advantage of separation

One advantage of making the lexical analyser a separate module is that it is a clean way of splitting up the translator. The lexical analyser does all the fiddling about with individual characters, thus allowing the rest of the translator to work in the more natural unit of a token. A further advantage of separating off lexical analysis is that it isolates the task of communicating with the user's input device. To some extent the use of a separate input/output module achieves this already, but some differences in input devices might have implications beyond this module. For instance your compiler might be wanted on a computer with an input device that supported delimiters such as IF and THEN as single keys. To cater for such a device you just re-write the lexical-analysis module—indeed you would just need to simplify it, given that some of its tasks are now done by hardware.

Disadvantage of separation

A possible disadvantage of a separate lexical-analysis module is that its textbook representation as a single self-contained subroutine does not always apply. Ideally the lexical analyser should have a set of simple universal rules for dividing text into tokens; the rest of the translator then deals with the job of analysing the syntax and semantics of these tokens.

However, consider the following sample lines in the BASIC language:

```
IF A = 300 THEN 300
REM IF OVERFLOW THEN STOP AT 300
DATA 300, THEN
PRINT "THEN"'
OLD THEN
```

All five lines contain the word THEN, but only in the first line is it used as a BASIC keyword. Similarly the number 300 is used with several different meanings. Thus the lexical analyser needs to do some syntactic analysis to distinguish between the different contexts, or it needs to communicate continually with the parser to find out what the context is. In BASIC, therefore—and the same applies to most other interactive languages—the idealized textbook model may be fine for teachers, but it is not perfect for people actually writing production compilers.

Specifying separate subroutines

If this applies to your source language, there is no need to despair of the concept of a separate lexical-analysis module. All you need to do is to abandon the idea that the lexical analyser is a single subroutine, GETTOKEN, but instead to make it a set of subroutines that are called from different points in the parser depending on context. Sample subroutines might be GETKEYWORD, GET-FILENAME and GETCOMMENT. Only the first of these would treat THEN as a keyword. For those unfamiliar with text scanning we give possible specifications of GETKEYWORD and GETFILENAME, together with a routine GETOPERAND. (They are actually functions rather than subroutines.)

(1) The function GETKEYWORD tries to match the characters beginning at the current position in the input buffer against entries in a table of keywords. If it finds a match it returns some indicator of what it has found; if it fails it returns a special value 'FAIL'.

(2) The function GETFILENAME gets the file name at the current position in the input buffer. This routine might scan ahead until some terminating character is found; if the text in between is not a syntactically legal file name it gives some error indication. Otherwise it returns a pointer to the first character of the file name, together with the length of the file name.

(3) The function GETOPERAND gets an operand (i.e. a variable name or a constant) from the input buffer. In a few compilers GETOPERAND might be allowed to build a preliminary dictionary entry for each new operand it finds, though usually there is a dividing line which says the lexical analyser should do the fiddly little tasks rather than major ones like building dictionaries.

Lexical analysis at a lower level

An alternative approach to the lexical analyser is to make it a less ambitious module, which simply scans and classifies individual characters, and leaves the parser to package these into tokens. Sample subroutines in the lexical analyser might then be as follows:

(1) The function NEXTCH gets the next significant character and classifies it—possible categories might be 'letter', 'digit', 'operator character', etc. The value of the function is the class of the character.

(2) The function TRYLETTER takes the next significant character and returns the value *true* if this is a letter.

Don't worry if you are confused by all this freedom of choice. Simply start by specifying a few lexical-analysis subroutines that appear appropriate to your source language. When you encode the parser, your set of lexical-analysis subroutines will slowly grow, and will eventually either 'come right' in that they converge to a stable and useful set, or 'go wrong' in that you never seem to have the right subroutine for the task in hand. In the latter case scrap everything, and try another tack.

There is even a completely different approach to explore if you like. This is the use of grammars, as described in Chapter 3 of Gries (1971). These can lead to quite neat methods, particularly when the textbook situation applies.

Other modules

The lexical analyser is the only part of the translator that we propound as a separate module. The modularization of the rest of the translator is dependent on the art of the reader and the philosophies he espouses.

Chapter 4.3

Grammars

An English grammar is a set of rules for determining whether an English sentence is syntactically correct. Thus the sentence 'the cat sat on the mat' obeys the grammatical rules whereas the sentence 'the cats sits on mat the' fails miserably. Grammar is concerned with form, not meaning. Thus the meaningless sentence 'desks eat religion' is quite acceptable grammatically.

A grammar for a programming language serves a similar function to a grammar for a spoken language; it determines whether programs are syntactically correct. (There are more advanced grammars concerned with the semantics of programming languages, but these need not concern us here as they are seldom used in production compilers.) Grammars were first used solely as an aid to specifying a language. If the user manual contains a precise grammatical specification of the source language, the user knows exactly what he can write and what he cannot. We shall discuss this use of grammars first.

Grammars for language definition

Unlike English, programming languages have grammatical rules that are precise and exact. Moreover the rules are independent of geographical location, unlike the English language which, after crossing the Atlantic, has gotten mangled. Most programming languages use English keywords (IF, PRINT, etc.). However even if these are changed to some other language the rules for writing programs remain unchanged—there is no change in the order of tokens or anything like that.

Because of their preciseness and universality, grammars for programming languages can with advantage be described in a formal mathematical notation. Nevertheless there are great dangers in the over-use of mathematical formalism. If a user manual looks like a mathematical thesis, most people will never look at it. Many languages have suffered from being presented to the world in a form the world does not understand. It is important to have a formal notation that is both precise and *easy for ordinary people to read*.

Backus–Naur form

The basis of most grammars used for specifying syntax is *Backus—Naur Form*, which is usually abbreviated to *BNF*. This was used in the original description of the Algol 60 language (Naur *et al*., 1960) and was a classic in its time. Recently it has been adapted to make it easier to read, and the use of some form of BNF to specify a language is extremely common in user manuals.

You may well be already familiar with such notations but in case not we shall give a brief explanation. We shall take as example the notation used to define BASIC in the ANSI standard definition.

A grammar can be defined by first defining the lowest-level objects, like variables and constants, and then defining successively higher-level objects in terms of these. At the very top of the hierarchy, the final goal is achieved by defining a program. Thus an expression is defined in terms of variables and constants, and then in turn a LET statement is defined in terms of expressions. Finally a possible constituent of a program is a LET statement.

In the notation used in the BASIC standard, objects that are defined in the grammar are given lower-case names (like 'expression') to distinguish them from fixed keywords such as 'THEN'. The lower-case names may include hyphens (e.g. 'gosub-statement'), and each name is chosen to be as meaningful as possible. An example of the definition of an object is

next-statement = NEXT simple-numeric-variable

We shall call this a *rule* of the grammar. The above rule defines the object 'next-statement' to consist of the keyword NEXT followed by a simple-numeric-variable. Elsewhere in the grammar there would be a definition of a simple-numeric-variable.

Some constructions in languages have alternative forms; others allow parts to be omitted and/or indefinitely repeated. The notation used to express these is as follows:

x/y/. . .	means	either x or y or . . . .
x?	means	x may optionally be omitted
x*	means	x may be repeated any number of times (including 0)

Using this notation the object 'digit' may be defined as

digit = 0/1/2/3/4/5/6/7/8/9

and then the object 'integer' may be defined in terms of 'digit' by

integer = digit digit*

meaning that an integer consists of one digit followed by indefinitely many further digits. In practice it is likely that a compiler would have some restriction on the size of integers, e.g. that they be less than 2^{31}. Restrictions like these are not normally specified in the grammar, partly because it is difficult to do and partly because the grammar is used to represent an ideal language rather than a subset for one particular computer. Such restrictions are usually specified in English rather than in the grammatical notation, and form an Appendix to the grammar.

In addition to the use of '/', '*', and '?' to specify grammatical rules, parentheses can be used to group objects together. For instance a BASIC INPUT statement can be defined as

input-statement = INPUT variable (, variable)*

meaning that after the first variable there may be indefinitely many repeats of the construct that consists of a comma followed by a variable. Similarly a RESET statement can be defined

reset-statement = RESET (# numeric-expression)?

meaning that the '#' and numeric-expression following RESET are optional (but if one is present they must both be).

The symbols used in specifying a grammar, such as '*', '?', '/' and the parentheses described above are called *meta-symbols*. These form part of the *meta-language*, i.e. the language to define a language. Ideally the meta-symbols should be distinct from the symbols in the language being defined. This is not true in BASIC because BASIC uses '*' for multiplication, '/' for division, etc., within the language. This potential ambiguity is resolved by using names such as 'asterisk' and 'slash' to represent the BASIC multiplication and division operators. Elsewhere there is a definition (in English) of what 'asterisk' and 'slash' mean. (In the definition of BASIC all punctuation characters are actually represented by names. Thus in the above example of 'input-statement' our explicit comma would have been written as 'comma'.)

Recursion

Some grammars involve *self-recursive definitions* where objects are defined in terms of themselves. Thus we could have defined an integer as

integer = digit integer?

meaning that an integer consists of a digit optionally followed by an integer. Such self-recursion is hard to read if you are not used to it, and can usually be avoided by the use of the asterisk meta-symbol, as in our previous definition of 'integer'.

A situation which is usually not avoidable is *mutual recursion*, where two objects are each defined, directly or indirectly, in terms of the other. An example is the following over-simplified grammar for an expression:

operator	= + / −
operand	= variable / constant
	/ left-parenthesis expression right-parenthesis
expression	= operand operator operand

Here an operand is defined in terms of an expression and vice-versa. (If you want to look ahead, the next chapter contains a more complete grammar for an expression, which contains relatively deep and complicated mutual recursion. It is in the section entitled 'Coding SCANEXPRESSION using recursive descent'.)

Given that most language definitions contain mutual recursion, it is something we must live with; it necessarily makes syntax definitions harder to read and has further implications on parsing, which we shall raise later.

Defects of BNF grammars

The main defect of BNF grammars is that they are incapable of describing certain interdependencies between different units in a program. In BASIC, for example, the variable name on a NEXT statement must match the variable name on the corresponding FOR; moreover if the name of a user-defined function is used it must be defined by a DEF statement somewhere in the program, and there must be only one such DEF statement for each function. BNF-type grammars are fundamentally incapable of describing rules like these. In technical terms BNF is a *context-free grammar*, whereas the above rules are examples where the syntax is context-dependent. Almost any real programming language contains context-dependent rules. Since such rules cannot be described in BNF, they are usually described in English in the language definition.

Interestingly the rules which BNF cannot describe are in practice the same ones that an incremental compiler cannot check when it analyses a single statement. (They would not be the same if there were context-dependent rules that applied *within* a statement, e.g. a statement which required the same variable name to occur in two different places within the statement. However, such things are rare in practice.) This is because the incremental compiler, like BNF, cannot examine the context in which a statement is used.

To avoid tedious repetition we shall assume in the rest of this book that when we say a language is specified by a grammar, we really mean that it is just the context-free part that is specified.

Summary of use of BNF for language definition

Given the limitation that BNF grammars can only specify part of the syntax of a language, are they worth using at all? The answer is a resounding yes; it is one of those cases where a partial solution is much better than no solution, and this has been proved by the success of BNF grammars in the field.

When you write your user manual, accept without question the need to specify syntax in a formal way, and use BNF to accomplish this unless you have strong reasons to the contrary.

There do exist more complex grammars that are capable of specifying context-dependence, but they do not interest us here. You may understand them yourself but the bulk of the readers of your manual will not.

Chapter 4.4

Using Grammars for Parsing

Given that the syntax of a language has been specified by a grammar, a further attractive possibility is opened. This is to use the grammar as an aid to writing the compiler. It can be done in several ways.

One is to use a general-purpose parsing program. You feed it the grammar of your source language, and it is then capable of parsing statements typed by the user to see if they conform to the grammar. A second possibility is a *parser generator*. A parser generator is likewise fed the grammar of your source language, but, rather than acting as a parser itself, it generates a parser for the given grammar. This parser is output as a program in some suitable programming language.

An enormous amount of effort has been spent in developing these automatic tools. The effort has been rather disproportionate, given that parsing is only a small part of a compiler. A huge number of automatic parsing tools have been written, most of which have been dead and forgotten within a few years of their birth. A few however are good and have stood the test of time. You may well find one available on your computer.

It takes a while to master the use of these tools. The grammars that they take as input may need to be encoded very carefully, and there may be several restrictions, particularly on the forms of recursion that are allowed. Moreover if you make a mistake in specifying a grammar—and you surely will—then it may be hard to find. However once the tool has been mastered it can offer two big advantages. Firstly the parser is relatively easy to write—it just consists of encoding the grammar; secondly, you can have reasonable confidence that the parser corresponds to the language you have specified in your user manual.

Because there ain't no such thing as a free lunch, there are, of course, some disadvantages. One is that many of these tools are slow and lumbering. Another is that few are geared to interactive work. A third is that when a user program contains a syntax error, the error reporting is often poor. Some automatically generated parsers only produce one form of error message. They just say 'syntax error' and the poor user has to figure out what is wrong.

To summarize, if you are already familiar with one of these tools and have confidence in it, by all means use it. This applies particularly if the syntax of your source language is complicated, and hence automation saves more work. On the other hand, if you have never used one of these tools, or have not got one available, you are not at a great disadvantage.

For a good tutorial paper on these tools see Feldman and Gries (1968).

An alternative to full automation

Our tone so far has been rather Philistine. The computer scientist's favourite research area has been dismissed as of marginal use and relevance, at least in our field of interactive compilers. We are not, however, advocating a complete return to the stone age, where parsers are written in a totally *ad hoc* manner, ignoring the grammar altogether. The chances of getting an *ad hoc* parser correct, in that it recognizes the exact syntax described by the grammar in the user manual, are remote. What we want to do is to present, to the reader who has not come across it before, the method of *recursive descent*. This is not an automatic method, but it does make direct use of the grammar of the language.

Recursive descent

In the method of recursive descent, a *scanning procedure* is written to correspond to each object defined by the grammar. The scanning procedure attempts to match that object against the current token(s) of the source line; if it fails it gives an error; if it succeeds it advances the scan of the source line beyond the object it has found.

Assume, for example, the source line is

$$\text{LET A1} = \text{X}+3$$
$$\uparrow$$

where the arrow indicates the position of the scanning pointer. Assume also that at this point the scanning procedure for the syntactic object 'variable' is called. This recognizes the token A1 as a variable and hence advances the scanning pointer to the position shown below

$$\text{LET A1} = \text{X}+3$$
$$\uparrow$$

It is best to use a systematic naming convention for scanning procedures, and make the names correspond to those used in the grammar. Thus we shall use the name SCANVARIABLE for the scanning procedure for a variable, SCANEXPRESSION for the scanning procedure for an expression, and so on.

With this convention, corresponding to the grammatical rule

let-statement = LET variable equals expression

the recursive-descent method has the scanning procedure

SCANLET /* call scanning procedure for LET */
. . .

SCANVARIABLE

. . .

SCANEQUALS

. . .

SCANEXPRESSION

. . .

SCANNEWLINE

Each occurrence of three dots (. . .) represents a possible semantic action. As we have said, we are assuming a one-pass translator with semantic and syntactic actions interspersed. We shall discuss, later in this chapter and in the next ones, the form that some of the semantic actions might take.

Each scanning procedure should try to match the largest piece of source it can. Thus SCANEXPRESSION, when trying to match the source 'X+3', *could* just match the X, since this is a valid expression, but it *should* match the entire 'X+3'. Then the next scanning procedure to be called, SCANNEWLINE, can find its right goal.

Alternatives and repetitions

Many objects in a grammar are defined in terms of alternatives, possible repetitions, etc. These are carried over into corresponding alternatives and repetitions in the scanning procedure. Thus corresponding to the rule

input-statement = INPUT variable (, variable)*

there would be a scanning procedure

SCANINPUT

. . .

SCANVARIABLE

. . .

WHILE BUFFER[PTR] = "," DO
BEGIN SCANCOMMA

. . .

SCANVARIABLE

. . .

END

. . .

SCANNEWLINE

where it is assumed that the source line is in a character array called BUFFER, and the index PTR points at the currently scanned character. (Thus PTR is advanced by the scanning procedures when they match something.)

The above procedure could, if desired, be re-coded to make it slightly smaller, e.g. to eliminate the double call of SCANVARIABLE. Provided such re-codings do not make the procedure hard to understand, they are to be welcomed and, indeed, are commonly used in practice.

As an example of alternatives, consider the rule

print-delimiter = , / ;

The corresponding scanning procedure would be

IF BUFFER[PTR] = ",". THEN SCANCOMMA
                         ELSE SCANSEMICOLON

A procedure at the lowest level

So far we have only shown scanning procedures which call other scanning procedures. At some stage this buck passing must stop, and a scanning procedure must actually do something. An example of such a procedure is SCANCOMMA, which might take the form

IF BUFFER[PTR] ≠ "," THEN ERROR ("MISSING COMMA")
ADVANCESCAN1

The ADVANCESCAN1 procedure advances the scan one character. Superficially you might think this operation is just PTR=PTR+1, and therefore hardly merits a procedure call, let alone one whose name is longer than the action it performs. However, the problem is that advancing the scan may have to skip non-significant characters such as spaces, and hence there is a bit of work to do. ADVANCESCAN1 is a procedure that forms part of the lexical analyser, which we have already discussed.

Eliminating redundant tests

When the SCANCOMMA procedure is used to look for a print-delimiter it is called in the context

IF BUFFER[PTR] ≠ "," THEN SCANCOMMA

Thus it is already known that a comma has been found when SCANCOMMA is called, but the first action of SCANCOMMA is to test again if the current character is a comma. The same thing applies to its use when scanning an input-statement.

This inefficiency may not be greatly important, but it has an air of untidiness about it, which is better swept away. We shall therefore use a new function with the name CHECKCOMMA which checks whether the current symbol is a comma; if not it returns the result *false*; if it is a comma, it advances the scan and returns the result *true*. Thus the code for CHECKCOMMA is

IF BUFFER[PTR] = "," THEN RETURN (FALSE)
ADVANCESCAN1
RETURN (TRUE)

We shall use similar procedures CHECKMINUS, CHECKPLUS, etc., to check other symbols. Given the existence of CHECKCOMMA the scanning routine for a print-delimiter becomes

IF NOT CHECKCOMMA THEN SCANSEMICOLON

Selecting the correct option

Consider a hypothetical superset of BASIC which allows any identifier to be used as a variable, and, moreover, allows the keyword LET to be omitted from the start of assignment statements. Thus a variable can be given the name IF and an assignment statement can be written

IF = 3

Compare this with the normal BASIC IF statement

IF A = 3 THEN 100

The recursive-descent parser must not, on scanning IF = 3, identify it as an IF statement. Once a wrong path such as this has been followed, and resultant semantic actions have been performed, there is no going back to try another possibility. Hence the condition used to select which alternative grammatical rule to take (e.g. whether to take the above as let-statement or as if-statement) must be guaranteed to pick the correct one.

There has been much theoretical study of "LL(1) grammars', which are grammars where you can guarantee to make the correct choice of path on the basis of *only looking at the current input token*. (Our above example is not an LL(1) language because you cannot decide what kind of statement it is on the basis of looking only at the IF.) This theory is not greatly relevant to recursive-descent parsers because restricting the field of view to the current token is not a game that they have to play. In an incremental compiler the entire source line is kept in the input buffer, and it is quite easy for the parser to look ahead (e.g. to see if the IF is immediatley followed by an equals sign). What must *not* be done, while making the decision on which option to take, is to call any of the scanning procedures, since these might perform semantic actions.

Recursion

Strictly speaking the name 'recursive descent' should really be 'potentially recursive descent'. Recursive descent is recursive only if the grammar it is following is recursive. Most grammars do, in fact, contain some recursion, so it helps, if you are coding a recursive-descent parser, if your encoding language supports recursion, i.e. it allows a procedure to call itself (either directly or indirectly). If not, you will need to program for yourself all the stacking and unstacking that recursion implies. This means saving return links for subroutines plus any local variables, though fortunately scanning procedures tend to use few local variables.

The most common occurrence of recursion is in the grammar of an expression. Paradoxically, the recursive-descent method is often replaced, in the part of the parser that deals with expressions, by an alternative technique. We discuss this later.

Errors

We have emphasized in this book that the error case is the normal case. Thus a parser should be regarded as a tool for pointing out syntactic errors in user's programs. Once in a while a user will produce a completely correct program, and will make use of the parser's secondary function—its use in helping to create the internal program.

Errors should be handled in a systematic way. In our snippets of code we have used a procedure to produce error messages, e.g.

ERROR("MISSING COMMA")

The argument to the ERROR procedure is a string giving the required message. In practice, the argument might not be the string itself, but a manifest constant indicating the error. Thus there might be a manifest constant NOCOMMA; its internal value might be an integer indicating where the required message could be found within an array containing all the error messages. We have said earlier that it is a good plan to keep all the messages together, and putting them in a single array is one way to achieve this.

The information that the ERROR procedure might produce, following the guidelines we introduced in Chapter 2.9, is as follows.

(a) An eye-catching message that there has been an error.
(b) A listing of the offending source line.
(c) An arrow pointing where the error was found. This is derived from the current value of the scanning pointer. Sometimes the scanning pointer will point *at* the offending character and sometimes just beyond it. Given this variation, it may be best to output a pair of arrows, or even three. This indicates to the user that the error occurs in a certain area of the line, and avoids the danger of pointing at the wrong character.
(d) A verbal explanation of the error.

In some cases (b) can be avoided, e.g. when the user has just typed the line at his terminal. However it might make it easier to get the arrows correctly positioned if the line is relisted.

An example of an error message, which is in an even more eyecatching form than the examples of Chapter 2.9, is

```
****ERROR***
*10 INPUT A B
*              ↑↑
*MISSING COMMA
```

It is very important that the verbal message be correct. Since producing error messages is the main task of the parser, it is a bad bug if a message is wrong. It is no good saying 'MISSING COMMA' if what is really meant is 'MISSING PRINT DELIMITER'. Getting messages correct may necessitate supplying extra parameters to scanning procedures in order to specify what error message it should produce if the match is unsuccessful.

Some systems have a HELP command, which enables the user to interact with the computer to get advice about his problems and, in particular, about his errors. Often such features are useless gimmicks, and if you want to provide a genuinely helpful HELP command you will need to put a lot of effort into it. Our own prejudice is that such effort is better put into improving error messages, the user interface and the user manual—then there is no need for a HELP command.

Error recovery

Having given its message, the next task of the parser's error procedure is to recover from the error. This means re-starting the scan in such a way that

(a) it *does not* give a lot of bogus error messages as a result of getting out of step;

(b) it *does* detect any further genuine errors in the program.

If the source line is a natural program unit, the simplest means of error recovery is to ignore the rest of the current line, and start again with a fresh line. Being the simplest, this is our preferred approach. However, in source languages where statements are ended with, say, a semicolon, one way of recovering from errors is to advance to the next semicolon (which is not within a character-string constant).

In some encoding languages, particularly those which ban GOTOs with fanatical fervour, the ERROR procedure may be hard to encode. As we have specified it, it does not return to its point of call, but GOes TO some fixed 'recovery point' in the parser, where the next source line is taken. If such a GOTO cannot be encoded, then it will be necessary for the ERROR procedure to return to its point of call. In this case the parser might have to suppress any further error messages from the current line, in case they are bogus ones, and make sure it advances the scanning pointer over the token that caused the error so that an endless loop of errors is avoided.

If you are interested in more subtle methods of error recovery, see the paper by Ammann (1978).

Routines not using recursive descent

An advantage of recursive descent is that it is a flexible method rather than a straitjacket. If you wish, you can abandon the use of recursive descent in some scanning routines, and code them in some other way.

This is often done in practice with scanning routines for the lowest-level syntactic objects, such as variable names, numeric constants and strings. Since these tend to be heavily used, it is better to code them to run as fast as possible; this might imply avoiding some of the potentially recursive procedure calls that recursive descent needs. (These low-level routines are often treated as part of the lexical analyser.)

Expressions

As we discussed on page 103, the normal precedence rules for arithmetic mean that the expression

$$4+6/2$$

gives the result 7. This is because we have been trained for years to regard the division operator as having *higher precedence* than the addition operator and thus to be done first. Most programming languages follow this same convention, though a few, notably the language APL, have adopted the attitude that the whole idea of precedence is illogical in programming languages and that all operators should have equal precedence. If this latter view is taken then there are no problems in analysing expressions, so we shall concentrate on the former case and discuss the significance of precedence.

The normal precedence rules for arithmetic expressions are

highest precedence :	$\uparrow$ (raising to a power)
next highest	:	*, /
lowest	:	+, −

Otherwise precedence is left to right. (Therefore $6-3-2$ is $(6-3)-2$ is 1.) Unary plus and minus may have precedence equal to their binary equivalents (e.g. $-3\uparrow2$ is $-(3\uparrow2)$), or they may have the highest precedence of all (e.g. $-3\uparrow2$ is $(-3)\uparrow2$). We shall assume the former. Some languages allow lots of other operators, such as logical operators. When this happens precedence rules may become quite elaborate, with say, eight different levels of precedence rather than just the three we have described above.

We first introduced the idea of precedence in Part 3 when we described Reverse Polish notation. One of the purposes of this notation is to eliminate precedence rules by making operators appear in the correct order. If the translator, via its semantic actions, is to convert the source program to Reverse Polish notation, it must unravel the precedence of source operators and then output them in the appropriate order. The procedure entrusted with this task is SCANEXPRESSION. SCANEXPRESSION can be coded using recursive descent. We shall consider this first and then an alternative.

Coding SCANEXPRESSION using recursive descent

If SCANEXPRESSION is coded using recursive descent, the grammar for the expression must reflect operator precedence. This is done by putting the

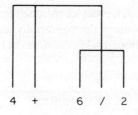

operators of lowest precedence in the highest-level grammatical rules. The figure above illustrates the parsing of the expression $4+6/2$. The result of $6/2$ is one component of the addition, which is at a higher level.

If we assume the operands in expressions can be variables or constants, then the grammar for an expression can be written

expression	$= (+/-)?$ term $((+/-)$ term)*
term	$=$ factor ((asterisk/slash) factor)*
factor	$=$ primary ($\uparrow$ primary)*
primary	$=$ variable/constant/
	left-parenthesis expression right-parenthesis

The corresponding scanning procedures can be encoded directly from this. It is worth discussing semantics at this point. We wish to convert our source to Reverse Polish, and we need to be sure when we select a parsing method that it is capable of generating Reverse Polish easily. With recursive descent, generating Reverse Polish is, in fact, a trivial matter. The following example shows how a typical routine, SCANFACTOR, can be encoded. Within this and subsequent examples, we use the notation INTERNAL($+$) to mean add the plus operator to the Reverse Polish translation of the line, and similarly for other operators.

```
SCANPRIMARY
WHILE CHECKUPARROW DO/* CHECKUPARROW looks for
                    "↑" */
BEGIN SCANPRIMARY
      INTERNAL ( ↑ )
END
```

When an operand is scanned it is copied directly over to the internal program by its scanning procedure. Thus the source $4\uparrow3\uparrow2$ is converted into the Reverse Polish internal form $4\ 3\ \uparrow\ 2\ \uparrow$. (In our examples of Reverse Polish, such as this, we shall continue to use the symbolic notation described in Part 3. When encoded inside the machine the constants 4, 3 and 2 might be represented as dictionary offsets, and the '$\uparrow$' operator by an internal numeric code, equated to a manifest constant with a name such as UPARROW.)

The end of the book?

As a slightly more complicated example, we shall show the encoding of SCANEXPRESSION. This takes the form

```
IF CHECKPLUS THEN
        BEGIN SCANTERM; INTERNAL (UNARYPLUS); END
ELSE IF CHECKMINUS THEN
        BEGIN SCANTERM; INTERNAL (NEGATE); END
        ELSE SCANTERM

EXPRLOOP: IF CHECKPLUS THEN
BEGIN SCANTERM
        INTERNAL (+)
        GOTO EXPRLOOP
END
IF CHECKMINUS THEN
BEGIN SCANTERM
        INTERNAL (−)
        GOTO EXPRLOOP
END
```

Maybe on seeing the above GOTOs you have burnt the book—if it came from the library they will have to buy a replacement and it all helps royalties. If, on the other hand, you are still reading, then by all means replace the GOTOs using your favourite looping construct, for example the somewhat repetitive:

```
WHILE BUFFER[PTR] = "+" OR BUFFER[PTR] = "−" DO
BEGIN IF CHECKPLUS THEN . . .
        ELSE IF CHECKMINUS THEN . . .
END
```

Recursion in the parser related to nesting in the source

If an expression contains a parenthesized sub-expression then SCANEXPRESSION is called recursively to scan the sub-expression. If, for example, SCANEXPRESSION is called to scan the expression (A+1)/3, the sequence is: SCANEXPRESSION calls SCANTERM calls SCANFACTOR calls SCANPRIMARY calls CHECKLEFT-PARENTHESIS and then SCANEXPRESSION again to scan the sub-expression A+1. The recursive call of SCANEXPRESSION automatically takes care of the nesting in the source language; there is no stacking or unstacking to be done other than that implied by the recursion.

Encoding SCANEXPRESSION in this way is nice and simple but it may be slow. A paper by Knuth (1971)—and a useful guide to computing literature is: 'If it's by Knuth it's good'—has shown that a high percentage of the expressions used in real programs consist of just one operand and no operators at all. To analyse this simple case, the above method involves procedure calls five deep (SCANEXPRESSION calls SCANTERM calls SCANFACTOR calls SCANPRIMARY calls SCANVARIABLE or SCANCONSTANT). If there are eight levels of precedence rather than three, the calls go ten deep.

If the time that all these nested procedure calls take worries you, you might be interested in the alternative method described in the next section.

Coding SCANEXPRESSION using precedence tables

The alternative method involves the use of a table giving the relative precedence of operators. This can be a matrix as illustrated below.

	+	−	*	/	↑
+	=	=	<	<	<
−	=	=	<	<	<
*	>	>	=	=	<
/	>	>	=	=	<
↑	>	>	>	>	=

In this *operator-precedence table* each entry gives the relative precedence of the operator named in the row against that named in the column. Thus, taking the third row and the first column, the operator '*' has greater precedence than the operator '+'.

An alternative is simply to assign to each operator an integer giving its precedence (e.g. '+' and '−' are 2, '↑' is 4).

Using the operator-precedence method, SCANEXPRESSION scans the source in the normal left-to-right manner. It essentially has two states: 'expecting operator' and 'expecting operand'. If it does not find what it expects it gives an error. As operands are scanned they are copied directly to the Reverse Polish, as in the recursive-descent method. When an operator is found it is placed on a stack; however before this stacking is done the precedence of the operator on top of the stack is compared with that of the current operator. If the operator at the top of the stack is greater or equal it is unstacked and put into the Reverse Polish; this process is repeated until the operator at the top of the stack has lower precedence than the current operator. The stacking of the current operator then takes place. Initially the stack is made to contain an imaginary 'end marker' operator (EM) with the lowest precedence of all. In addition it is convenient to assume that there is an imaginary operator at the end of the source expression; we shall represent this by a dot. This imaginary dot operator has lower precedence than any real operator—though higher than the imaginary operator EM—and its purpose is to clear the real operators off the stack.

The following example illustrates the algorithm. It shows the source expression being scanned token by token, and the state of the stack and the Reverse Polish at each stage.

Source to be scanned	Reverse Polish	Stack
A+B−C*D.	Null	EM
+B−C*D.	A	EM
B−C*D.	A	EM +
−C*D.	A B	EM +
C*D.	A B +	EM −
*D.	A B + C	EM −
D.	A B + C	EM − *
.	A B + C D	EM − *
Null	A B + C D * −	EM

If a unary operator is encountered it is copied directly to the stack without ever removing anything from the stack first; a unary operator has an associated precedence, just like any other operator, and it is copied over to the Reverse Polish when a non-unary operator of lower or equal precedence occurs. Some languages only allow unary operators at the start of expressions (i.e. 2↑−3 is wrong) whereas others allow a single unary operator to precede any operand (i.e. 2↑−3 is acceptable). In the latter case a unary operator is acceptable to the parser on entering the 'operand expected' state.

Sub-expressions in parentheses can be dealt with either by calling SCANEXPRESSION recursively as in the recursive-descent method or by a simple direct method. If you use the recursive method think carefully about the state of the stack before and after the recursive call. The simple direct method is to treat a left parenthesis as an operator with a very low precedence. When found, the left parenthesis is put straight onto the stack, without taking anything off first. (The same action as for a unary operator.) Once a left parenthesis gets on the stack, no other operator can knock it off, since all real operators have higher precedence. The parenthesis therefore 'protects' everything below it on the stack.

A right parenthesis clears the stack down to a left parenthesis, and then removes the left parenthesis as well. If no left parenthesis lies on the stack, an error is diagnosed; such an error would arise from an unmatched right parenthesis, e.g. 'A+B)'. When the end of an expression is reached, a check is made that no left parentheses are left on the stack; if so they were not properly matched by right parentheses, e.g. as in the illegal expression '(A+B'.

The following example illustrates both unary operators and parentheses. The unary minus is represented in the Reverse Polish as *NEGATE*.

Source to be scanned	Reverse Polish	Stack
−A*(B+C).	Null	EM
A*(B+C).	Null	EM *NEGATE*
*(B+C).	A	EM *NEGATE*

(B+C).	A	EM *NEGATE* *
B+C).	A	EM *NEGATE* * (
+C).	A B	EM *NEGATE* * (
C).	A B	EM *NEGATE* * (+
).	A B C	EM *NEGATE* * (+
.	A B C +	EM *NEGATE* *
Null	A B C + * *NEGATE*	EM

A possible order of precedence including all these new operators is

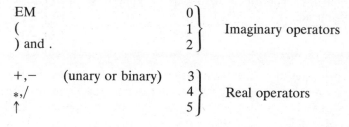

The real power of operator-precedence tables

The operator-precedence method is much more powerful than our example of SCANEXPRESSION shows. It can be used to analyse entire programs, just like the recursive-descent method. Moreover, even when the method is used in SCANEXPRESSION our description above only gives a pale glimpse of the true power. A lot more information can be put into the precedence matrix than we have described. Firstly, our imaginary operators EM, '(', ')' and '.' can be added to the table. Secondly, operands, as well as operators, can be introduced into the table, and this can aid error checking. This is done by placing a special code meaning 'error' at points in the table that represent errors. (The table might then be used to diagnose that an operand followed by another operand is an error, or even that a numeric operator applied to a string operand is an error.) Finally the table can be used to show the left-to-right rule for operators of equal precedence (i.e. 2−1+3 is (2−1)+3), and could even cater for special operators whose precedence was right to left.

The effect of all this is to reduce the size of the code of your compiler at the expense of increasing the size of the precedence table. The compiler becomes 'table-driven'. The advantage of a table-driven compiler is that it is relatively easy to extend or change.

'Top down' and 'bottom up'

The recursive-descent method is an example of *top down* parsing. It starts by calling the scanning procedure for the highest-level syntactic object, the statement, and then calls lower and lower level procedures until it gets down to recognizing individual tokens. The operator-precedence method, on the other hand, gives the flavour of a *bottom up* method. It builds up a parse of the expression from working with individual tokens.

There is a host of alternative top down and bottom up methods in addition to the ones we have mentioned. If you are interested in these and their relative merits, read Gries (1971). There is a lot to read.

A final word before leaving grammars. Grammars are one of the baits that have led the innocent into the *eleventh deadly sin*: to rate the beauty of mathematics above the usability of your compiler. Do not get too carried away by all the beautiful neat models of compilers you read about in the technical journals.

Chapter 4.5

Checking and Resolving Data Types

It is the duty of the translator to check, where it can, that data types are correct and to signal a *type violation* if they are not. In the BASIC language each of the following lines contains a type violation involving the wrong use of string or numeric objects.

```
10  LET A = A$
20  PRINT −A$
30  PRINT "X"&"Y"&23
40  ON A$ GOTO 100
50  LINPUT A
60  PRINT A$(B$)
```

Most type violations, including probably all the above, should lead to error messages. However, as we discussed in Chapter 3.2, certain type violations may lead to an operand of the wrong data type being automatically 'coerced' to the correct data type; if and when this applies in your source language your translator should insert the appropriate coercion operator rather than give an error message.

A second duty of the translator is to associate a data type with each polymorphic operator. Thus

LET A$ = B$ becomes   A$ B$ *LETSTR*

whereas

LET A = B   becomes   A B *LETNUM*

These two duties involve actions by the translator that are partly syntactic and partly semantic, and thus fall naturally into a chapter which comes between syntactic actions and semantic ones.

Specifying data types

We shall now expand on the material, introduced in Chapter 2.10, on how data types are specified in programming languages.

Most languages support more than one data type. For the purpose of example we shall assume the language supports numeric and string data types, together with arrays and functions, and that the scope of all variables is global.

There are two possible ways a source language can associate a data type with its variables. One is to make the data type manifest, either from the name of the variable or the context in which it is used. This method, which we shall call *manifest data types*, is generally adopted in BASIC, where the names of all string variables end with a dollar sign to distinguish them from numeric variables. Names of arrays in BASIC can be the same as names of scalar variables, but the former are always followed by a left parenthesis (or, in some extended BASICs, occur in MAT statements), whereas the latter never are (e.g. LET X(3) =X). Manifest data types were also used in early versions of the FORTRAN language, where the first letter of a variable name indicated its data type; the concept has since become more blurred.

The second approach is to allow any name for any type of variable, and to declare somewhere in the program which type is associated with each variable name. Thus the name X can be used for either a numeric variable or a string variable, and there is a declaration such as

STRING X   or   NUMERIC X

to say which it is. This technique, which we call *declared data types*, is the one most frequently used in modern batch languages. It is not good for interactive languages because a statement such as

LET X = Y

cannot be completely parsed on its own. It is an error if X and Y turn out to have separate data types, but this cannot be detected by looking just at the statement itself. Moreover the statement cannot be translated into the internal language under our requirement that internal operators specify the data type of their operands.

Manifest data types are therefore much the better choice for interactive languages, and we shall assume that they are generally used. However, as the source language becomes more complex, manifest data types become increasingly infeasible. This is particularly so if the language includes data structures with named sub-fields (such as the PASCAL records we showed in Chapter 2.11). Then it becomes necessary to resort to declared data types, and to check data types in the pre-run module or the run-time system. Even in BASIC, some of the subsidiary information about data types is not manifest. In particular this applies to the dimensionality of arrays and to the number of arguments that a built-in function possesses. In the program

```
10 DEF FNA = 3
20 DIM A(4,4)
30 LET A(2) = FNA(3)
```

statement 30 contains two errors—the array A has the wrong number of subscripts and the function FNA has the wrong number of arguments—yet neither of these errors can be diagnosed from looking at statement 30 alone. The errors, since they depend on context, can only be detected on a pre-run or run-time check. A similar situation arises if a function is used in a program but not declared at all.

In richer source languages the crude facilities for functions found in simple BASICs are much augmented. Typically both functions and subroutines can have any identifier as their name, and can be defined to have any number of arguments of any data type. If your source language provides decent facilities like these, your compiler needs to do a good deal of context-dependent error checking.

The outcome of all these exceptional cases is that, although we stand by our assumption that your source language contains manifest data types, we realize that there is probably further checking to be done. We consider this when describing the pre-run module. This chapter concentrates on the task of dealing with manifest types.

Implementing type checking for manifest data types

The ordinary recursive-descent mechanism can be used to check data types that are manifest. This is done by having separate grammatical rules for each data type. Thus one object in the grammar might be a string-expression and this could have a completely different syntax from a numeric-expression; similarly with a string-variable and a numeric-variable. Arrays and functions present no special problems, apart from the context-dependent aspects described above. The rule

numeric-variable = numeric-scalar-variable/
numeric-array left-parenthesis
numeric-expression right-parenthesis

is an example of the way in which array elements can be used.

We should, however, remember the requirement that the parser must be able to pre-select the correct alternative in each situation. If the parser tries to match the source text X(3) against the above rule, it cannot decide which of the two alternatives applies by looking only at the X. This is because X could be a numeric-scalar-variable or it could be a numeric-array. In this case, a simple look-ahead to the next symbol resolves the pre-selection problem: X is the name of an array if and only if it is followed by a left parenthesis.

The above rule also illustrates type checking. The array subscript is specified to be a numeric-expression. Thus A("W") is rejected because "W" does not fit the syntax of a numeric-expression.

The pre-selection problem with array names is easily resolved but with polymorphic operators the problem can be much harder. Consider the statement

IF ((((A$& . . .

IF is polymorphic as it can be followed by a string-expression or a numeric-expression. Our requirement says we must pre-select the correct option. In the above example, it is necessary to look ahead a long way in order to select the correct alternative, since the parentheses that follow the IF give no help—it could be

$$\text{IF} \quad (\,(\,(\,(A+1 \ldots$$

Only on reading the A\$ is the selection resolved. It is hard to find a simple and safe rule that resolves all such cases. Try to find one for yourself; remember that finding a dollar sign is no guarantee that the expression is a string-expression, as exemplified by IF(LEN(A\$)) . . .

If the source language has automatic coercions, this is likely to lead to the same kind of difficulties as with polymorphic operators.

Your may begin to feel that the look-ahead difficulties for your source language will get out of hand if you try to distinguish data types in your grammar. There are dangers from pathological examples you have not thought of, and of slight changes in the source language invalidating your elaborate strategies.

A method to avoid look-ahead

'If you come to a difficulty, give up; if you come to a danger, run away'. If this motto were generally adopted, popular novels would be less exciting and there would have been a dearth of film parts for John Wayne. Yet it is a good motto for software writers. There is a proviso that, having left the difficult or dangerous path, you must search relentlessly for the simple and safe one.

We shall therefore abandon the use of recursive descent for type checking of polymorphic operators, if the going gets at all rough. Instead we shall use the nice simple and safe method described below. We shall describe its use in performing complete type checking for numerics and strings (or any similar scalar data types); the method takes this dangerous task away from the grammar, so that the grammar no longer distinguishes between strings and numerics. The grammar thus has all-embracing objects such as 'variable' and 'expression'. We assume the grammar makes sure arrays and functions are correctly used, but, if not, our method could be adapted to deal with these too.

The method uses two internal variables, CURRENTTYPE and NEWTYPE, to keep track of the data type. CURRENTTYPE indicates the data type resulting from the preceding analysis, whereas NEWTYPE indicates the data type of the current token. Initially CURRENTTYPE is given the value 'unset'. After each source symbol has been scanned CURRENTTYPE and NEWTYPE are compared and one of the following actions is taken.

(1) If CURRENTTYPE and NEWTYPE are the same, then all is well and the

scan can proceed. This also applies if NEWTYPE is 'unset', as it may be if the current token is a polymorphic operator.

(2) If CURRENTTYPE is 'unset', it is set to the value of NEWTYPE.

(3) If CURRENTTYPE is unequal to NEWTYPE, and it is not 'unset', then a type violation is diagnosed. This in turn leads to an error message or perhaps a coercion.

In most languages all operands have a fixed associated data type (although this is not known at translate-time unless data types are manifest); some operators also have a fixed data type, wheras others are polymorphic. Examples from BASIC are

Operands	numeric:	A1, 1.3
	string:	A1$, "PIG"
Operators	numeric:	+, −, ON, arguments to SIN, COS
	string:	& (concatenation), LINPUT
	polymorphic:	LET, IF, most I/O operators

For everything except polymorphic operators, NEWTYPE is set to the associated data type.

For a polymorphic operator, if it accepts all our data types, NEWTYPE is given the value 'unset'. If a polymorphic operator accepts only a subset of the available data types, then a partial check is needed to make sure CURRENTTYPE is within the subset (e.g. in some languages the operator '+' might accept integers and reals, but not strings). In all cases, when the translator comes to output the polymorphic operator to the internal line, the operator is 'qualified' by CURRENTTYPE. Hence the LET operator is output as *LET-NUM* or *LETSTR* depending on whether CURRENTTYPE is numeric or string.

Nested and intermixed data types

When a nested expression is encountered, CURRENTTYPE needs to be stacked and reset for the scanning of the inner expression. Its old value is restored at the end. This applies particularly to array subscripts and function arguments. For example in A$(X+3)&B$, CURRENTTYPE is set to 'string' after scanning A$. Before the inner expression X+3 is scanned, the existing value of CURRENTTYPE, i.e. 'string', is stacked and CURRENTTYPE is reset to 'numeric', since a numeric subscript is required (A$(A1$) must given an error). After X+3 has been scanned and, since it is numeric, passed as acceptable, the old value of CURRENTTYPE is unstacked for the scanning of the rest of the expression. A similar example is a string function that takes a numeric argument, e.g. CHR$(X) in some BASICs.

In statements such as PRINT, where intermixed data types are acceptable, e.g.

PRINT A, A$,B

158

CURRENTTYPE is reset to 'unset' before each element is scanned.

An example

The following exampie shows the use of CURRENTTYPE and NEW-TYPE to analyse the (incorrect) statement

$$IF - A = A\$ \text{ THEN} \ldots$$

Symbol	CURRENTTYPE beforehand	NEWTYPE	Resulting CURRENTTYPE
IF	unset	unset	unset
–	unset	numeric	numeric
A	numeric	numeric	numeric
=	numeric	unset	numeric
A$	numeric	string	*type violation*

Exceptional languages

Our descriptions are peppered with qualified terms such as 'most languages', 'usually', 'generally', 'could'. This is because there are languages that are rugged individualists, refusing to follow the way the sheep are going. One such is SNOBOL4 (Griswold *et al.*, 1971), and anyone interested in languages will find it an enjoyable study. It is also a very useful tool in its field of string manipulation. One way SNOBOL4 differs from the crowd is that *operands* can be polymorphic, and, what is more, the data type of an operand can vary during a run—one moment X is a string and the next moment it is a number. Hence all we have said in this chapter, and in many others too, is invalid.

Another rugged individualist is the APL language, and this equally makes lively acquaintance.

Chapter 4.6

Semantic Actions

If your internal language is simple in structure then your semantic actions will be equally simple. The semantic actions to produce Reverse Polish consist simply of outputting operands then operators. Using the recursive-descent method, the form of a scanning procedure for a binary operation is as follows.

> Scan first operand
> Output first operand to Reverse Polish
> Scan binary operator
> Scan second operand
> Output second operand to Reverse Polish
> Output binary operator to Reverse Polish

Operators and operands are converted from their source form to appropriate internal codes. If an operator is polymorphic it has several possible internal codes, and the appropriate code must be selected according to the data type of its operands.

Operands

When Reverse Polish is created, each operand is immediately output to the internal line when the appropriate scanning procedure recognizes it. However, our use of symbolic Reverse Polish in previous examples has disguised some of the work needed to process operands. Thus we represent A+B in symbolic Reverse Polish as A B + , whereas inside the computer, if the method of Chapter 3.3 is followed, it might consist of the three bytes:

> OPERAND + *dictionary subscript for A*
> OPERAND + *dictionary subscript for B*
> OPERATOR + *internal code for plus*

In this case, the scanning procedures for operands have the task of converting operands from source form into dictionary offsets. This involves a search of the appropriate dictionary to find if the operand is already there, and if not to create a new dictionary entry for it.

If the operand is a built-in function name, the scanning procedure may extract information about the data type of its argument(s) from its dictionary entry. Consider, for example, the two built-in functions SIN(X), which finds the sine of X, and LEN(X$), which finds the length of the string X$. The translator must know, for these as for every other function, not only the data type of arguments but also the number of arguments. Both LEN(X) and SIN(X,Y) must be taken as errors.

Default semantics

Many source languages have 'default semantic actions' (which should not be confused with the default declarations we have mentioned earlier). A popular default semantic action is to supply a step size of one on a FOR statement. Thus if the user writes

FOR X = A TO B

it is assumed he really means

FOR X = A TO B STEP 1

There are two possible ways the translator can treat such defaults: it can 'expand them out' or it can carry them over to the internal language. We shall discuss each in turn.

Expanding out defaults

An example of expanding out a default is to create the internal line as if the above implied STEP 1 had been explicitly written. Expanding out defaults has the advantage of simplicity in subsequent processing. It obviously helps if there is only one possible internal format for FOR statements.

If defaults are expanded out and the source is then re-created, it is a matter of choice whether default material is (a) always omitted; (b) always made explicit; or (c) made dependent on the original source. The following example illustrates the three approaches.

Original source   FOR X = A TO B
                        FOR Y = C TO D STEP 1
(Here the user has employed a default in the first line, but has made the STEP 1 explicit in the second.)

Re-created source (a) FOR X = A TO B
                         FOR Y = C TO D
Re-created source (b) FOR X = A TO B STEP 1
                         FOR Y = C TO D STEP 1
Re-created source (c) FOR X = A TO B
                         FOR Y = C TO D STEP 1

With approach (c) the internal line needs to contain a record of whether the source line contained an explicit STEP. One way of doing this is by representing the default constant 1 for a STEP size in a different way to the explicit constant 1, by making them different dictionary offsets, for example.

Carrying defaults over to the internal language

In many languages default semantics is extensively used in input/output statements. There may be default files, default output formats and default error actions. In such cases, where there is a host of defaults, the policy of expanding them out may make the internal line excessively long. The alternative policy of carrying defaults over to the internal program is then more attractive; it is left to the run-time system to figure out what default actions to take.

Semantics local to a line

We have assumed all declarations of variables are global, but we also wish to allow declarations that are local to the unit of compilation, i.e. the line. References to local variables are likely to need different semantic actions from references to globals.

Consider the BASIC program

```
10   DEF FNA(X) = X*X+Y
20   LET Y = 10
30   LET X = 1234
40   PRINT FNA(2),X
```

The parameter X in line 10 is an example of a local declaration. (In many BASICs this is the only kind of local declaration there is.) Within line 10, X has a special meaning which is quite distinct from any X that may exist outside. In the above example, statement 40 prints the value 1234 for the value of X. The local use of X in the call of FNA has no effect on the value of this global X.

If the only use of local variables is as function parameters, and if functions can only have one parameter, there are many simple ways of dealing with them. One is to reserve the first dictionary entry for the local variable name. Normally this is set to a null name, because there is no local variable in existence. When a DEF is encountered the name of the current local variable—X in the above case—is copied into the first dictionary entry and stays there until the complete statement has been processed. When a dictionary look-up is made, any reference to the local variable X is matched against this local declaration because, being the first entry, it is the first one scanned (assuming a sequential dictionary look-up). The result is that, within any DEF statement, references to its parameter are always translated into references to the first dictionary entry, which the run-time system must interpret to mean the argument of the current function.

A similar technique can be used if there can be a maximum of, say, two or three local variables. If the potential number of local variables is almost boundless, a more general technique must be used. However, the same general principle applies; the dictionary is temporarily augmented by some new entries which are deleted when the local context ends; on every dictionary look-up these temporary local entries are scanned before the global ones, thus ensuring that if a local has the same name as a global, the local takes precedence. See Gries (1971) for details—but beware the extra complications introduced if global variables are not declared: in the above example, statement 10 not only introduces a new local, X, but it also introduces a new global, Y, which must *not* be deleted from the dictionary at the end of the statement.

Where there may be several local variables, the form of operands in the internal language may be adjusted to include an extra bit to say whether the operand is local or global.

In those source languages, like Algol 60, which allow several levels of locality, the problems are much greater than for the single level of locality we have been discussing. If you have such a language you are again referred to Gries (1971).

Re-creating local variable names

If the source is being re-created, the temporary dictionary entries corresponding to local variables will have disappeared by the time the re-creation is done. The original names are thus lost from the dictionary. To combat this the names should be preserved somewhere in the internal program so that they can be temporarily restored during re-creation. Thus the internal form of a BASIC DEF statement might contain the source name of the parameter.

Part 5

THE RUN-TIME SYSTEM

Chapter 5.1

Error Detection and Diagnosis

The run-time system is entered when the user types a RUN command or an immediate statement. The program to be run will already have been converted to the internal language, and the pre-run module will have processed context-dependent features. (We discuss the pre-run module in a later chapter, when we have seen what the run-time system itself is like.)

Since the error case is the normal case, the main tasks of the run-time system are (a) to report to the user those errors in his program that can only be shown up by running it; and (b) to help the user find out what caused each error. Occasionally the run-time system may be called on to perform its secondary function of running a program to completion and producing correct answers! If your compiler is used mainly for production work rather than development work, the successful runs may be more frequent, but it is even more important to detect the errors.

Complete detection of errors

The specification of your source language prescribes the syntactic and semantic rules of the language. All syntactic errors should be detected by the translator or the pre-run module (or, as a last resort, by the run-time system) and the run-time system should make sure that all semantic errors are detected. The *twelfth deadly sin* is to let any error go undetected. Sometimes this sin is committed in the language specification, which may say: 'The effect of breaking this rule is undefined'. This means that user programs that inadvertently breach the rule are not portable, since they are almost certain to give different answers with different compilers.

Examples of semantic errors that can arise in almost any source language are the following.

(a) Numeric overflow (a number too large for the machine to hold) or division by zero.
(b) Array subscript out-of-range (i.e. too large or too small).
(c) Unassigned variable. We discuss this below.
(d) Incorrect selection in ON or CASE statement.
(e) String too long.

165

(f) Storage exhausted; subroutine or function calls too deep.
(g) Failure in input/output device or filing error.
(h) Wrong input data.
(i) Error in argument to built-in function, e.g. an attempt to take the square root of a negative number.

Unassigned variables

Probably the most common error in programming is the use of an unassigned variable, i.e. the attempt to take the value of a variable for which no value has been set. In languages that do not require variables to be declared this error may be caused by mistypings, e.g. in the BASIC program

$$\vdots$$

LET A1 = . . .

$$\vdots$$

LET X = A2   (should have been LET X = A1)

Not only does the unassigned variable result from clerical errors, but in most source languages it is often the first manifestation of serious logical errors (e.g. one routine is supposed to create an array for a second routine to manipulate; however the second routine finds one of the array elements is unassigned).

If your compiler detects every usage of an unassigned variable as an error, this is a huge help for your users in finding their bugs. Some source languages throw away this advantage by specifying that all variables are initialized to some arbitrary value, such as zero for a numeric variable. Programs that use this feature intentionally are hard to read, and programs that use it unintentionally are hard to debug, because they produce no error message but give a mystifyingly wrong answer. Other source languages specify that the initial value of variables is undefined, which is worse still. If you have any say in the matter, make the user manual for your source language say: 'It is an error if you try to refer to the value of a variable when that variable has not previously been given a value'. You might make an exception when values of variables are to be printed; the printing routines might simply print the word 'UNDEFINED' for an unassigned variable, but not give an error; this can be useful in printing arrays during debugging.

Detecting unassigned variables

Having made the brave statement that unassigned variables are errors, you are landed with the task of implementing it. If you are very lucky your encoding language will provide an automatic means of detecting such errors, and then handing control to your compiler so that it can relay a suitable error message to the user. The chances are, however, that you will not be so lucky and will need to do the detection work yourself.

There are two obvious ways of doing this. One is to initialize every variable to an 'impossible' value. On each attempt to reference the value of a variable a check is made to see if it has this impossible value, and if so an error is diagnosed. If this method is infeasible, as it may well be for some data types, then the second method must be used. This involves having a bit in the dictionary entry for each scalar variable to record whether it has been defined; this bit is checked on every reference to the variable. For arrays a corresponding array of these 'check bits' is needed.

If you are interested in more subtle methods, which run faster than the two above, read Barron (1971).

Giving the error message

When the run-time system gives an error message it needs to tell the user where in the program the error occurred, e.g.

*** ERROR: DIVISION BY ZERO IN LINE:
*** 190 LET X = P/Q

In order to provide this information it may be necessary for the compiler to keep a record of which line it is executing. If this is thought too expensive, as it might be for a true compiler, an alternative method is to deduce the offending line from the point of failure. At any error it is known which internal language instruction was being executed. If there exists a dictionary of line-numbers, this can be used to find the line-number that most closely precedes the error, and this in turn can lead to the offending line.

Generally it is best for the run-time system to give up after the first error. In many cases any attempt to continue would lead to further errors of an almost random nature. An exception occurs when a user makes an error in typing a line of input at an interactive terminal; here he should be given another chance. This cannot, however, apply to input from a file or a non-interactive device such as a card reader.

Exception handling

Some run-time errors may be detected by mechanisms completely outside your compiler. The hardware itself will detect some errors, such as numeric overflow and perhaps subscripts out-of-range, and will give an interrupt when one occurs. The encoding language—strictly speaking, its run-time system—may detect others; for example if your user tries to access a non-existent file, the result may be that your run-time system, in trying to access the file, executes an illegal statement, and this error in turn is detected by the run-time system of your encoding language.

All this free error checking by outsiders sounds good, but the advantage is lost if your compiler does not have complete freedom of action after such errors. In particular it is lost if the encoding language gives an error message after such errors, and ends the session. The result is that your user is confused by the message, which is not in terms of his program, and, worse still, he loses his program unless he has just previously saved it. What the encoding language should do is to provide *exception handling* facilities whereby your compiler can, on option, handle all errors that occur, whether they arise from interrupts or not. Your compiler can then print an error message in the user's terms and await further commands from him. The exception handling should not only cover errors, but also break-ins and exceptions resulting from signals from peripheral devices.

You will probably find that your encoding language does not provide adequate exception handling features—very few do. Before launching a virulent attack on the moron who designed your encoding language, you might stop to consider what exception-handling facilities you are providing for your own users. We have just suggested your compiler gives a fixed message—not under the user's control—after an error and then stops the run, exactly the mechanism that is to be condemned in the encoding language.

Thus turn your energies towards thinking about the design of your source language. Would it be possible for the user to override your compiler's action for an error and perform his own? He might, for example, like to write

```
AT 'DIVISION-BY-ZERO'
PRINT 'BAD LUCK -- TRY AGAIN'
GOTO   200
```

Some efforts have been made to provide users with exception-handling facilities, and the subject is now beginning to get the attention it deserves. One early effort was in the language PL/1 with its ON statement (no relation to the ON statement in BASIC). In addition, Ormicki (1977) has produced a BASIC compiler that allows the user to handle those exceptions that arise from hardware interrupts; his system is geared to handling peripheral devices rather than errors.

When the user does his own exception handling, he needs to know where the error occurred, what variable or file it applied to, and so on. You might consider therefore how this information could be provided.

Unfortunately, if you consider the full implications of providing good exception handling, you will find that it is extremely difficult to implement unless it is severely restricted. Your anger may be diverted from the designer of your encoding language to the moron users who clamour for such features without understanding the problems of implementation.

All this talk does not solve your immediate problem: dealing with exception handling if your encoding language does not provide it. One answer is for your run-time system to perform the necessary checks before the outside mechanisms do. Before attempting a divide operation, for example, you could check that the divisor is not zero. You can probably cover most exceptions this way but not all; for the remaining hard core it might even be necessary to modify or somehow by-pass the run-time system of your encoding language, so that you, rather than it, are in control.

Whatever you do, make sure it is only errors by your user which require such exception handling. Within your compiler itself such things as division by zero and subscripts out-of-range should be impossible. If, for example, a dictionary subscript within your compiler goes out of range, shoot the person who wrote the dictionary routines. And make sure a statement such as

LET A = 1E500   (assumed to be too big a number)

does not knock the translator out.

Error diagnosis

Having told the user about his run-time error, the second task of the run-time system is to give the user help in finding *why* the error occurred. If the source statement is

PRINT   X(11)

and the array X has only 10 elements, then the reason for the error is obvious. If the statement

PRINT   X(K)

gives a similar error because K has the value 11, it might be entirely unclear why K does not have its expected value, which is, say, 3.

We discussed error diagnosis in Chapter 2.8, and our prejudice was that the best tools were symbolic dumps and program profiles. The user should be able to ask for either of these by using a command or statement in the source language, e.g. DUMP or LISTPROFILE. Neither facility is hard to implement.

A symbolic dump is a list of all current variables and their values. Usually the dumps are restricted to scalar variables. To output a dump it is necessary for the run-time system to access the dictionaries created by the translator. The simplest way to produce a dump is to proceed sequentially through the dictionary of variable names, printing each name and its corresponding value represented as a constant of the appropriate data type, e.g.

X = 3
X$ = "ABC"

Variables with unassigned values should be left out of the dump; this in turn weeds out any redundant dictionary entries. If you want to impress your users you can sort the dumps into alphabetical order. You can also supplement your dump with other relevant information that your compiler has to hand, like a count of statements executed or the return links of currently active subroutine calls. If arrays and other data structures are omitted from your dumps, your source language should provide an easy way—ideally a single statement—of printing individual structures (e.g. MAT PRINT X in some BASICs).

A profile is even easier to produce. It is simply necessary for the run-time system to keep, for each statement, an *execution count* of the number of times the statement is executed. These execution counts are attached to program lines when the program is listed. Fancy options could allow the user to list all statements whose execution count exceeded some threshold—e.g. the top 10%. When producing execution counts make sure no quirk of your system makes them inconsistent; looping statements require special care.

Chapter 5.2

Executing Reverse Polish

A prime reason why we based our internal language on Reverse Polish notation is that it is easy and fast to execute. The method of execution is delightfully simple. All that is needed is a stack on which operands can be placed. We call this the *operand stack*. The task of executing the Reverse Polish internal language is then to scan it sequentially, performing the following action for each element:

— for *operands*, stack them on the operand stack.
— for *operators*, unstack the necessary number of operands, apply the current operator to them, and put the result back on the operand stack. (Some operators have no resultant value to stack. This usually applies to operators that come at the end of a statement.)

The following example shows how the expression

$$6\ 5 * 8\ 2\ NEGATE\ /\ -$$

is evaluated. Its source program equivalent is $6*5 - 8/(-2)$.

Element scanned	Stack before	Stack after
6	empty	6
5	6	6 5
*	6 5	30
8	30	30 8
2	30 8	30 8 2
NEGATE	30 8 2	30 8 −2
/	30 8 −2	30 −4
−	30 −4	34

If, in the encoding language, the procedure UNSTACKVALUE(X) is written to unstack an item and place its value in X, then the action of the run-time system to perform the binary operation of subtraction is

```
UNSTACKVALUE(OPERAND2)
UNSTACKVALUE(OPERAND1)
STACK(OPERAND1−OPERAND2)
```

171

Note that it is the second operand that is unstacked first. The UNSTACKVALUE procedure could be made to check for the error of an unassigned value.

Addresses and values

The example above has a small element of over-simplification in it. Items placed on the stack are said to be values, but in practice they are usually represented indirectly by the addresses in which the values are stored. To understand why, consider the assignment statement LET X=Y, which is X Y *LETNUM* in internal language. Here it is no good stacking the value of X; it is the address of X that the operator *LETNUM* will need.

Our philosophy of the internal language is that operands that represent addresses are not distinguished from operands that represent values. It is the operators that determine whether they want the address of an operand or its value. Thus *LETNUM* takes the address of its first operand and the value of its second. It is easy to derive a value from an address but not vice versa. Hence it is best for the operand stack to contain addresses; if it turns out that a value is needed, the value can be found simply by looking at the contents of the address. This tiny complication can easily be allowed for by making UNSTACKVALUE extract the value corresponding to the address it unstacks. *LETNUM* uses UNSTACKVALUE for its second operand, but, for its first operand uses a procedure UNSTACKADDRESS (A), which sets its parameter A directly to the address it unstacks. If we assume that all the values of variables are stored in an array VALUES, then the address of a variable is represented as an index to VALUES. Thus if variable P is stored as the 20th item of VALUES, then the address of P is 20. Given this environment, the action for *LETNUM* is

```
UNSTACKVALUE(OPERAND2)
UNSTACKADDRESS(INDEX)  /* Get address of first operand */
VALUES[INDEX] := OPERAND2
    /* If multiple assignment were allowed, OPERAND2 should be
       put back on the stack so that any further assignments could use
       it */
```

Note that even if an operand is a constant, as in the source statement LET P=6, the address of the constant, not its value, is placed on the operand stack.

Given that the operand stack contains addresses, it is relatively easy to produce good error messages. When an error occurs, for example an unassigned variable, it should be simple to use a dictionary to deduce the name of the offending variable from its address, and then to produce a really good error message, such as 'VARIABLE Q HAS NO VALUE'.

Temporaries

The shrewd reader has doubtless taken our public relations exercise in extolling the advantages of addresses as a preparation for some nasty aspects to come. We had therefore better come clean.

There is a very tiny problem with intermediate results. Consider the Reverse Polish expression A B 5 + *LETNUM*. The first operator, the plus sign, adds 5 to the value of B and puts the result back on the operand stack. Our rule says it cannot put the value of the result on the stack but must use its address. Therefore it must find some storage location in which to store the value, and put the address of this location on the stack. Such storage locations used to contain intermediate results are called *temporaries*. Temporaries can be stored in a separate stack, or, with the usage of special markers, can even be incorporated into the operand stack. As an example of the latter, all entries on the operand stack can be prefixed with a bit which says 'address' or 'value'. Intermediate results can be represented as values, and other items as addresses. This scheme escapes our earlier straitjacket of 'addresses for everything'. Variables still need to be stored as addresses, but constants can, if desired, be represented directly as values.

Finally if you do not like any of these schemes, you can put markers in the internal language to say which operands are addresses and which are values. As a result, you shift some complications away from the run-time system at the expense of adding much more complication to the translator. (Consider translating a multiple assignment statement LET A=B=3 and compare it with LET A=B. B is an address in the first case and a value in the second, but the translator cannot tell this until it has scanned beyond the B.)

Calls of user-defined functions

Our basic method of executing Reverse Polish using an operand stack not only covers the ordinary arithmetic operators, but caters for all other operators as well. In this section we consider calls of user-defined functions, using the example

10   DEF FNA(X) = X∗X
.
.
.
200 LET P = 3∗Y+FNA(C)/Z

In the internal language, statement 200 above is represented as

P 3 Y ∗ FNA C *CALLUD1ARG* Z / + *LETNUM*

When the time comes to execute the operator *CALLUD1ARG*, the operand stack contains the following four items:

$$\text{top of stack} \rightarrow \text{C}$$
$$\text{FNA}$$
$$\text{result of } 3*Y$$
$$\text{P}$$

The action of *CALLUD1ARG* is to take its two operands (C and FNA, in this case) from the stack, and execute the function call. At the end, the result of the function is put back on the stack and the execution of the original statement is resumed. Before executing the DEF of the function, the value of the argument C is copied into the storage reserved for the parameter X so that, within the function, any reference to X uses the value of C. (We assume parameters are 'called by value'; 'call by reference' would differ slightly.) Before entering the DEF it is necessary to preserve the following information:

(a) the *return address*, i.e. where execution is to resume when the function has finished.
(b) any information relevant to statement 200 which the function might overwrite. We call this the *environment of call*. It is discussed further below.

The best place to put this information is on the operand stack. (Strictly speaking it need not be put on a stack if one function is not allowed to call another.)

User-defined functions are much easier if functions can only consist of a single arithmetic expression as in our DEF in line 10. 'Multi-line functions', where a function consists of several statements, are not only more difficult for the translator, since the parameter name has a local scope straddling several lines, but also for the run-time system. To see why, consider the BASIC statement

PRINT # 6: USING L$: X,FNA(Y),Z

(Here '# 6' means PRINT on output device number 6, and USING L$ requests a special format for printing.) If FNA is a multi-line function, it can contain a line such as

PRINT # 5: USING M$: . . .

The result is that, in the middle of the original PRINT on device 6, a new PRINT, using a different device and a different format, is executed, and then a return is made to the original one. Worse still, the function might even execute a GOTO and never return to finish off the original printing—an action so upsetting to compilers that many forbid such a GOTO and take great trouble to enforce the restriction.

All this relates back to preserving the environment of call. With multi-line functions you need to preserve (and later restore) a huge amount of information. In the above PRINT statement, for example, you need to preserve the output device number and the printing format. In your own source language, there may well be many situations similar to this.

Overall the life of the compiler writer is much happier, therefore, if there are no multi-line functions. The source language can offer a facility that is almost as good for the user, and much easier to implement, by providing a good subroutine-calling mechanism.

To return again to the environment of call, assuming that there are no multi-line functions, the stacked environment of call is likely to consist only of the following two items:

(a) the indicator of the current line; this is kept for possible use by error routines.
(b) if all function parameters are stored in the same place, it is necessary to preserve the old parameter value before setting the new one. This is necessary for example in the BASIC statement

$$\text{DEF FNB(Y)} = \text{FNA(P)} + \text{Y}$$

The call of FNA must not destroy the value of FNB's parameter Y.

Executing user-defined functions

Execution of a single-line function, such as our previous example

$$10 \text{ DEF FNA(X)} = \text{X} * \text{X}$$

is quite straightforward. The value of the expression $X*X$ is calculated using the top of the operand stack in the normal way. Note that if calls of functions (or subroutines) can go arbitrarily deep, the operand stack can get arbitrarily big, whereas its size inside the compiler must be limited. Hence when using the operand stack, as for every other stack that has no pre-defined limit on its size, it is necessary to check for possible overflow before stacking each item.

On return, a function leaves its resultant value on top of the stack. This value must be copied into a temporary if it is not already in one. (If this is not done, consider the effects of DEF FNA(X) = X; here the function value, if not put in a temporary, would be in the parameter, which may then be destroyed.) After the return, the environment of call is restored (the function value should be repositioned, if necessary, so that it remains on top of the stack after the environment of call has been unstacked), and execution of the original statement resumes at the point specified by the return address. Subsequent execution will use the value of the function.

Built-in functions

Built-in functions are even easier than user-defined ones. For example the action for calling the SIN function might be

```
UNSTACKVALUE(OPERAND1)
STACK(SIN(OPERAND1))
```

This assumes SIN is also available as a function in the encoding language. If not, with any luck it is available in a subroutine library that can be accessed from within the encoding language. Usually the first person to write a compiler for a machine writes subroutines for the standard built-in functions, and all the later compiler writers use them. Let us hope you are not the first.

The only problem with built-in functions is likely to be error responses. It is related to the exception-handling problem that we discussed in Chapter 5.1. If your user asks for the square root of a negative number, you do not want the encoding language to print an error message and then stop. Instead you want it to relay control to your compiler, which can give the error message in the appropriate terms.

If your source language supports a random-number generator as a built-in function, and you need to code this yourself, you would do well to consult the relevant literature. Those of us who have little knowledge of statistics can do terrible things if we write our own random-number generator. Good references are Volume 2 of Knuth (1973), and Algorithm 266 of *Communications of the ACM* (published in 1965).

Subroutine calls

In principle, subroutine calls are similar to calls of user-defined functions, but simpler because they occur as a statement on their own, rather than within another statement. The only 'environment of call' information that needs stacking on a subroutine call is the return address. If subroutines have an explicit RETURN statement, as in BASIC, it is necessary to make sure there are not more RETURNs than calls.

In practice, many interactive languages, unlike minimal BASIC, provide elaborate ways of passing arguments to subroutines, thus making them better languages but harder to compile. (Some interactive languages carry these elaborate facilities over to function calls, too.) Among the facilities that may be provided are:

(a) arguments passed 'by value' or 'by reference';
(b) unrestricted numbers of arguments;
(c) arguments of any data type, including array names, function names and line-numbers.

Our mechanism for user-defined functions caters for a single numeric argument called by value, but this could be extended to cover some of the more elaborate cases. Another possible mechanism is to treat subroutine parameters as global variables, but to stack the previous value of the variable each time the subroutine is called. On exit the value is restored. Within the subroutine the parameter is assigned the value of the corresponding argument. The advantages of this method are that (a) parameters are treated as ordinary variables, thus allowing them to be translated in a context-independent manner, and (b) recursive subroutine calls present no special problems. The following example shows the method at work.

```
10   LET X = 20
20   LET Y = 30
30   LET Q = 17
40   CALL SUBNAME(3,Q+1)
      .
      .
      .
90   REM The subroutine is declared below. It uses X and Y as
     parameter names
100  SUBROUTINE   SUBNAME(X,Y)
110  REM   On entering the subroutine the old X and Y are
     stacked
120  REM   X and Y then take the new values 3 and 18
130  IF X = Y THEN . . .
      .
      .
      .
200  RETURN
201  REM At the return the old X and Y are restored
```

When X and Y are stacked both their addresses and their values are placed on the operand stack, i.e.

```
top of stack → Address of Y
               30
               Address of X
               20
               0 /* means end of argument list */
```

The run-time system then knows which values to restore at a return. If necessary, the data type of each variable can also be stacked. The mechanism is then general enough to cover indefinitely many arguments, with varying data types, though, as we have described it, each argument must be called by value.

In the most elaborate cases, the treatment of parameters can be one of the key problems of a run-time system. Nevertheless we shall not discuss any more details here, as source languages vary so much in the facilities offered and the problems that arise in consequence.

Minimizing the effect of compiler bugs

One of the arts of programming is to ensure that if your program does contain a bug it stops before the effects of the bug pervade the whole system. If a bug can multiply by producing further side-effects, the original bug may be almost impossible to find.

During the testing of your compiler, you should eliminate most if not all of your bugs. Even so, there will be bugs arising throughout the life of your compiler, if only because some lesser mortal has changed it, or it has become corrupted in the store of the machine.

Most modules of the compiler either process each statement independently of all others, or make a sequential scan of the whole program. The run-time system, on the other hand, jumps all over the place, depending on the behaviour of the user's program. Bugs are, as a result, particularly hard to trace.

To combat multiplying bugs, it is invaluable to put checks throughout your compiler, and especially in the run-time system, to make sure everything is as it should be. It is infeasible to check everything. The run-time system must have some faith in its colleagues, such as the translator, and in itself. It is, for example, too slow and time consuming to check that each operand really has the correct data type, given that the translator should already have done this. However the operand stack provides some examples of checks that are cheap and valuable to perform. One is to check that return addresses really are return addresses. A return address may be placed on the operand stack, and some time later removed. In the meantime the top of the stack may have been heavily used, and it is just possible that an error in your compiler might cause it to get out of phase. For example an operator may have unstacked one too many operands. The result is that, later on, when the run-time system thinks it is picking up a return address, it is, in fact, picking up something else. After this, the bugs would multiply exponentially.

To prevent this it is useful to 'put a signature' on return addresses, and only accept them if they bear the signature. Crudely, this can be done by stacking, before each return address, some unique pattern of bits (i.e. the signature), and then checking, when a return address is unstacked, that this bit pattern is attached to it. At a higher level, some encoding languages may allow you to designate return addresses as a data type which cannot be confused with objects of any other data type.

A second check you might make on the operand stack is to ensure, before you unstack something, that the stack is not empty. This check is simpler than the one above, but rather more expensive in run time.

If any of these checks on your compiler fails, you should generate a *system error*. This is discussed in Chapter 7.1.

Code generation in true compilers

Rather interestingly, the actions of executing Reverse Polish closely mirror the actions of the translator in a true compiler. Many true compilers use Reverse Polish as an *intermediate language*. Phase I of the translator converts source language to Reverse Polish, and Phase II converts Reverse Polish into machine code. The activities of Phase II closely follow those we have described in this chapter, except that where we perform an action, like adding two of the user's variables together, Phase II emits machine code to perform that action. Unlike our run-time system, Phase II is exclusively concerned with addresses rather than values, because the latter are not, of course, known until run-time.

As an example, the action of Phase II for a 'plus' operator might be

> UNSTACKADDRESS(OPERAND2)
> UNSTACKADDRESS(OPERAND1)
> Emit machine instructions to add OPERAND1 to OPERAND2

This relates to a remark made in Part 4. If your internal language is closer to the source than Reverse Polish, then part of our translator is in your run-time system; if your internal language is further from the source than Reverse Polish, and in particular if it is machine code, then part of our run-time system is in your translator.

Reaching the end of a statement

During execution, the flow of control usually proceeds from one statement to its successor. This sequence is only interrupted when a statement explicitly changes it (e.g. a GOTO, IF or looping statement).

We have suggested, in Chapters 2.13 and 3.3, that each internal statement is preceded by a 'header' consisting of two integers. The internal form of the statement follows the header. If such headers are present, execution cannot 'fall through' from one statement to its successor.

Consider the two statements

> 20 LET A = B
> 30 LET C = D

which are encoded in the precise internal language suggested in Chapter 3.3 as

> Header for statement 20
> OPERAND + dictionary subscript of A
> OPERAND + dictionary subscript of B
> OPERATOR + *LETNUM*
> Header for statement 30
> OPERAND + dictionary subscript of C
> OPERAND + dictionary subscript of D
> OPERATOR + *LETNUM*

After executing the *LETNUM* from statement 20, the run-time system must not take the next byte and execute it as if it were Reverse Polish. Instead it must do the following.

(1) Recognize that the *LETNUM* marks the end of a statement.

(2) Skip over the header of statement 30; it should remember where the header is in case this is needed later, e.g. in an error situation.

(3) Initiate execution of statement 30 by executing its first element (which takes the operand C).

There are two possible ways of recognizing the end of a statement. One is that, assuming the length of each internal statement is known (our proposed header gives this information), a check can continually be made for falling off the end. The alternative is to make each statement 'self-terminating', in the way discussed in the next section.

A more radical alternative is to eliminate the headers, or to incorporate them within the general framework of the internal language (e.g. the two integers that form the header can be made the operands of a binary operator, called, say, *HEADER*).

Whatever scheme you use, you must ensure that, at the end of a statement, the operand stack is not left containing 'garbage', which is then carried over to the next statement. If so, this garbage would gradually accumulate until the operand stack blew up. An example of such a time-bomb would arise if every assignment statement left behind the address of its first operand. We shall say more about this in the next section.

Self-terminating statements

Consider the 'multiple assignment' facility (e.g. LET A = B = 3 in BASIC). Some source languages support such a facility, whereas others only support assignment to a single variable. In the latter case, it is known, when the assignment operator *LETNUM* is performed, that the execution of the statement is complete. Such statements are said to be *self-terminating*. If, on the other hand, multiple assignment is possible, it is indeterminate whether an assignment operator represents the end of a statement. If you want to make multiple assignment statements self-terminating, you can replace each assignment operator by one of two alternative operators: a 'final' assignment operator (e.g. *LETNUMLAST*) for the end of the statement, and a 'more to come' assignment operator (e.g. *LETNUMMORE*) for other cases. (This division also helps avoid the garbage problem mentioned in the last section; *LETNUMLAST* clears the operand stack, whereas *LETNUMMORE* leaves a value on the stack.)

In most source languages some statements are naturally self-terminating whereas others are not. The latter can be made self-terminating if extra internal language operators are introduced in the way we just suggested. Alternatively, a catch-all method is to introduce a single new operator called *ENDSTATEMENT*.

Chapter 5.3

Allocating and Referencing User Variables

When we discussed, in Part 3, the encoding of the internal language, we said it would be valuable if each operand directly referenced the position where its value could be found. Thus the internal language might refer to variable 17, and its value could be found in the 17th position of some vector of values. A good way of achieving this is to set up a one-to-one correspondence between values and dictionary entries, e.g. the 17th value corresponds to the 17th dictionary entry. Then, given a reference within the internal language to variable 17, both the value of the variable and its properties (e.g. its name) can be found directly.

The internal program is produced by the translator, so an implication of our proposed scheme is that the translator must fix the order in which variables are to be stored, and use this information when it generates the internal program. It need not always fix the exact storage locations in which values are to be stored, but only their relative position within a vector of values.

Kinds of variable

In this chapter we look at the different kinds of variable and examine (a) how storage is allocated for them, and (b) how this storage can be referenced from within the internal program.

The simplest variables to deal with are global variables of a fixed and uniform size. These can be represented in a vector of values, as we mentioned in Chapter 3.3, and the translator can allocate each variable a position within the vector. Storage for the vector can be reserved at any time before a run starts, though if the translator plants constant values into the vector, then the vector must be allocated before or during translation.

Local variables of a fixed and uniform size can be dealt with by similar mechanisms, though the storage for these is not actually reserved until the program is running. We have already discussed one type of local variable, the function parameter, and have suggested a somewhat *ad hoc* scheme to deal with this. More general kinds of local variable are not covered in detail in this book, but the techniques for allocating them are well-established and can be found in Gries (1971) or almost any other book on batch compilers.

The biggest problems for storage allocation and referencing are variables whose size varies during a run. We shall discuss this in the context of global string variables, since these are by far the most common instance of such variables. Other objects of varying size can be processed in a similar way.

Strings

When humans communicate with one another, the most popular medium is words. Sometimes the words are supplemented by numbers, pictures, visual signals, missiles, etc. If an interactive compiler is to communicate with humans it, too, should be capable of dealing with words. To do so, interactive languages frequently support a data type called 'string', which is a sequence of characters. In practice the values of strings are often words or sentences in some spoken language, though they can, of course, be any sequence of characters.

When you compare string operations with numeric operations, there is a surprising disparity. Everyone agrees that the fundamental operations on numbers are addition, subtraction, multiplication, etc. If you write an expression such as

$$X/(P+2)$$

it is acceptable to almost any programming language. With strings, on the other hand, no-one agrees about anything. Each source language provides different operators, and, at the lower level, machine codes are equally diverse. Languages do not even agree on what a string is. To some a string is an array of single characters; to others it is a single indivisible object; to still others it is a single object which can be chopped up and/or stuck together with other objects.

In consequence, our discussion of the implementation of strings cannot present firm rules, but instead must show several alternative methods.

String variables

When discussing strings it is usual to refer to the size, i.e. the number of characters in a string, as the *length*, and we shall follow this convention. There are essentially three attitudes that source languages can take concerning the length of string variables.

The *fixed-length* method is to insist that each string variable has a fixed pre-defined length. For example a given variable may be declared to have a length of ten characters; its value then has to be a string of exactly ten characters. This method is relatively easy to implement, but severely limiting to the user, and we shall concentrate our attention on more powerful methods.

The *maximum-length* method is to insist that each string variable has a pre-defined maximum length, and to allow its value to vary in length up to this maximum.

The *free* method is to impose no pre-defined limit on the length of strings (though, of course, since computers have a finite size, there must be some absolute maximum).

The following BASIC program provides a simple (and semantically absurd) example of a string variable that varies in length; it could be related either to the maximum-length method or to the free method.

```
FOR K = 1 TO 10
  LET S$ = "X"
  LET S$ = "A STRING OF 25 CHARACTERS"
NEXT K
```

Here the length of the string variable S$ is continually alternating between 1 and 25 characters.

Allocating storage for strings

Most compilers store strings as a single contiguous sequence of characters, and we shall assume this is so. (A few compilers store strings as linked lists.)

If all string variables have a pre-defined maximum length, storage allocation is quite easy. It is simply necessary to reserve enough storage for each variable to accommodate its maximum length. If its actual length is less than the maximum, the excess storage is left unused. Thus the user should keep his maximum as small as he can. If he declares all his strings as having a maximum of a million characters, he will suffer. If the maximum length is an all embracing one (e.g. all strings must be less than 256 characters) rather than one associated with each individual string variable, then the amount of wasted storage will tend to be larger, and it might be better to allocate storage dynamically as described below.

In cases where there is no reasonable limit on the size of each string, storage must be allocated dynamically according to the current size of each string variable. When a string variable is assigned a value, enough storage to contain this value is *borrowed*; the storage containing its previous value, if it existed, is *returned*. In the BASIC example in the previous section, when the string S$ is first assigned the value 'X', a storage area of one character is borrowed. When S$ is subsequently assigned a value of 25 characters, the 1-character area is returned and a new 25-character area borrowed. When S$ is assigned a value of 1 character again, the same process happens in reverse.

More on dynamic storage management

When we considered storage management in Chapter 2.12, we restricted ourselves to storage areas that behaved like stacks. The scheme we have just discussed, where storage is continually being borrowed and returned, is much more general. It therefore requires a different storage management strategy; this might be applied as a sub-strategy for management within one of the dynamic areas we discussed in Chapter 2.12.

The management of storage for our string variables is an interesting and potentially difficult one. Our storage manager starts with one large contiguous block of storage and continually chops off pieces of diverse sizes to satisfy the requests of borrowers. Periodically some of these pieces are returned and can be re-used. Inevitably, as more and more borrowings are made, the available storage becomes increasingly chopped up. This leads to the problem of *storage fragmentation*. The problem comes to a head when there is a request to borrow an area of, say, 100 characters, but the unused storage consists of lots of tiny pieces smaller than 100 characters, although the sum total of all these pieces might be as much as 500 characters. A secondary problem of storage fragmentation is that, even if requests are satisfied, the time taken to satisfy them may become unacceptably long as a result of searching through lots of little pieces.

To combat fragmentation, it is necessary to balance the chopping mechanism by a compensating mechanism that sticks pieces together again. Two adjacent unused pieces, for example, can be combined into a single bigger piece. To illustrate this, assume a request is made to borrow 150 units of storage. This request is satisfied by taking these 150 units from an unused piece of storage of 200 units, thus leaving 50 units still unused. If the 150 units are subsequently returned, and the 50 units are still unused, then the two can be stuck together again to get back the original single block of 200 units. (It may even be that the pieces each side of the 150 units are both unused, thus allowing a double sticking operation.)

If you are interested in dynamic storage for strings, what you should do is this. First have a go at designing your own method, so you get to know what the problems are; then read Gries (1971) to see if there is a better method. Another good book is Volume 1 of Knuth (1973).

Finally, we would like to make three points about managing strings. Firstly, your encoding language may contain built-in storage-management strategies that you can exploit to make your task easier. Secondly, if you create a management scheme to cover strings, you could use it for other aspects of the compiler; for example the internal program is continually having lines added and deleted and thus has some similarity to string variables. Thirdly, in all your work with strings, beware null strings (e.g. LET S$ = " " in BASIC); they are too much for weak compilers to take.

Descriptors for strings

Irrespective of whether your storage allocation for strings is dynamic or static, you will probably find *descriptors* useful. A descriptor is a small fixed-sized object which describes a value. A descriptor for a string usually consists of two items:

(a) the length of the string;
(b) a pointer to the start of the string.

Either constituent of a descriptor may change its value during a run. Descriptors have two big advantages. The first advantage is that, being of a fixed and uniform size, they solve the problem of referencing the value of a string. The layout of the storage used for descriptors of string variables can be fixed in advance by the translator, just like the storage for numeric variables. Thus a descriptor can be referenced directly by operands in the internal program (e.g. the 17th string descriptor, just like our example of the 17th variable).

The second advantage arises when strings are manipulated. These manipulations will probably be performed by subroutines which are passed, as arguments, the strings they have to work on. It is much easier to pass a descriptor as an argument than the value of the string itself.

This ends our present discussion of strings. However string temporaries present a special problem, which merits a chapter to itself, Chapter 5.5.

Descriptors for other variables

Our discussion of the allocation and referencing of variables started with the simplest case, variables of uniform pre-defined size, and then went on to the hardest case, variables whose size changes during a run. It is now time to mention the intermediate case: variables which have differing sizes, but whose sizes are fixed before a run starts. An example of this, in many source languages, is the array. The storage for these can be allocated by the pre-run module, when their size is known, but not by the translator, which does not generally know their size. Hence the descriptor mechanism again comes in useful. The internal program can reference the 17th array descriptor, without knowing where the array itself is, or what bounds it has.

The descriptor for a one-dimensional array typically consists of the following.

(a) A pointer to where the values of the array elements can be found. (We discuss the layout of these in the next section.)
(b) The *upper bound*, i.e. the highest possible value for a subscript (together with the *lower bound* if the source language allows this to vary between arrays).

For a two-dimensional array there is a second upper bound. If the source language only supports one-dimensional and two-dimensional arrays, it is probably best to make all array descriptors the same size. A one-dimensional array could be distinguished by giving the second upper bound an impossible value, perhaps a negative integer.

Descriptors are implemented in the hardware of many modern computers. Here they serve not only the purposes we have described but also aid storage protection and virtual storage mechanisms. This is done by giving an interrupt if an attempt is made to reference an element that is not accessible.

Referencing arrays

An array, like a string, is usually allocated as a contiguous area of storage. (We discuss the actual allocation when we consider the pre-run module in Chapter 6.1.) The main scope for design choice in the layout of this storage comes with two-dimensional arrays, and, *a fortiori*, with three-dimensional arrays if thay are allowed. If an array X has three rows and two columns, there are two possible ways of laying out its elements (we assume subscripts start at 0):

'Row-major' order		'Column-major' order
(0): value of X(0,0)		(0): value of X(0,0)
(1): value of X(0,1)		(1): value of X(1,0)
(2): value of X(1,0)	or	(2): value of X(2,0)
(3): value of X(1,1)		(3): value of X(0,1)
(4): value of X(2,0)		(4): value of X(1,1)
(5): value of X(2,1)		(5): value of X(2,1)

In many situations it is arbitrary which of these you choose. However, there are some cases where it matters: one case arises if your language has a horrible facility whereby the user can supply only one subscript to the two-dimensional array X, and index it as if it were a one-dimensional array. Thus X(4) picks up X(2,0) or X(1,1) depending on which representation you choose. A more important case arises if your run-time system, or the user's program, communicates with outside subroutines, in a library, say. If arrays are passed to these, there will be rules as to how the arrays are represented.

When a reference is made to an array element, e.g. X(0,1), the appropriate address must be found. If we assume row-major order this is done by multiplying the first subscript by the number of columns in the array and then adding the second subscript. Thus X(0,1) can be found in position $0 \times 2 + 1$, which is 1. Your run-time system must, of course, check all subscripts to make sure they are within the bounds of the array; this can be done using the bounds stored in the array descriptor. Note that when an array element is referenced its address, not its value, is placed on the operand stack.

Some compilers regard a calculation such as $0 \times 2 + 1$ as too taxing, since it involves a multiplication—a slow operation on many computers. They therefore represent arrays in a different way which, although it uses more storage, allows elements to be accessed without doing a multiplication. One way of achieving this is to represent a two-dimensional array by means of a vector of descriptors, where each descriptor represents a row of the array. The following picture shows the layout.

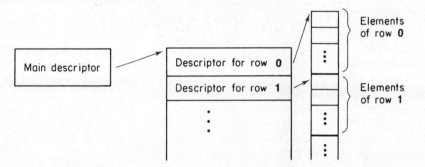

Given this, the element (1,3) is accessed as follows. The row number, 1, and the main descriptor are used to find the descriptor to row 1. The column number, 3, is then used in conjunction with this descriptor to find the correct element.

If your source language allows arrays of strings, you can use a similar method. The layout of a one-dimensional array of strings would look almost identical to the above picture—just substitute the term 'string' for the term 'row'.

Uniformity of addresses

When addresses are placed on the operand stack they may represent such diverse objects as scalar variables, array elements, constants or temporaries. We have suggested that the address of a scalar variable be represented as the offset of that variable within the vector in which all such scalar variables are stored. Similar principles apply to the addresses of other objects. To avoid potential ambiguity (e.g. between the 17th variable and the 17th temporary) it may be necessary to add special markers to addresses. Alternatively the ambiguity may be resolved as a consequence of the method of storage allocation. In practice all the compiler's storage, whether for scalars, arrays, temporaries, etc., will be taken from a single 'master' vector of storage. (After all, the underlying computer usually has a single vector of storage.) If addresses are represented as positions within this 'master' vector they are unambiguous.

Chapter 5.4

Execution of Statements

In Chapter 5.2 we discussed the general principles of the execution of internal language programs and we made more detailed studies of function and subroutine calls. In Chapter 5.3 we suggested some principles for storage allocation and referencing. Given these general principles the execution of perhaps 80% of the statements in a typical language becomes quite straightforward. A few statements, however, present additional problems and in this chapter we discuss four of these: non-executable statements, immediate statements, input/output, and loops.

Non-executable statements

Consider the BASIC program

```
10 LET A = 1
20 DEF . . .
30 DIM . . .
40 REM . . .
50 DATA . . .
60 LET B = A+1
```

When the program is run, the effect is as if statement 60 follows immediately after statement 10, because the intervening statements are *non-executable*.

It is best if the internal form of each non-executable statement begins with an operator, e.g. the first element of a REM statement could be the operator *REM*. The run-time system can then treat all such operators as meaning 'proceed to next statement'. Note that, in many source languages, the user's program may be allowed to GOTO a non-executable statement.

Take care with DEF statements because they are executed when the corresponding function is called. Such execution should start with the second element, thus ignoring the 'proceed to next statement' operator at the start.

Immediate statements

You can treat the execution of an immediate statement in a similar way to a normal run. Indeed if the immediate statement jumps to the first line of the main program the effect is identical to a normal run. Take care with error messages from immediate statements, since they do not, in most languages, have line-numbers. Make sure that, when the immediate statement has finished, control returns to the user; you might do this by appending an internal 'return to user' statement after the immediate statement. (This pseudo-statement is a useful return point if there is an immediate subroutine call.) Make sure the translator rejects absurdities like an immediate DEF statement, so they do not upset the run-time system.

Immediate statements should not be incorporated as part of the main program, and their headers normally take a different form from ordinary statements. After they have been executed they should be deleted; this applies irrespective of whether they execute successfully or produce a run-time error.

Input and output

Input and output operations are simple in principle but in practice often bring up a host of annoying difficulties and special conditions. The following are some of them.

Line overflow

You need a consistent strategy for dealing with the case where an output line is too long. Assume, for example, that output lines consist of 72 characters, and 60 characters in the output buffer are already filled. What do you do if the user tries to print a 13-character string, or even a 73-character string?

Formats

If your source language supports real numbers, converting between internal and external format can be a heavy task. Consider, for example, the job of inputting the constant 50.09324E-17, and then outputting it again. On output, numbers do not have a unique representation (for example 5, .5E1, +5, 50E-1, 5.0, all represent the same number), but your source language will, if properly defined, contain rules prescribing how each number is to be printed. Even if these rules are framed to make the task of the run-time system as easy as possible, the task will certainly not be trivial. Also beware overflow; make sure your routines can deal with the biggest number the machine can hold, and give a sensible error response if the user inputs a number bigger than this.

End-of-file

It is valuable to the user to be able to specify some action to be performed if the end of an input file is reached (e.g. AT 'END OF FILE' GOSUB . . .). Similarly the user may wish to control other 'exceptional' I/O conditions, and generally increase his freedom of action in error situations.

Differing media

Some languages allow input to come not only from the user's terminal or a file, but also from other media such as the source program (the DATA and READ facility in BASIC) or from the value of a string variable. It is usually easy to combine all such facilities into a single input routine (e.g. READ and INPUT in BASIC can be combined into one if DATA lines are represented like input lines), but take care to give the correct response to error conditions.

Deadlocks

Comprehensive input/output facilities give the user plenty of rope to hang himself. Save him from the noose. Make sure that whatever stupid thing he does (like taking input from a non-existent device, using a paper tape reader with no paper in it, setting his line width to zero) he can escape, say by typing the break-in key.

A second chance

A principle of interactive systems is immediate error detection. If the user is asked to input a number, for example, and he types one of the following incorrect numbers

        X
        3X7
        2.3.1
        3E999 (a number which we assume is too big for the machine to
               hold)
        − −1

then the error should be pointed out and the user given a second chance. If his input is syntactically correct but logically wrong, like a value of 1000 for his age, the detection of the error will, of course, be the duty of the user's program rather than the input routines.

Graphics

If your source language supports some form of graphical input/output, our assumption that the input/output module works in lines of characters may be inadequate. General advice in this area is hard to give, because of the great variability of languages and devices. It is well worth putting effort into graphics, if you have a suitable device, because they give the user an extra dimension in communicating with the machine, and therefore add fundamentally to the power of your compiler.

Looping statements

Almost every language contains looping statements, and some of these can cause problems for the run-time system. The most frequent kind of looping statement is the FOR statement, as exemplified in BASIC by

> FOR K = 1 TO X/3 STEP Y
> .
> .
> .
> NEXT K

Here K is called the *controlled variable*. Many newer languages supplement FORs by a WHILE statement. If your source language supports a WHILE this is good news; it is an excellent facility for the user and the problems of executing it are less than for a FOR. We concentrate here on the problems of the FOR.

In most (but certainly not all) source languages the following rules apply to FORs.

(a) The *step* and *limit* (i.e. Y and X/3 in the above example) are evaluated once at the start of the loop. Thus in our example, if X changed its value during the execution of the loop this would have no effect on the FOR statement.

(b) If the initial value is beyond the limit (e.g. FOR K = 1 TO N where N is zero, or FOR K = 1 TO N STEP − 1 where N is 2) then the loop is not executed at all.

(c) It is legal to jump out of the loop before it has finished, e.g.

> FOR K = 1 TO 100
> .
> .
> .
> IF . . . THEN 200
> .
> .
> .
> NEXT K
> .
> .
> .
> 200 . . .

The consequences of (a) above are that the step and limit should be calculated in advance and placed in temporaries. It is not, for most source languages, a good plan to put these temporaries on the operand stack because of the danger of their being left there as permanent garbage. This could happen, for example, if there was a jump out of the loop as in (c) above. The temporaries are best placed in a special block of storage called a *FOR-block*. Each FOR statement has its own FOR-block—we shall discuss how these might be allocated later.

Given these rules, the tasks of a FOR statement on first entering a loop are the following.

(a) Set the controlled variable to its initial value.
(b) Evaluate the step and limit and place their values in the FOR-block.
(c) Test if the controlled variable is over the limit, and if so, abandon the loop by jumping to beyond the NEXT. If the step is negative, the test should abandon the loop if the controlled variable is under, not over, the limit.

Be careful to do (a) and (b) in the correct order. Some source languages say that (b) should be done first. It does make a difference as the following example shows:

    LET K = 3
    FOR K = 1 TO K

When the loop controlled by a FOR statement is entered, it becomes *active*. When the NEXT statement is executed the step is added to the controlled variable, the testing against the limit is repeated and, if the loop is to continue, execution resumes at the statement beyond the FOR; otherwise the loop becomes *inactive*. The significance of an inactive loop is that it should not be jumped into from outside, as we shall see later. (For a WHILE–NEXT loop there is no need for temporary variables and the NEXT is usually simply a jump back to the WHILE. The condition controlling the loop—e.g. WHILE A+B>C—must be re-evaluated each time round.)

Allocating FOR-blocks

FOR-blocks are best allocated by the pre-run module, which can count the number of FOR statements and then reserve the necessary number of FOR-blocks. The Nth FOR statement could use the Nth FOR-block. We call the value of N the *FOR-block number*. To help the run-time system, the internal form of a FOR statement might start with a special operator, *FORSTART*, which is followed by two context-dependent fields giving (a) the FOR-block number, and (b) a pointer to the statement after the NEXT.

A clever pre-run module might share the same FOR-block between more than one FOR statement, but such cleverness is rarely worth while.

The internal form of each NEXT statement should have a context-dependent field pointing at the corresponding FOR, so the run-time system will know where to go back to.

The following picture shows how a loop might be represented internally.

FOR K = . . .
      header
      OPERATOR + *FORSTART*
      *FOR-block number
      *pointer to statement beyond corresponding NEXT
      OPERAND + dictionary subscript for K
      ⋮

      (internal form of the rest of the FOR statement)
NEXT K
      header
      OPERAND + dictionary subscript for K
      OPERATOR + *NEXT*
      *pointer to header of corresponding FOR

The fields marked with an asterisk are the context-dependent ones filled in by the pre-run module. On executing the NEXT, the run-time system can find what FOR-block is in use by looking at the corresponding FOR. If the loop is to be repeated, it jumps to the statement beyond the FOR.

Jumping into loops

Consider, if you can, the following horrible program.

    ⋮
    GOTO 100
    ⋮
    FOR K = 1 TO 10
    ⋮
100 . . .
    ⋮
    NEXT K

Any good source language should ban programs such as this, which jump into a loop from outside. Sometimes the syntax of the source language makes these jumps impossible, but more often the run-time system is left with the task of enforcing the restriction. Remember that all source language rules must be enforced, and if no other module acts as policeman then the run-time system must do the job.

Happily the use of FOR-blocks can make enforcement simple. A good method is to set the step in every inactive FOR-block to an impossible value, which we shall call UNASSIGNED; then, when a NEXT statement accesses the step, it checks whether it is UNASSIGNED and, if so, gives the appropriate error message. To ensure that the step of every inactive FOR-block is UNASSIGNED, it is necessary to initialize all steps to UNASSIGNED at the start of the run; moreover whenever a FOR loop becomes inactive, as a result of the controlled variable passing its limit, the step is set back to UNASSIGNED. In principle the approach is to shut all the gates at the start of a run, and to make sure that all gates are shut after they have been used; trespassers into FOR loops are then stopped and punished (at least when they reach the NEXT).

This strategy does not treat the following program as an error:

```
     FOR K = 1 TO 10
       .
       .
     GOTO 200
       .
       .
 100 ...
       .
       .
     NEXT K
       .
 200 GOTO 100
```

Jumping out of an active FOR and then back again, although horrible programming according to most people's aesthetics, at least has a consistent and well-defined meaning, and there is thus a case for allowing it.

Make sure the definition of your source language squares exactly with the rule you enforce. The rule we have enforced is not, in fact: 'You must not jump into a FOR loop from outside'. It is: 'You must not execute the NEXT of an inactive FOR loop'.

Chapter 5.5

String Temporaries

This is a specialized chapter dealing with the problems of allocating temporary strings in languages that offer powerful operations on strings of varying size. (Similar problems apply to other objects of varying size.) If these problems do not affect your source language, you are fortunate enough to be able to skip this chapter, with all its low-level detail.

The need for string temporaries

String temporaries are needed during the execution of string expressions in the same way as numeric temporaries are needed during the execution of numeric expressions. Consider as an example the BASIC string expression

$$\text{SEG\$(A\$\&B\$,X,Y) \& SEG\$(C\$\&D\$,P,Q)}$$

where, following normal conventions, the operator '&' is used to denote concatenation, and the built-in function SEG$(*S,M,N*) takes the substring of the string *S* from the *M*th character to the *N*th (e.g. SEG$ ('PIGGY',2,4) is 'IGG'). During the execution of this expression the first operation performed is A$&B$. The result needs to be placed in a temporary. This temporary is subsequently passed as an argument to the routine that implements the SEG$ built-in function—we call this routine SEGROUTINE. The result of the call of SEGROUTINE (i.e. the substring of A$&B$ from the Xth to the Yth character) is returned in another temporary. Then C$&D$ is calculated, yielding another temporary, which is subsequently passed to a second call of SEGROUTINE. This again yields a result that is placed in a temporary location. Lastly the two temporaries returned from the calls of SEGROUTINE are concatenated, forming the final result of the expression, which itself will probably be placed in a temporary.

If strings are addressed via descriptors in your compiler, then it is obviously sensible to address temporary strings likewise. In this case a temporary descriptor is created alongside every temporary string.

Use of stacks

String temporaries, like numeric temporaries, can be organized as a stack. Every time a new string temporary is needed the requisite space is taken from the stack; when the value of the string temporary has been used, the space is returned. For this to work it must be guaranteed that the temporary string on the top of the stack is the next one to be used.

The string stack may or may not be a separate one from the operand stack, which we have suggested is used for numeric temporaries. (Our apologies for this vacuous advice, but the choice of method depends on your encoding language and your storage allocation strategy.) It may be that string descriptors including, of course, temporary descriptors, use the operand stack, whereas string temporaries themselves have a separate stack. For the purposes of this discussion we shall assume a separate string stack.

There are special problems with string temporaries. Consider the expression

$$B\$ \ \& \ SEG\$(A\$,X,Y)$$

Assume that B\$ has the value 'PROB' and that SEGROUTINE has returned the result 'LEM' (being the value of the call of SEG\$) in a temporary string. The concatenate routine—we call this CATROUTINE—is then called with the stack of string temporaries containing the single string 'LEM'. When CATROUTINE gets to work, it needs to build up its result in a temporary. If it reserves the storage for this temporary before the temporary containing 'LEM' has been released, then 'LEM' is no longer at the top of the stack and cannot therefore be released. On return from CATROUTINE the stack contains the two strings 'LEM' and 'PROBLEM'. If no remedial action is taken 'LEM' forever remains on the stack as garbage.

If, on the other hand, the temporary 'LEM' is released earlier, there is a danger that it may be overwritten by the result of CATROUTINE before it has been used. This is because CATROUTINE would most naturally work by moving its first argument into the temporary to be used for the result, and then adding the second on the end. If it does this. 'PROB' is moved on top of 'LEM', thus destroying 'LEM' before it is used.

The reasons that such problems do not happen with numeric operations are two-fold. Firstly, there is often no need for the run-time routine to build up the result in stages; thus for a multiply operation the hardware might produce a complete answer in one go. This answer could then overwrite the multiplicands, which are no longer needed. Secondly, if the result does need building up, it can be done in some fixed place, perhaps a machine accumulator or a fixed variable, that does not interfere with the temporary stack.

It may be possible to carry this second advantage of numeric operators over to strings by having a special piece of storage called the *string accumulator*. Each string operation uses this to build up its result. When the result is complete it can be copied, if necessary, to the temporary stack. If temporaries are passed as arguments to string operations, their storage can be released when they are passed, as there is no danger of their being overwritten until they are no longer needed. The string-accumulator concept is most attractive when strings have a reasonably small maximum length.

Other possible solutions

If you decide not to use a string accumulator there are at least two other possible methods to explore, each of which might eliminate the problems of garbage being left on the stack of string temporaries.

One method is for routines like CATROUTINE and SEGROUTINE to take special action when they find they have temporary strings as arguments. With our 'LEM' example, CATROUTINE might take special action when the second argument was a temporary (with an even more special action if the first argument was also a temporary). One possibility is to copy the second argument into its final position before copying the first argument, e.g. first add four characters to the temporary that contains 'LEM'—then copy 'LEM' into the last three characters of this temporary—then copy 'PROB' into its first four characters.

A second method is to clean out, at the start of each new statement, any garbage left on the string stack. Note that there is a special danger of garbage accumulating after errors, break-ins and other exceptions.

Functions

Consider the BASIC statements

    10 DEF FNA = LEN(C$&D$)
        ⋮
    50 LET V$ = SEG$(A$&B$, FNA,10)

where LEN is the built-in function that returns the length of its argument. In executing statement 50 the result of A$&B$ is first put in a temporary string, and then the function FNA is called. FNA needs its own temporary string for calculating C$&D$. Care must be taken that temporaries needed in such function calls do not interfere with those of the calling statement. This requires special wariness if multi-line functions are allowed.

Optimization

A clever compiler can, by looking at string operations closely, avoid lots of redundant work. Thus the BASIC statement LET A$ = A$&B$ just requires adding B$ to the end of A$. No temporary string is needed for A$&B$. Even with LET A$ = B$&C$ the result can be built up in A$, without the need for a temporary string.

Even though there are large savings to be made, such optimizations are only really practical in large and expensive compilers. The cases that are suitable for optimization are surprisingly hard to recognize, and there are always nasty cases that are liable to upset optimization strategies, e.g. LET A$ = X$&A$ cannot be accomplished by moving X$ into A$ and then tacking A$ onto the end.

Assignment to sub-strings

Some languages that really go to town on string manipulation allow assignment to sub-strings, e.g.

LET SEG$(A$,2,4) = "PIG"

replaces characters 2 to 4 of A$ by the string 'PIG', leaving the rest of A$ unchanged.

Such features make the implementor's task much harder. Use of functions such as SEG$ in the above context requires completely different treatment from their use in string expressions. To prevent complete anarchy, it is desirable to enforce a restriction that it is only permissible to assign to a sub-string of a string that already exists. If not, in the above example, characters 2 to 4 of A$ might exist after the execution of the LET statement, whereas the rest of A$ would not. In such circumstances checking for unassigned values becomes difficult, and properties such as the length of a string become hard to define.

The message that comes out of this is really one for language designers: if you are going to allow assignment to sub-strings, be sure you understand the full implications of what you are doing—and spare a thought for the implementors.

Part 6

OTHER MODULES

Chapter 6.1

The Pre-run Module

The task of the pre-run module is to process all the context-dependent aspects of the source language. It bridges the gap between the translator, which works on a line-by-line basis ignoring context, and the run-time system, which requires a completely integrated internal program to run. Its task can be divided into two separate aspects:

(1) checking for context-dependent errors in syntax.
(2) filling in context-dependent fields in the internal program and its associated tables. In some compilers the pre-run module builds entire tables from scratch, such as a table of array declarations.

These jobs are done when the program is complete and ready to run. In BASIC compilers, the pre-run module is usually quite small but, in languages with more structure and more data types than BASIC, the pre-run module may be nearly as big as the translator or run-time system.

A further task which the pre-run module might profitably do is to allocate storage for the user's variables. We discuss this towards the end of the current chapter.

Examples of context-dependent errors

To give a feel for the checking task of the pre-run module, it is worth looking at an example which shows the kind of errors that should be detected in BASIC. In the following program every single line is acceptable to the translator, but nevertheless all but three of them contain context-dependent errors.

10	DIM X(20),Y(6,7)	A correct line
20	DIM X(10)	Double declaration of X
30	PRINT FNA	Undefined function
40	PRINT Y(6)	Wrong number of subscripts
50	IF P = Q THEN 42	Non-existent line-number
60	DEF FNB = 6	A correct line
70	PRINT FNB(3)	Wrong number of arguments
80	NEXT K	NEXT without FOR
90	FOR K = 1 TO 3	A correct line

```
100 NEXT P          Unmatched NEXT
110 FOR U = 1 TO 3  Unmatched FOR
```

As we said in Chapter 4.5, BASIC generally has manifest data types and therefore .can do most of its checking in the translator. Source languages with less manifest data types leave a heavier burden of type checking to the pre-run module. This checking is likely to be similar to that required in BASIC for array and function declarations, but extended in scope. It is unlikely to require any fundamentally different mechanisms. Likewise the structuring represented in BASIC by matching FORs and NEXTs can be considerably extended in other source languages by the wide use of constructs such as BEGIN . . END and IF . . FI. Again this is an increase in the volume rather than in the fundamental nature of the checking.

In this chapter we base most of the discussion and examples on checking function calls and matching FOR with NEXT. It should be a simple matter to adapt these methods to cover other context-dependent constructions in your source language, such as array references, subroutine calls, and BEGIN . . . END.

Delaying checking until run-time

In some compilers the pre-run module passes the buck by leaving some of its error-checking tasks to the run-time system. The pre-run module does not, for example, check each call of a user-defined function (or subroutine) to make sure that it is declared and has appropriate parameters. Instead, when each function call is actually executed on a run, the run-time system does the checking. In this case, an error in a function call that is not executed on a given run remains undetected; it remains in the program as a landmine, waiting for the day the unwary user finally treads on it.

In compilers that are written by more than one person, such buck-passing may be a matter of personalities. The run-time man may, for example, be the archetype of the 'before' picture in the muscle-building adverts, and thus gets imposed upon by everyone else.

There is, however, a wider justification. This is that the buck-passing avoids the overheads of the pre-run module making a detailed scan of the internal program to identify function calls, array references, etc. The run-time system already contains routines to perform certain actions at function calls, array references, and so on. Adding an extra task to these routines involves no further scanning overhead.

Nevertheless even if the buck-passing makes the overall compiler slightly simpler, we are still against it because it makes the compiler a worse product for the user. There has been a powerful movement in computing to make programs more reliable, thus ensuring that a 'tested' program does not suddenly collapse in a heap during a production run, because it has run into a situation which it never encountered before. This movement is greatly to be welcomed. One way to help reliability is to move error checking earlier in the development cycle. An error detected when a statement is typed in is better than the same error being detected during a production run; in an ideal world programs would be proved correct before they were even fed to the compiler, thus removing errors at an even earlier stage. The buck-passing described above goes against this movement; it leaves more errors to be detected at run-time and thus makes user programs less reliable. If you are ever in a space ship controlled by a computer, make sure its program has full error checking in the pre-run module.

Filling in context-dependent fields

Even if it passes the buck on some of its error checking duties, the pre-run module should never shirk its task of filling context-dependent fields. Even if the run-time system is to check a function call, it must be told, in the dictionary of function names, whether the function is defined and, if so, where and with what parameters; otherwise the run-time system needs to search the entire internal program at each call, trying to find the definition.

There is an important principle here, which carries over to all the work of the pre-run module. This is that any context-dependent field in which no information is placed must be set to a special value meaning 'undefined'. It applies to fields in dictionaries and in the internal program; it even applies to any fields which are actually to be filled in by the run-time system. For example, if no definition is found for a function whose name is in a dictionary, the dictionary field that points to its definition must be explicitly marked as undefined. It is no use leaving the field unchanged; the function may have been defined previously, and the field may be left pointing at a definition that has been deleted. It is not necessarily an error if an object used in a dictionary is undefined. The dictionary entry may be a redundant one, as we discussed in Chapter 2.11. If an undefined object is actually referenced in the internal program, this is, of course, an error.

Thus the first task of the pre-run module is likely to be to mark all context-dependent fields as undefined. Its next task is to find all the declarative statements in the internal program and copy the relevant information into the appropriate context-dependent fields within dictionary entries. However, rather than perform this task in isolation, it is better to integrate it with other tasks.

The single scan

Many of the tasks of the pre-run module are concerned with searching for particular constructions within the internal program, and taking appropriate actions at each occurrence. Usually it is possible to perform all these tasks in a single sequential scan of the internal program. The likely tasks include the following.

(a) Copying declarative information into dictionaries, as we have just indicated.
(b) Matching FOR with NEXT, and other operations concerned with block structure.
(c) Joining together of related statements. In BASIC, for example, it is useful to connect all DATA statements together. This can be done by inserting a context-dependent field, within each DATA statement, to point to the next DATA statement in the internal program (if any). This helps with the execution of READ statements, which need to take DATA statements in sequence. Similar principles apply to any other case where a sequence of related statements can be scattered throughout the internal program.
(d) The error-checking tasks concerned with data types.

With task (a) it helps if the internal form of declarative statements is very close to the format of dictionary entries. Then the task is simply one of copying information across—remember that the translator will already have checked that the declarations are syntactically correct. Before copying anything across, the pre-run module must, however, make sure the object has not already been defined. If so, the same object has been declared twice in the user's program—an error in almost any language.

Tasks (b) and (c) are straightforward. We used task (b) as an example in Chapter 2.1 when explaining the use of stacks.

Tasks (a), (b) and (c) only involve scanning a few selected statements in the internal program, whereas task (d) usually necessitates a complete analysis of every statement. This is why it is this task, rather than the others, that may be the victim of buck-passing. Nevertheless we assume that you, the implementor of the pre-run module, have saintly qualities and do not stint your own efforts if the result is a better product. Alternatively the assumption is that the implementor of the run-time system has taken his muscle-building course. In either case the buck stops, and we discuss in this chapter how to deal with it.

Scanning and pseudo-execution

Given that the buck stops, the pre-run module must scan the entire internal program from beginning to end. To check function calls, it needs to identify every occurrence of operators such as *CALLUD1ARG* and *CALLUD0ARG*, and find the operands to each. One of the operands is the function name. The dictionary entry for the function name is consulted to make sure the function has been defined (we assume, for the moment, that declaration precedes use), and to find what argument(s) are expected. The actual arguments are then checked against this expectation to make sure there are no errors. Similar actions are performed for array references, subroutine calls, GOTOs and any other context-dependent operations.

The methods for scanning Reverse Polish internal language have already been covered in Chapter 5.2 in the context of the run-time system. The pre-run module can share the same scanning routines and the same area for the operand stack. It differs from the run-time system in that it does not execute any operators; instead it performs checking, where necessary, and *pseudo-execution*. Pseudo-execution consists of putting symbolic markers on the operand stack to represent the result of operators, rather than genuine values. These symbolic markers give the nature of the result (e.g. NUMERICEXPRESSION, STRINGEXPRESSION) in case this is needed for further checking. As an example consider the function call FNA(X + Y) which in internal form is represented as

$$\text{FNA X Y} + CALLUD1ARG$$

Immediately before the '+' operator is pseudo-executed, the operand stack contains the three operands: FNA X Y. Afterwards the stack contains the two operands: FNA NUMERICEXPRESSION. The operator *CALLUD1ARG* is then applied to these two operands, and the requisite checking is done. The pseudo-result of this function call is NUMERICEXPRESSION.

The operators that require special actions by the pre-run module are usually in a minority. Most operators, and these normally include all the arithmetic operators, do no more than produce a pseudo-result.

Note that the pre-run module cannot, in general, check for errors that depend on the run-time behaviour of the program, such as a subscript too big or division by zero. Thus it cannot check whether X/Y would give an error. It can, however, perform such checks when operands are constants (e.g. X/0), but this is not generally worth doing. It is better to leave the responsibility for such errors squarely with the run-time system.

A few languages support a 'dynamic' GOTO, such as

$$\text{GOTO X+3}$$

which is allowed in a few dialects of BASIC. These cannot be checked until run-time. Our feeling is that such facilities are best banned because they make source programs unreadable and unreliable, but if they exist in your source language, you will need to put the necessary checking in your run-time system. If you follow the philosophy we have just espoused with the 'division by zero' example, you will then put *all* checking of GOTOs into the run-time system. It is even possible that your source language might support a similar dynamic feature with function names, where the name of the function can be calculated at run-time (e.g. "FN" & X$, where X$ might have the value 'A', making the function name FNA). If your source language is built upon such shifting sands, your pre-run module might as well give up the struggle.

Declaration after use

Some languages require objects to be declared before they are used, whereas others allow declarations to appear anywhere in the program. Languages that allow GOTOs almost invariably allow the position of the designated line to be declared after its use—this is simply a forward GOTO. Fortunately, declaration after use is not a major problem for the pre-run module. It is not even necessary to abandon the strategy of making a single scan through the internal program. It suffices to adapt the strategy as follows.

If, during its scan of the internal program, the pre-run module finds an object that has not been declared, it cannot give an error message in case the object is declared later. Instead it marks the dictionary entry for the object as 'must be declared'; if the reference is, say, to a function call with one argument, it also fills into the dictionary entry the information that the function has one argument. When a declaration of the 'must be declared' object is found, this declaration is processed in the normal way, except that an additional check is made to make sure the declaration matches any information placed in the dictionary as a result of the previous reference to the object (e.g. if the previous reference was to a function with one argument, the declaration must also specify one argument). If a second reference to the object is found before its declaration, the same additional check is made to ensure this second reference has consistent properties with the first. At the end of the scan the dictionaries are checked to see if any objects have the property 'must be declared'. If so an error message is given. (Any objects that remain in their initial state of 'undefined' rather than 'must be declared' are redundant ones, since they cannot have been referenced in the program. They can therefore be deleted from the dictionary if this is thought worth doing.)

Error detection and error recovery

The translator, when it finds an error in a line, is entitled to give up as the line will need to be re-typed. The pre-run module, on the other hand, should continue its work in order that it can find all the errors in a program. Occasionally it may give a few spurious errors because a genuine error earlier in the program has upset it. The following two examples illustrate this point.

Example 1	*Example 2*
FOR J . . .	FOR J . . .
.	.
.	.
FOR K . . .	FOR K . . .
.	.
.	.
NEXT J	.
.	NEXT J
.	
NEXT J	

In Example 1 the user has written NEXT J rather than NEXT K. In Example 2 he has omitted NEXT K altogether. In each case, when the pre-run module comes to the (first) NEXT J it gives an error. At this stage, one strategy for error recovery is to cancel the offending NEXT against the most recent FOR and continue the scan; this does well on Example 1, but gives a spurious error on Example 2 because it thinks that the FOR J is unmatched. An alternative is to try to match the offending NEXT against other FORs that are still unmatched; this does well on Example 2, but gives a spurious error on Example 1 because it thinks that the second NEXT J is unmatched.

Such spurious errors are unfortunate but inevitable; they merit an explanation in the user manual, and a certain caution in the wording of error messages (e.g. 'NEXT' MAY NOT MATCH 'FOR'). It would be even more unfortunate if the pre-run module gave up after the first error. In this case the user would have a tedious time detecting and correcting his errors one by one.

When the pre-run module has completed all its checking, it should refuse to run the program if any errors have been found. The run-time system then has the advantage of knowing that, when it is entered, it always has an internal program that is completely correct in syntax (assuming no bucks are passed) and thus does not require any further checking in this regard.

All error messages must give the line-number of the offender. This applies particularly to errors that are only detected at the end of the scan. Sample messages might be:

*** ERROR: UNMATCHED FOR STATEMENT IN LINE 200
*** ERROR: FUNCTION FNA IS NOT DECLARED; FIRST USED IN
    LINE 300

Even better is to list the offending line, e.g.

*** ERROR: UNMATCHED FOR STATEMENT IN LINE:
*** 200 FOR U = 2 TO 7

In order to give the line-number it is necessary to record it. Thus when a dictionary entry is marked 'must be declared', the line-number of the first reference to the object should also be placed in its dictionary entry in case it needs to be used in a subsequent error message.

Default declarations

Every feature introduced by the language designer has, of course, an impact on some part of the compiler. There is one feature by which the language designer can give sleepless nights to the implementor of the pre-run module. This is the 'default declaration', a feature whereby the declaration of an object may optionally be omitted and, if so, certain properties are assumed for it.

The definition of standard BASIC (at the time of writing) contains the devastating sentence: 'Unless explicitly declared by a DIM statement, subscripted variables are implicitly declared by their first occurrence in the program'. It then goes on to say that the upper bound is assumed to be 10 in this case. It is not clear what 'first' means. If it means the first usage during a run of a program, then consider the example.

```
10 INPUT N
20 IF N = 0 THEN 50
30 LET X(1) = 0
40 GOTO 60
50 LET X(1,1) = 0
60 . . .
```

Here it is not known whether X is one-dimensional or two-dimensional until the program is run and it is found whether N is 0.

If 'first' is taken to mean the first occurrence in a static scan of the program (or even the first that is typed in) possible problems still remain. Many BASICs (though not standard minimal BASIC) have MAT statements for manipulating whole arrays; thus MAT X = Y copies the array Y into the array X. Consider the program

```
10 DIM Y(3,3)
20 MAT X = Y
```

Here the pre-run module has presumably got to be clever enough to deduce that X is two-dimensional because Y is. Its deductive powers would need to be cleverer still if the DIM statement for Y had come after the MAT statement.

The moral to language designers is that default declarations are not the harmless things they look; they require extremely careful thought, particularly if it is the language designer who also has the task of writing a compiler. Let us hope your source language has no default declarations of arrays or other data aggregates and that you can laugh at the problems we have raised (and shall raise again soon).

Immediate statements

The execution of an immediate statement counts as a run, and causes the pre-run module to be entered in the normal way. Note that the pre-run module does not just examine the immediate statement itself; instead it must process the complete internal program (if one exists). This is because, assuming immediate statements can use any facility of the source language, they can reference objects in the internal program or jump to a line of the internal program.

Allocation of storage for variables

Two points made in earlier chapters have an important bearing on the pre-run module. Firstly, values of variables need to be carried over from one run to a subsequent immediate run, so that the user can print values of variables to aid his debugging; some compilers go further and carry the values of variables over from one run to the next irrespective of whether it is immediate. Secondly, the storage for arrays cannot be reserved until the pre-run module has finished processing declarations of array bounds; in Chapter 5.3 we considered how the storage for arrays could be laid out (e.g. in row-major order, accessed via a descriptor), but we did not discuss how the actual reservation was made.

We shall finish this chapter by trying to clear up these matters, with particular attention to arrays and the carrying over of values between runs. If you do your storage allocation at run-time rather than in the pre-run module, the same principles apply. Likewise they may apply to other data structures as well as arrays.

The carrying over of values from one run to another places extra demands on storage allocation strategies. An attractive strategy is to decree that if values of all variables are to be carried over from run 1 to run 2, then no further storage allocation is done for the second run—everything is just left as it was at the end of the first run. Unfortunately this strategy will not work for most source languages. Even if the second run is an immediate run it could introduce new scalar variables and new arrays. Examples from BASIC are the immediate statements.

$$\text{LET } X = A+B$$
$$\text{LET } Y(3) = A+3$$

where neither X nor Y previously existed. (By the BASIC default rule Y should be created as a vector with an upper bound of 10.) Thus at the beginning of run 2 there may be a task of allocating new variables and consolidating them with the old.

Worse still, the program could be edited between run 1 and run 2, and the declared bounds of arrays could be changed or even deleted (thus making an array revert to default size). Most compilers, not unreasonably, thrown up their hands at this and make the rule that if an array changes size then all its previous values cease to exist.

As a final straw, default declarations can wreak further havoc. Consider the following successive BASIC immediate statements

$$\text{LET } X(1) = 3$$
$$\text{LET } X(1,1) = 3$$

Presumably X should be created as a vector for the first statement and then, when the second statement is executed, the old X is thrown away and a new two-dimensional X is created.

Since most of the problems are with arrays, we shall consider how arrays can be allocated. Scalars are relatively easy to allocate (and the job may even be done by the translator, as we have already mentioned). In formulating our strategy for arrays we shall assume that

(a) if an array changes size, all its previous values are lost and its new values set to 'unassigned'.
(b) within the dictionary entry for an array, there is a field which contains a pointer to the start of a contiguous area where the array elements are stored. (The pointer may actually be part of a descriptor.) If the array has not yet been allocated this field is set to a special marker meaning 'no storage exists'.

When the pre-run module comes to copy bounds into the dictionary entry, it looks to see if storage already exists for the array. If so, it checks that the new bounds are the same as the previous ones; if they are, all is well and the previous values are left alone; if they are not, the existing storage is released and new storage allocated with its contents set to 'unassigned'. (There may be more problems with default declarations here, particularly if a default declaration is overridden by an explicit declaration of the same size—but enough of such nightmares.) If an array is marked as 'no storage exists', new storage is allocated for it with its contents set to 'unassigned'.

The allocation of the storage areas in which the values of the array elements are actually stored comes under the compiler's overall storage management strategy. We have assumed that each array occupies a contiguous area of storage and that space for the whole array is reserved in one go. A few compilers, such as SOBS (Rees and Oppenheimer, 1977), allow 'sparse arrays', where storage is only allocated for the elements that are actually used. One crude way to allocate arrays is to place them end to end within a steadily growing contiguous area. If an array is de-allocated for any reason (e.g. because its size has been changed), the space released can either be left to lie fallow, or, at the cost of some extra complication, the array(s) beyond it can be shifted up or down to make the space the right size for the new array bounds. The pictures below show these two strategies. An array Y is assumed to have been re-declared to have a different size.

Array X		Array X		Array X
Array Y		Unused		New Array Y
Array Z		Array Z		Array Z
Array P		Array P		Array P
		New Array Y		

| 1. Before re-allo-
cation of Y | 2. Case where
old Y is left
unused | 3. Case where new Y
re-uses space of
old Y |

In all cases where a new variable is allocated, whether a scalar or an array, the variable should be given the initial value(s) of 'unassigned'.

An optimization

The pre-run module has a fair amount of work to do, which will take a perceptible amount of computer time. If the internal program is re-run without any change, little or none of this work needs to be repeated. It is therefore a useful optimization if this case can be detected and the pre-run module given a rest from its labours.

Putting stops on the end

A final job that the pre-run module might usefully do is to insert an artificial 'stop' instruction at the end of the internal program. This prevents the run-time system from falling off the end.

Chapter 6.2

The Re-creator Module

An interactive system requires a facility for the user to list or save (in a disc file, say) all or part of his source program. If the user's program is maintained in source form this is a trivial task, and if your compiler does this you can skip this chapter.

If the source is re-created from internal form the task of re-building the source requires some thought, and the more the internal language differs from the source, the more thought and effort is needed. Even so, the re-creator module, which performs this task, is rarely very large.

The re-creator will, like the translator, work one line at a time. If it is providing a complete listing it will go sequentially through the internal program from beginning to end. Sometimes, it will take a sub-set of the internal program, and this might even consist of a single line. A single line is required, for example, if the re-creator is called to list the offending line in an error message. Each re-created line is listed at the terminal, or, if the re-creator has been called to implement a SAVE command, sent to a file.

We shall assume here that a line corresponds to a statement as we did for the translator. As in the translator, it would not be hard to adapt our methods to deal with a language where several statements are written on one line.

Spacing within re-created lines

Most internal languages contain no information about the spacing in the original source line. The re-creator therefore imposes its own standard spacing on the re-created source line. For example, the original line might have taken either of the forms

```
10LETA=3
10 LET A  =  3
```

but the re-created line would always take the standard form, such as

```
10 LET A = 3
```

If your compiler imposes standard spacing, you are free to design the layout according to your own ideas of what is most visually attractive, subject, of course, to any constraints imposed by the source-language definition. The following hints may help you in your choice.

(a) Do not under any circumstances make your spacing up as you go along. Think out a consistent scheme in advance.
(b) Many people like extra spaces around the assignment symbol and around relational operators on IF statements, e.g.

$$\text{LET A1} = \text{A1}+1$$
$$\text{IF B}\uparrow 2 > 4*A*C \text{ THEN} \ldots$$
$$\text{DEF FNA} = X+3$$

(c) Use indentation to show block structure, e.g.
```
FOR K = 1 TO 30
    FOR J = 1 TO 10
        PRINT K↑J,
    NEXT J
    PRINT
NEXT K
```
Beware, however, crazy source programs such as those that contain 100 nested blocks, or more ends of blocks than starts (e.g. more NEXTs than FORs). The latter is, indeed, quite likely if only part of the source program is being listed.

(d) Remember that the re-created lines might be longer than the original ones. In particular your compiler might limit source lines to, say, 80 characters, but the re-created version of a correct source line might be more than 80 characters. Many compilers treat this as an error, because if the line is SAVEd it may not be possible to restore it again. Such an error is an unusual kind of error—one that only arises if the program is SAVEd.

Re-creation of individual tokens

The re-creation of individual tokens (e.g. variable names, constants, keywords) is normally a simple task.

In the internal language a keyword such as RETURN might be represented as a single byte, say with the internal value 15 (being the value of the manifest constant representing the internal operator *RETURN*). Translating 15 back to RETURN can be done with the aid of a table, possibly the same table—we called it a dictionary—that is used to convert RETURN into 15.

Variables might be represented internally as references to a dictionary of variable names, so it should be a simple matter to re-create the name by examining the appropriate dictionary entry.

Some tokens may have more than one possible source representation. The source language might, for example, allow the operator 'greater than or equal to' to be written either as '>=' or as '=>'. Moreover a numerical value, such as 3, might have a large number of alternative representations, such as 3., 3.0, 03, .3E1, etc.. In such cases the simplest approach is to re-create the same standard form, irrespective of the form used in the original source.

Re-ordering tokens

If tokens in the internal language are in the same order as the corresponding tokens in the original source, then re-creation is simply a matter of converting back each token in turn. However in an internal language such as Reverse Polish notation the source line

$$LET\ A = 3$$

becomes

$$A\ 3\ \mathit{LETNUM}$$

and here the tokens are clearly in a different order from the source. Moreover two original symbols, LET and '=', have been transformed into the single Reverse Polish element *LETNUM*. Hence the re-creator has the added task of reversing all such transformations done by the translator.

We consider this in some detail in subsequent sections, confining our discussions to our suggested internal language based on Reverse Polish notation.

Re-creating Reverse Polish

Several algorithms have been presented for re-creating source language from Reverse Polish notation. Possibly the first is due to Hamblin (1962). The fastest algorithms rely on the ability to scan the Reverse Polish backwards. Unfortunately, if the Reverse Polish has elements of variable size, it is not possible to scan it backwards (unless extra information is added at the end of each element to say how long it is). Thus we shall concentrate on algorithms that work forwards. The relative slowness of such algorithms rarely matters, as it is usually completely swamped by the slowness of the output device on which the LISTing or SAVing is being done.

For some reason the algorithm that most appeals to us is the one presented in a paper by Brown (1977), and it is this which we shall describe. (The same paper also contains an introductory survey of some backwards algorithms, if you are interested in looking these up.)

The algorithm works for all types of operator, whether the usual ones such as binary or unary, or the more bizarre such as ternary, nonary (having no operands), etc. We shall thus talk in terms of *N-ary* operators. If N is two, for example, this means a binary operator.

In source form an N-ary operator is represented as

PREFIX1 *operand1* PREFIX2 *operand2* ... *PREFIXN operandN* SUFFIX

For most operators the SUFFIX is null, and for other than unary operators PREFIX1 is often null too. For example, the binary operator '+' which is written

$$operand1 + operand2$$

has '+' as PREFIX2, and PREFIX1 and SUFFIX are null. However, the binary operation of assignment, in a language where each assignment statement ends in a semicolon, might be written

$$\text{LET } operand1 = operand2;$$

This has LET as PREFIX1, '=' as PREFIX2 and ';' as SUFFIX, and therefore has no null parts.

The re-creating algorithm needs a table of the prefixes and suffix corresponding to each operator in the internal language. We call this the *re-creation table*. The re-creation table can usually be encoded quite concisely, say with one byte for each prefix or suffix. The majority of entries will be null. If an external name is more than one character (e.g. LET or '< >') and hence will not fit into a single byte, then this name should be placed in a separate table of source names; its entry in the re-creation table should give its offset within this other table.

Subsidiary routines of the algorithm

We shall shortly describe the complete re-creating algorithm, but before doing this we shall specify the subsidiary procedures and functions that the algorithm needs. The way you encode these depends closely on the precise details of your internal language. The algorithm uses a 'scanning-pointer', which progresses sequentially through each element of the internal line to be re-created. (Sometimes it is set back to a 'restart-point' to make a second scan over some elements.) Where the word 'element' is used in the names of subsidiary routines, it means the element currently referenced by the scanning-pointer. The following are the specifications of those routines whose names may not quite be self-explanatory.

end-of-Polish returns the value *true* only if the scanning-pointer has advanced beyond the end of the current internal line.

element-is-operator returns the value *true* only if the current element is an operator rather than an operand; *element-is-operand* returns the value *true* if it is an operand rather than an operator. (Similar routines are *element-is-binary-operator*, etc.)

suffix-for-element returns the character string, possibly a null one, representing the suffix for the current element, which is an operator. The functions *prefix1-for-element, prefix2-for-element*, etc., are similar, but deal with prefixes rather than the suffix.

name-of-operand returns the character string giving the source representation of the current element, which is an operand.

The algorithm uses a stack of character strings, all of which are prefixes to the current operand. In practice this stack is doubtless best implemented as a stack of pointers to the strings, rather than the strings themselves. The procedure *stack*(S) adds the string S to the stack, and the two following functions also work on the stack.

stack-not-empty returns the value *true* only if the stack is not empty.

unstack unstacks the string on top of the stack and returns this as its value.

When you come to encode the above routines, you will probably find that some of them are so simple that they can be represented by in-line code.

The algorithm

We can now show the algorithm itself. It is described in the imaginary encoding language that we introduced in our 'Policy on examples' in Chapter 4.1. You will, it is hoped, both understand it and be able to convert it directly into your own encoding language. The algorithm is presented as a procedure called 'printpolish'. It uses a PRINT statement to output the source line, token by token; strictly speaking, this PRINT should be modified to allow either SAVing in a file or direct printing at a terminal.

```
PROCEDURE printpolish
BEGIN
    Set scanning-pointer to start of Reverse Polish
    WHILE NOT end-of-Polish DO
        WHILE element-is-operator DO
            BEGIN/*loop to find next operand, printing all suffixes on the way */
```

```
      PRINT suffix-for-element
      advance-scanning-pointer-to-next-element
      IF end-of-Polish THEN RETURN
   END /* WHILE loop to find next operand */
```

/* Now an operand has been found. Scan ahead to find all the operators that give rise to prefixes for it. These prefixes are stacked since they need to be printed in reverse order. (Consider, for example, the expression A/–B, which is represented as A B *NEGATE* / in Reverse Polish.) */

```
   level := 0
   restart-point : = scanning-pointer

   WHILE level > = 0 DO
   BEGIN
      advance-scanning-pointer-to-next-element
      IF end-of-Polish THEN BREAK /* Go to the end of this WHILE
                                                            loop */
      IF element-is-operand THEN level : = level+1
      ELSE BEGIN
         IF element-is-binary-operator THEN level : = level−1
         /* In general if it is an N-ary operator that produces one result
            then: level : = level −N +1 */
         IF level = 0 THEN stack(prefix1-for-element)
         IF level = − 1 THEN stack(prefix2-for-element)
         /* In general: IF level = −(N − 1) THEN
            stack  (prefixN-for-element) */
      END /* ELSE clause */
   END /* WHILE loop to scan for prefixes */


   /* Now print all the prefixes stacked above */
   WHILE stack-not-empty DO PRINT unstack
   scanning-pointer : = restart-point
   PRINT name-of-operand
   advance-scanning-pointer-to-next-element
   END /* outer WHILE */

END /* printpolish */
```

An example

The following example shows how the algorithm works. It includes two binary operators, assignment (represented internally by *LETNUM*) and exponentiation (represented internally by *EXP*), and also the unary minus operator (represented internally by *NEGATE*). In addition there is an unusual unary operator whose source representation is LH(*operand1*). (If you want to imagine a meaning for it, think of it as 'lower half'. Assume for instance that operands are stored in four bytes, and it is possible to reference the 'lower half' consisting of the last two bytes.) We shall assume *LOWER* is the internal representation of the unary LH operator. Our example consists of the source line

$$\text{LET LH(X)} = -Y{\uparrow}Z$$

which is represented in symbolic Reverse Polish as

$$X\ LOWER\ Y\ Z\ EXP\ NEGATE\ LETNUM$$

The re-creation table for these operators is as follows

Internal representation	External representation		
	Prefix1	Prefix2	Suffix
LOWER	LH(	not applicable	)
NEGATE	–	not applicable	null
EXP	null	$\uparrow$	null
LETNUM	LET␣	␣=␣	'newline'

where the '␣' symbol represents a space.

When re-creating the source from the above internal line, the algorithm first finds the operand X. It then scans ahead to find all the prefixes associated with X. In doing this *prefix search* it must only use prefixes of operators that come immediately before the operand X in the source form. The *NEGATE* operator, for example, has a prefix '–', but this operator is *not* associated with X and therefore must not be picked up in the prefix search for X. To accomplish this, the variable 'level' is used; 'level' is increased by one for any operand found on the prefix search, and decreased by one for any binary operator. It then turns out that the prefixes that apply to an operand are those that result from operators with the same 'level'.

Given this use of 'level', the prefix search for X first finds 'LH(' from the *LOWER* operator and then 'LET ' from the *LETNUM* operator. These two strings are first stacked and then unstacked and printed, thus reversing their order and producing the output

$$\text{LET LH(}$$

The operand X is then printed.

The algorithm then goes back to the beginning of its outer WHILE loop and searches for the next operand, which turns out to be Y. It finds Y after scanning past the operator *LOWER*. *LOWER* causes its suffix ')' to be printed, and thus the output line is now

LET LH(X)

The algorithm then performs the prefix search for Y, and finds null (from *EXP*), '−' (from *NEGATE*) and ' = ' (from *LETNUM*). These are printed in reverse order as they are unstacked. Then Y itself is printed and the output line has become

LET LH(X) = −Y

The outer WHILE loop is again repeated to process the next operand, Z. The prefix search for Z yields '↑' from *EXP*. Thus after printing Z the line is

LET LH(X) = −Y↑Z

Finally a search is made for another operand. This fails since it reaches the end of the Reverse Polish and RETURNs. The suffix 'newline' (from *LETNUM*) is printed before the end is reached, thus completing the output line. (In practice, since every line must end with a newline, there is little point in putting this in the re-creation table. Instead a newline can automatically be added on after the RETURN from printpolish.)

Parentheses

It is generally agreed that parentheses in the source should be re-created exactly as the user typed them, even if the parentheses are, in fact, redundant. Thus if the user writes

(B∗C) − (P/2∗H)/N

he would be upset to get back

B∗C−P/2∗H/N

even though it means the same.

Fortunately, re-creating parentheses is easy. They can be treated as if they were unary operators, with an internal name such as *PARENS*. Thus the above expression can be represented as

B C ∗ *PARENS* P 2 /−∗ *PARENS* N / −

The run-time system treats *PARENS* as a null operator—it is there solely for the needs of re-creation. The re-creator translates *PARENS* back into a prefix '(' and a suffix ')'.

The above discussion was concerned with the use of parentheses to group together operators and operands in expressions. Many languages use the same parenthesis symbols in other contexts, such as to surround the argument lists of functions or the subscripts of arrays. It should be regarded as a coincidence that the same parenthesis symbols are used in different ways, and the re-creating mechanisms can be entirely different. For example if the array element X(K) is represented as

X K *ARRAYSUB1*

then the source can be re-created by treating the *ARRAYSUB1* as a binary operator with a null first prefix, the symbol '(' as its second prefix and the symbol ')' as its suffix. There is no need to use the *PARENS* operator. Our use of LH in the above example has already shown this.

The *PARENS* mechanism can easily be generalized to cover any other kind of bracketing that is used in the source language.

Sub-parts of statements

Consider the INPUT statement

INPUT X,Y,Z

which appears in Reverse Polish as

X *INPUTNUM* Y *INPUTNUM* Z *INPUTNUM*

This Reverse Polish is a somewhat bastardized form, where the statement has effectively been split up into three separate parts, each of which is a complete piece of Reverse Polish in itself. (A 'purer' way of representing the statement might have been

X Y Z *INPUTNUM INPUTNUM INPUTNUM*

but this would, in fact, make the task of the run-time system more difficult.)

One way of re-creating the source is to treat *INPUTNUM* (and similar operators such as *INPUTSTR*) as unary operators which produce INPUT as a prefix and a 'null' as a suffix. The re-created source then reads

INPUT X INPUT Y INPUT Z

which is, of course, wrong. (The same problem of wrong re-creation is likely to arise even with the 'pure' form of Reverse Polish.) To get the correct source form, the prefix must be printed as INPUT if it comes at the start of a re-created statement, but otherwise as a comma. Thus the prefix has *alternative forms*. In most source languages there will be a number of prefixes with this property.

When a prefix with alternative forms is re-created it will be necessary to execute a *selection routine* to print the appropriate alternative. The re-creation table entry for the prefix must take a special form; one possibility is for it to consist of a marker meaning 'execute a selection routine' plus an index that specifies which selection routine to call.

Omitted parts of statements

A further re-creation problem arises when parts of source statements are optional. We shall illustrate this in terms of an INPUT statement in BASIC which has an optional channel number. Possible forms of the statement are

INPUT#3: X,Y
INPUT X,Y
INPUT#2+1: X,Y

In the case where the channel number is omitted, the standard input device, channel 0, is assumed. Assume that the optional channel number is allowed on several different kinds of statement (e.g. PRINT, LINPUT), and is always represented in Reverse Polish by the channel number followed by the operator *CHANNEL*. Thus the above INPUT statements might be encoded as

3 *CHANNEL* X *INPUTNUM* Y *INPUTNUM*
X *INPUTNUM* Y *INPUTNUM*
2 1 + *CHANNEL* X *INPUTNUM* Y *INPUTNUM*

Again this is a bastardized form of notation that might be convenient to the run-time system. (In a 'pure' notation *CHANNEL* is a binary operator that combines a channel number with a list of items to be printed.) The bastardized notation presents a problem of re-creation because it is difficult to fix what kind of operator *CHANNEL* is. One possibility is to treat it as a unary operator with prefix '#' and suffix ':'. However, this causes the first line to be re-created as

#3:INPUT X,Y

and the third line is in a similar wrong form. Our own experience is that there is no neat way round such problems. The nature of the Reverse Polish notation tends to be dictated by the run-time system, in order to achieve a reasonable execution speed. When this causes a bastardization of the notation the task of re-creation becomes more clumsy, but it may be a price worth paying.

There are numerous dirty devices that can be used to solve problems such as those above. One is to introduce extra operators, which, like *PARENS*, are recognized only by the re-creator. One such operator could be the nonary operator *INPUTSTART*, inserted at the very start of each INPUT statement. On re-creation it would generate the suffix INPUT. Such an operator might even be useful to the run-time system, for example to warn it to perform certain initialization tasks. Given the existence of *INPUTSTART*, the operators *INPUTNUM* and *INPUTSTR* would no

222

longer need to re-create the INPUT prefix; their prefix would therefore be null at the first occurrence, and then a comma. Lines would then re-create correctly, with the channel after the INPUT.

A second device, which is hardly dirty at all, is to treat as *semi-terminators* all those operators that terminate a self-contained sub-section of a statement. A semi-terminator then stops the look ahead for prefixes. To accomplish this in the encoding of the algorithm, change the line near the middle which reads

IF end-of-Polish THEN BREAK

to the new form

IF end-of-Polish OR element-is-semi-terminator THEN BREAK

This speeds up re-creation and can, in some bastardized notations, prevent incorrect prefixes being picked up.

Re-creating output statements

Output statements often have a syntax that is foreign to the rest of the language. This is particularly true of operators, functions and statements that control the format of output.

In BASIC, for example, the format of output is controlled by commas (and semicolons) within the list of values to be printed. Sample statements are

```
PRINT
PRINT A,B
PRINT ,,A,,B,,
```

These are particularly nasty because they represent a case where operands can optionally be omitted, thus casting doubt on whether the associated operators are unary, binary, etc. (Our previous examples of optional constructs consisted of an operand *with an associated operator*.) A good way round this is to represent the comma internally as a nonary operator, called, say, *PRINTTAB*. When an operand appears, an extra unary operator *PRINTNUM* (or *PRINTSTR*) is introduced to print it. Given this convention the last of the above PRINT statements is represented in Reverse Polish as

PRINTSTART PRINTTAB PRINTTAB A PRINTNUM PRINTTAB PRINTTAB B PRINTNUM PRINTTAB PRINTTAB

This is likely to be convenient for the run-time system and easy to re-create.

Re-sequencing

If he has edited his program a lot, the user may find that his system of line-numbering is beginning to creak, and he may want his program to be automatically re-numbered, starting from scratch. This is called *re-sequencing*. If line-numbers are also used within programs as objects of GOTOs and the like, then re-sequencing can be a difficult operation; when a line-number is changed, all the references to it in the program need to be changed correspondingly. The following example from BASIC illustrates this:

Original program	*Re-sequenced program*
15 INPUT A	10 INPUT A
17 IF A > 99 THEN 100	20 IF A > 99 THEN 40
25 IF A < 9 THEN 15	30 IF A < 9 THEN 10
100 PRINT A*A	40 PRINT A*A
150 END	50 END

It is easier to re-sequence the internal form than the source form. Thus if your compiler re-creates the source from the internal form this is good news. It may be that your compiler can achieve re-sequencing simply by changing the names of line-numbers within a dictionary of line-numbers. Alternatively you may find that it is necessary to make a search of the entire internal program to find all the relevant references to line-numbers, and thus re-sequencing presents a rather tedious problem.

If you have this problem it can be greatly eased by combining re-sequencing with re-creation. We have already observed that the source can be re-created with a different, and hopefully better, spacing than the original. It may also be easy to change the source in other ways. There could, for example, be an option to change keywords to a foreign language, to round constants to n significant figures, or, of particular relevance here, to re-sequence the program. Such options could be requested by the user through extra arguments on commands such as SAVE.

Re-sequencing a program as it is re-created is often an almost trivial task. All that is necessary is to create in advance a table giving all the old line-numbers and the corresponding new line-numbers. Then, whenever a line-number is output during re-creation, it is looked up in the table and the new version substituted for the old. (If a line-number is not found in the table, the user should perhaps be warned that his program uses a non-existent line-number, for example as an object of a GOTO.)

Although combining re-sequencing with re-creation has the advantage of simplicity, it does have the disadvantage that only the re-created program is re-sequenced; the internal program remains unchanged. Hence a re-sequenced LIST is downright confusing to the user, as his internal program continues to work with the old line-numbers and these are the line-numbers used in error messages. Thus the re-sequencing option should be confined to commands such as SAVE.

Chapter 6.3

The Command Module

The tasks of the command module are

(a) to perform initialization at the start of the session;
(b) to decode commands and to pass control to the appropriate routine to execute each command;
(c) to provide a stable base to which other modules can return after an error or a break-in;
(d) to clear up at the end of a session.

Most of the command module should be straightforward to code, but the following few points may help.

Initialization

Initialization involves setting up the compiler's variables and data areas, initializing input/output devices and printing an introductory message to the user (if desired).

Unless initialization is successfully completed the compiler must not be used. Thus any errors detected during initialization must cause an immediate abandonment of the session. The same applies to any break-ins occurring during initialization. Ideally these should be inhibited; if not, a break-in should cause the session to end.

Errors will arise during initialization when there is something amiss in the environment in which the compiler is to run. For example a user may have forgotten to switch on a peripheral device, or he may be trying to run your compiler on a machine with insufficient storage to hold its data areas. All too often when compilers have an error in initialization they just go dead, giving the user no clue to what is wrong. This is inevitable, perhaps, if the user has forgotten to switch on the only output device on the computer, but in other cases the compiler should be able to give a helpful error message.

In many systems the user has a command that can re-initialize the compiler (e.g. NEW in BASIC). Within the compiler a few of the initialization tasks will only be done at the very start, whereas the majority will also be done on re-initialization. You must be careful to put each task in the correct category.

226

Re-entrant or serially re-usable compilers

This is a good point to discuss how your compiler might be shared and re-used. If you run in a time-sharing environment your compiler may be shared by several different users. If so, there should only be one copy of the code of the compiler, but each user must have his own separate data area(s) in which his program is compiled. If the code of your compiler can be shared in this way it is called *re-entrant* (because a second user can enter it when one user is already in it). In the old days, when compilers were written in assembly language, great care had to be taken to make programs re-entrant. Nowadays, with improved design of machines, encoding languages and operating systems, re-entrancy often comes for free, without the compiler writer having to think much about it. The only action necessary may be to borrow the requisite data areas for the current user during initialization (and return them at the end). If you are very lucky it will even be possible to share constant 'read-only' data areas, such as a built-in table of statement names.

If your compiler only has one user at a time, re-entrancy is irrelevant. What is valuable, however, is for your compiler to be *serially re-usable*. This means that it can be re-started from scratch at any time without having to re-load it, which has obvious advantages if loading takes a relatively long time.

Your method of initialization largely controls whether your compiler will be serially re-usable. Consider the case of a data item (either within a data structure or as a stand-alone object) which has an initial value of, say, six; this value may be changed during the run of your compiler. If your compiler is to be serially re-usable it must place the value six into the data item during initialization; what it must not do is to rely on the loader to place the initial value in the data item.

If you are writing your compiler in assembly language for an old-fashioned machine it may be possible for the compiler to overwrite its own code. This is a terrible thing to do, and means that your compiler is neither re-entrant nor serially re-usable; you will be lucky if it is usable at all.

Decoding the commands

In some systems, commands are treated as entirely separate entities from statements in the source language, whereas in others there is little distinction between the two. At one extreme would be a language where commands had a totally different syntax from source statements and were prefixed by a special symbol (a dollar sign is a frequent choice). At the other extreme would be a language where a 'command' such as LIST was treated the same as any other statement in the source program. Normally LIST would be used as an immediate statement, but the user could, if he wished, put a LIST statement in his program, to be executed when the program was run.

The more that commands are likened to ordinary statements, the more the command module becomes enmeshed with the other compiler modules, until, at the extreme, it almost loses its identity.

A stable base

It is vital, in an interactive compiler, that there be some stable base to return to after an error, break-in or other exceptional happening. It is also vital that on returning to the stable base, the user does not lose his program or the values of his variables, and that he can communicate with the compiler in the normal way so that he can investigate the cause of his problem, correct it, and continue his work.

The provision of the stable base is a task that makes implementing interactive compilers much more difficult than batch compilers, which tend to give up when the going gets tough. It is a task that requires great care and discipline; you must continually ask yourself the question: 'If something goes wrong at this point will the compiler recover?'. The alternative is that mechanical devices are left whirring or spewing out paper, storage is corrupted, or the source program is turned to nonsense. We have already discussed the problem of unstable states when, in Chapter 2.15, we considered break-ins, the most difficult of the exceptional conditions.

Clearing up

The complexity of the clearing-up operation at the end of a session is directly related to the complexity of the operating system, if any, under which the compiler runs. In many operating systems, you need to return all the resources, such as storage and peripheral devices, that you borrowed at the start of the session. Here you must be careful if the session is abandoned because of an error or break-in during initialization; you must return any resources you borrowed but avoid returning resources that you never actually got around to borrowing.

Part 7

TESTING AND ISSUING

Chapter 7.1

Testing the Compiler

Your aim must be to eliminate all the bugs from your compiler before the first user touches it. The thirteenth deadly sin is *to leave the users to find the errors in your compiler*. This is really such a stupid sin to commit that one wonders why it is so frequent. The costs of the sin are huge. One immeasurable cost is that user attitudes change to your disadvantage. Not only are users likely to be angry when they find errors in your compiler, but they also lose confidence in your product. When they next encounter something they cannot explain, they assume it is another compiler bug and bring it to you to sort out. After spending a good deal of time on it you may find it was the user's mistake after all. Even if you yourself are the user, detecting bugs is much harder if there are two equally likely sources of error to investigate: the compiler and your program. If, on the other hand, you have confidence in the compiler (and this confidence is soundly based), one of the unknowns is eliminated.

When users meet, compiler bugs are a frequent source of conversation. Indeed it is rather depressing that, if one enters a tea-room full of computer people, although one hopes the conversation might cover many an exciting topic, it is usually just moans about software bugs. It does not take many bugs in a compiler for that compiler (and indirectly its writers) to become a laughing stock, the butt of a host of ironic jokes.

The costs of the sin are even worse than having all your friends and colleagues laugh at you behind your back. It is actually a lot more work for you to correct bugs found by users than bugs you find for yourself at the testing stage. If, when writing your compiler, you thoroughly test each section of code soon after you have written it, then any bug that is revealed should be relatively easy to correct, because the workings of the code that contains the error are still fresh in your mind. Consider the effects of the same bug being found by a user one year later. We shall assume you have issued your compiler to several outside sites and your user is working at one of these. When the bug is found, the following actions take place.

(1) The user contacts you to report the bug.
(2) You mount, on your machine, the version of the compiler he is using.

232

Remember that you may have sent him the compiler several months previously, and his version may differ from the one you are using or developing.

(3) You re-create his bug. This is no mean task if the bug arose in a big program or after a long series of interactive commands.

(4) You identify the part of your compiler that is likely to contain the bug. Sometimes this is obvious, sometimes it is mystifying. (If you test the compiler as you write it, you can be fairly sure—though not absolutely sure—that a new bug is caused by the most recently added code.)

(5) You bring back to your mind the workings of the errant part of the compiler. This will involve consulting your compiler documentation, particularly the implementation manual. If this is poor or out of date you really have got problems.

(6) You eventually find the bug and correct it. You run a test to make sure the correction works.

(7) You also correct the bug in your current version of the compiler, and test this too.

(8) You report that the bug has been corrected and issue the correction to all users.

Given the above sequence of events, a bug found by a user will cost at least ten times more of your time than if you had found the bug at the compiler-testing stage. Because of this factor of ten many organizations that produce compilers get into the *deadline trap*. This happens as follows.

The first version of the compiler is supposed to be ready by some deadline date. It is really a month behind schedule, but, by cutting out a month's testing, the compiler is issued on time. There is much rejoicing among the compiler writers that the target date has been met. They then start working towards their target date for the next version. But gradually they become less happy. The wretched users start reporting bugs in increasing numbers. These bugs, which would have been found in one month of testing, take ten month's work to correct. If we assume the compiler writers correct their own bugs, this time is taken from the work on the next version of the compiler. Now this version becomes ten months behind schedule. By cutting out three months of testing, the compiler writers manage to keep it to seven months late. As a result of this . . . .

Avoiding the sin

Given the terrible consequences of the thirteenth deadly sin, both in your own time and in your loss of face, how are you going to avoid issuing a compiler with bugs in it?

The most important aid is to take a positive attitude, as portrayed by the first sentence in this chapter. It you take a negative attitude and say that it is inevitable that your compiler will be issued with bugs in it, your prophecy will be self-fulfilling. Your only hope of success is to take a positive view and be absolutely determined to catch all the bugs. Even then you will probably fail. But though you may not achieve the summit of absolute freedom from bugs, only by striving for it will you know the exhilaration of getting close. And your life thereafter will be a happier one than the life of those who gave up the climb far below.

Comprehensive test programs

Given your positive attitude, you will put great efforts into writing test programs to reveal bugs. This part of your climb is long and tedious, and only your determination to reach the summit will keep you going. You must produce a comprehensive *test suite* that covers every facility of the source language. You must test combinations of facilities that are likely to upset one another—a function call within a subroutine may be a simple example. Obviously you cannot test all combinations of facilities, because this would take you into thousands and even millions of possibilities. Thus you must, in your testing, take account of how your compiler works and prise away at its weak points. For instance if function calls share the same operand stack that is used during expression evaluation, call functions at points in expressions where the operand stack is already in use.

Test nesting. Put a function call within a function call, a FOR statement within a FOR statement, the result of one exponentiation as the operand to another, e.g. $3\uparrow(4\uparrow2)$.

Test at the boundaries. If your compiler rules that array bounds must lie between 1 and 999, try bounds of 1 and 999. Also try bounds of 0 and 1000 to make sure they give errors. Then try outrageous bounds, like a huge negative number or a positive number too big for the machine to hold; make sure these give decent error messages, too. Test artificial boundaries in your compiler; if you know that constants less than 256 are stored in a special way, test the constants 255 and 256.

Test the null case. Run a null program, input a null line, call a subroutine that just returns, run a program consisting of a FOR loop with nothing before, nothing inside, and nothing after.

Test as near as you can to the infinite case. Run a program that uses 500 different scalar variables; run one that has FOR loops nested 100 deep (assuming your compiler has no limit on this); input the largest possible positive and negative numbers. Most test programs of this nature will need to be artificially generated; after all, you do not want to write 100 FOR statements yourself.

Test the error case. At least half your testing should be devoted to ensuring that your compiler gives the correct response to errors.

Test outrageously wrong syntax. See what your compiler does when fed a program in the wrong source language.

Relate your testing to the formal grammar for the source language, as provided in your user manual. This helps make testing more systematic and comprehensive.

Ordering the tests

There are many good methodologies for determining which parts of the compiler to write first. The best for testing is probably the following. First produce a skeletal input/output module, so that you can communicate with your compiler. Then encode the part of your compiler that processes error messages—the compiler will initially contain bugs that make it give error messages when it should not, so any help with locating such bugs is valuable. If the error message points at the position in the line where the error (was supposed to have) occurred, this helps greatly. After error messages are working, get PRINT statements to the stage you can actually run them. This will involve writing part of the translator and part of the run-time system, plus an embryo pre-run module (which perhaps does nothing but enter the run-time system), and a similar embryo command module.

Now move on to the debugging facilities that you will provide for the user. Such facilities are also useful to you, the compiler writer, during the debugging stages of writing the compiler. An example is a symbolic dump.

At this stage you can write simple test programs and can gradually build on these as you add more and more facilities to your compiler.

Try to organize your compiler so that, at each stage of development, if an unimplemented feature is used this produces an error message 'NOT IMPLEMENTED YET'. Then you can feed real programs to the compiler without fear of unimplemented features knocking it out.

Building up the test suite

There are actually two stages in testing a compiler. In the first stage you test each new section of code as you write it; in the second stage you apply your test suite to the complete compiler.

Your early test programs in the first stage will not have any lasting value. An early test program might, for example, only cover printing constants of one digit. As you progress in writing your compiler, you should start producing comprehensive test programs for each new feature. These can then be used later as part of the test suite. If possible, write a comprehensive test program for each new feature even if the compiler cannot quite handle it at the time. As an example of this, assume your compiler has just reached the stage where it can process input statements in the source language, but it cannot yet process two-dimensional arrays. Obviously a comprehensive test program for input statements must include the case of inputting an element of a two-dimensional array. If you write the full test at the current stage, your compiler will not be able to run the whole thing, but, if well written, it will produce the message 'NOT IMPLEMENTED YET' for the two-dimensional array case. Later on, when two-dimensional arrays are working, you can re-run the input test (as part of the test suite) and it should work in full.

Relying on others

When you are really exhausted from writing test programs it becomes very attractive to lessen your own task by taking advantage of the work of others. If you are on a professional project, your organization may have a department called 'product test' or 'quality assurance', whose very task is to find your bugs. Alternatively you may be able to get test programs from elsewhere. Attractive as these outside aids may be, place no reliance on them. Simply regard them as a useful back up. You are the person who knows most intimately how your code works and what its weaknesses are, and you are therefore the only person who can give it proper testing.

An example

The following example illustrates a possible section of a test program. It shows tests of the '=' and '< >' operators on IF statements in BASIC.

```
10    REM Some variables used in the tests:
20    LET A$ = "TESTSTRING"
30    LET X3 = 29
40    LET A(3) = 10
50    DEF FNA(X) = A(3)+X
90    REM ---------- Test successful comparisons ----------
95    PRINT X3;
100   IF 34 = X3+5 THEN 120
110   PRINT "**** FAILURE 1 ON ="
120   IF 0 = -0 THEN 140
130   PRINT "**** FAILURE 2 ON ="
140   IF A$ = "TEST"&"STRING" THEN 160
150   PRINT "**** FAILURE 3 ON ="
160   IF SEG$(A$,2,1) = ""&"" THEN 180
170   PRINT "**** FAILURE 4 ON ="
180   IF FNA(X3) <> 39.1 THEN 200
190   PRINT "**** FAILURE 1 ON <>"
200   IF "PIG" <> "PIGG" THEN 220
210   PRINT "**** FAILURE 2 ON <>"
220   IF "." <> "" THEN 240
230   PRINT "**** FAILURE 3 ON <>"
240   PRINT " SHOULD BE";X3
250   REM The above line should print 29 SHOULD BE 29
260   REM Further tests should cover special cases in the source
270   REM language and compiler. For example some source languages
280   REM have special rules for spaces, e.g. spaces on the end of
290   REM a string may be ignored. Some compilers, especially true
300   REM compilers, may treat comparison with zero as a special case.
500   REM ---------- Test unsuccessful comparisons ----------
510   IF SQR(9) = -3 THEN 8000
520   IF A$ = A$&"+" THEN 8000
530   IF FNA(ABS(-X3)) <> A(SQR(9))+2*13+LEN("XYZ") THEN 9000
540   IF SEG$(A$,2,12/3)&"" <> "ES"&"T" THEN 9000
550   IF "" <> "" THEN 9000
560   IF A$ <> A$ THEN 9000
600   REM ... Then test a backward jump; all the above were forward ...
610   REM ...
620   REM ...
999   PRINT "TEST OF = AND <> COMPLETED"
1000  STOP
1010  REM ---------- Error actions ----------
8000  PRINT "**** WRONG JUMP ON ="
8010  GOTO 530
9000  PRINT "**** WRONG JUMP ON <>"
9010  GOTO 999
9090  END
```

If your compiler passes this test and if you have been careful with your tests for the special cases mentioned in line 260, then you should have reasonable confidence that '=' and '< >' are working.

Interactive testing

A number of people who write interactive compilers 'test' them by sitting at a console and typing in whatever comes into their heads. Such testing is worse than useless, as all it can give is a false confidence in the product. Everything that we have said has been geared to producing tests that are comprehensive and systematic, and your testing procedure must be likewise. Thus you should have a pre-defined file full of commands that exercise each of the test programs. While the compiler is being written, you should not only test the new parts, but also run all the previous tests to make sure the new code has not upset its elders. When your compiler is complete, together with its test suite, you should re-run the entire test suite every time you make a major change to the compiler.

Ideally you should exercise the complete test suite even after a minor change in your compiler, but sometimes this is impractical because of the time taken or the volume of output produced (particularly error messages). Thus it is useful to have a single 'mini-comprehensive' test, which contains an example (a relatively complicated one) of each statement, command, and operator in the source language. This test can be run after *every* compiler change.

If a bug in the compiler is found after the compiler has been issued to users, this really represents a bug in the test suite as well as in the compiler itself. Thus augment the test suite at the same time as you correct the compiler bug.

We have suggested that systematic testing should not be done interactively. There are a few facilities, however, that are inherently interactive in nature. The most important is break-in. A secondary one is response to errors in run-time input; we have suggested that, when input is interactive, the user is given another chance, whereas non-interactive users are not. You may have to test these facilities interactively, but an alternative is to simulate the interactive environment; you might, for example, simulate the effect of random break-ins. (A paper by Brinch Hansen (1978) is of some relevance here.)

The output from the test suite

If your test suite does too much printing you will be left with thousands of lines of output to check each time you run the suite. There are two ways of avoiding this. Firstly you could produce an automatic checker which compares the output from the tests with a master copy that contains the output that the tests *should* produce. Any differences are reported as errors. This approach sounds attractive, but does not seem to work well in practice. One problem is the effect of minor changes in output format, e.g. a different spacing, a change in the version number, or a change in the text of an error message. It is hard to keep the master version up to date with such changes.

An alternative is to make the test self-checking. As a trivial example, a line to test BASIC might read

100 IF 2+10 < > 3*4 THEN 5000
:
5000 PRINT "ERROR IN LINE 100"

Obviously a test cannot be completely self-checking and produce no output at all. Otherwise the compiler could contain a terrible bug whereby every single statement was completely ignored, yet it would still satisfy the test.

Given that there must be some output, it is useful to make the output directly checkable by a human reader without reference to any 'master copy'. This can be achieved by printing suitable messages. For example a test line might read

10 PRINT 2+2; "SHOULD BE 4"

Then if the human reader, scanning through the output, saw the line

293 SHOULD BE 4

he would be alerted that something was seriously wrong.

Several tests can be combined into one line of output. For example

10 PRINT 2−1;6/3;4−2+1;16↑.5; "SHOULD BE";
11 PRINT −3+4;8*.25;(2−1)*3;(3−1)↑2

should produce the line

1 2 3 4 SHOULD BE 1 2 3 4

Where error messages should occur in the output the reader should be warned. For example

10 PRINT "+++ THE FOLLOWING LINES ARE ALL ILLEGAL
                                              FOR STATEMENTS"
20 FOR A(1) = 1 TO 3
40 FOR A$ = B$ TO C$
:
90 PRINT "+++ END OF ILLEGAL FORS"

A sop to the users

There is a powerful psychological aid which can help both you and the users. It is suggested in a paper by Rain (1973), and consists of offering a free beer to the first user to find each bug in your compiler. This softens user attitudes—they are pleased, not angry, when they find a bug—and it hardens your determination to produce a bug-free compiler, and thus be able to spend your money on beers for yourself rather than others. Your users may actually be trying to find bugs, so your product will have to be all the better to keep them at bay.

This beer offer is almost standard practice at the author's place of work, and no compiler writer has yet suffered unduly from it. If certain computer manufacturers made the same offer they would need to take over a brewery to satisfy the user demand.

Using your product

Incredibly, in professional projects it sometimes happens that the compiler writers never seriously use their product before it goes out to customers. This always leads to trouble.

Before you issue your product, put yourself in the place of the user and develop a program on your compiler. The purpose of this is not so much for testing—your suite of test programs will be much better at this than an ordinary user program. Instead it is to make sure the user interface is as friendly as it should be. You will almost certainly find, when you first try your compiler as a user, that there are plenty of ways whereby intercommunication between user and compiler can be improved.

The user interface is one thing that can only be investigated by actual interactive usage working on a real programming problem.

Finding the errors

Your tests will show that bugs exist, but in some cases you will need help in finding a bug. We have emphasized that your compiler should be strong on debugging aids for its users; let us hope that your encoding language is equally helpful to you, when you act as a user.

Nevertheless, even if your encoding language has good debugging aids, you still need to add your own enhancements. As an example of this, assume that your encoding language gives a symbolic dump of all scalar variables. (Remember that this gives the scalar variables *that you defined when encoding your compiler*; your compiler's symbolic dump will in turn give the scalar variables *that your user defined*.) Good as this dump may be, you will sometimes need to enhance it by dumping further information, such as data structures. As a specific case, you may suspect that your compiler's dictionary is being corrupted and you will then want to have it printed out.

One way of making such enhancements available is to add some *secret commands* to your compiler. Such commands are secret because they are for your use, not for the ordinary user of your compiler. One secret command might print out the dictionary in a symbolic format, another might print the internal program, and so on. When the compiler is working, these secret commands can perhaps be removed from the issued version. Do not, however, remove them irretrievably. You will doubtless be changing your compiler later and bugs will re-appear; you will therefore still need all your debugging aids. Some encoding languages have a special feature that allows the optional inclusion of parts of the program, such as the debugging routines of a compiler. This is called *conditional compilation*. It consists of an IF statement which is executed by the translator of the encoding language. We shall assume this is written '%IF' to distinguish it from an IF statement in the program itself. Given this, part of your compiler might be

> %IF DEBUG=1 THEN
> BEGIN
> *Code for optional debugging routine*
> END

At the start of your compiler you set the manifest constant DEBUG to zero or one. You set it to one when you want the debugging routine included as part of the compiler; you set it to zero when you do not.

If your encoding language has no conditional compilation facility, you can use another tool, a macro processor, to achieve the same effect.

System errors

We suggested in Chapter 5.2 that the compiler should include checks that everything is as it should be. Such checks should be included wherever they are cheap and easy. If a check fails, the compiler should generate a 'system error', thus indicating there is something wrong. The advantage in catching system errors early is that bugs are easier to find, since the bug may not have had time to cause lots of side effects that obscure the root problem.

The detection of system errors should be included in all compiler modules. A situation where they are particularly appropriate is in CASE statements (or, the equivalent at a lower level, a table of jump instructions). Often there will be cases that are never used. For example a variable used on a CASE statement might have possible values 1, 2, 3 and 6, but never 4 or 5. Cases 4 and 5 should therefore cause a system error.

The action at a system error should be to print a message to the user such as

> THERE IS A BUG IN THE COMPILER.
> PLEASE REPORT IT (AND CLAIM YOUR BEER).

and then stop. The compiler might automatically invoke your secret debugging commands, if these are present.

Performance testing

As well as testing your compiler for bugs you need to test its performance. Specifically you will be interested in how fast it translates and how fast it runs. Times may be measured in *real-time*, i.e. the amount of time the user waits, or in *CPU time*, the amount of computer time actually used. Both matter. To aid performance measurement it is helpful if your compiler has an optional facility whereby the times for each activity are automatically printed out at the end of that activity.

It is valuable to compare the performance of your compiler with that of other, similar, compilers. Do not worry about the possibility of yours being worse; the exercise of dreaming up favourable reasons why this is so (e.g. because the other compiler does not do proper error checking, or because of some peculiar temporary quirk in the hardware) will give you some training for being a software salesman. In any case you would be very unimaginitive if you could not find some test that showed your compiler in a good light; many academic papers describing some purported advance in computer science are based on extremely carefully chosen examples.

If, however, you are interested in objective testing—and of course you should be—have a look at the synthetic benchmark of Curnow and Wichmann (1976).

Summary

Countless people have put great efforts into producing compilers, based on excellent compiling techniques, yet the compilers have totally failed because the implementors skimped the 'boring' task of testing.

If you avoid everything that is boring and tedious, you will never achieve anything in software. Therefore do your testing properly. It is a hurdle that will knock out three-quarters of your competitors.

Chapter 7.2

Issuing

If your compiler is to be used by anyone other than yourself, you have the problem of issuing it. On a professional project there is the crucial task of marketing the product, but this is an area beyond the scope of this book.

There are three possible types of issuing.

(1) An issue to your colleagues, who have access to your computer. Here, 'issuing' is simply a matter of giving out documentation.

(2) An issue to outside users who have the same kind of computer as you. Here you have the task of physically transferring the compiler and its documentation.

(3) An issue to outside users with a different kind of computer. Unless you have written your compiler to be portable there is no chance of doing this at all. Even if your compiler is portable, you are likely to need at least a month of work to make a transfer. Most of the time will be spent in sorting out nasty little incompatibilities between computers and between different compilers for your encoding language.

Whichever situation applies, resist the temptation to issue your compiler before it is ready. Even if you say to a user: 'My compiler is not quite ready, but give it a try', the user's view of your compiler is still governed by his first impressions. If he finds your trial version to be half-baked and full of bugs, this impression will stick.

Choosing a medium on which to issue a compiler to outside users is no easy task. For a discussion of some of the available choices and the problems with each, see the paper by Waite (1975). Since Waite's paper was written, further devices have become available, particularly on small machines, but the problems have not gone away. However for the amateur, at least, one problem may disappear; if he has only one suitable peripheral on his machine, say a floppy disc, there is no problem in selecting which medium to use. There is, however, still the problem of selecting the format in which to write information.

There is no point in discussing further details here, as these change over time. You must simply survey your likely market at the time you issue

241

your product, and choose the medium and formats that most closely match your resources and manner of working with those of your users.

In some environments there may be pressure to put your compiler into a PROM, and it may also be sensible to issue it in this form. As with all aspects of issuing, be careful not to rush into this before you are sure the compiler is in an established stable form.

Copyright

You may wish to present your compiler as a gift to the world. This will make you feel good and avoid a lot of problems, except perhaps those of bankruptcy.

Alternatively you may wish to limit the use of your compiler, for example to those who have paid for it, and protect it from being stolen or being given away to third parties. One way of protecting it is to copyright it. Unfortunately the copyright laws in many countries were not designed with computer software in mind, and, given that lawyers are not famed for their speed of action, the laws have been slow to change. Moreover the interpretation of laws varies from country to country.

It is therefore necessary for this book again to retreat from giving firm advice, and simply make the vacuous comment that you should refer to the current laws of your own country. In addition you might read papers by authors bold enough to make more definitive statements, such as Mooers (1975) or Niblett (1977).

A compromise that avoids many problems is to issue your compiler free (or rather just for the cost of copying it), but to make a comparatively large charge for its documentation, so that you can make your profits on this.

If you wish to copyright your documentation this is easy. You just write a line of the form

©1979, P.J. Brown

at the start of your work.

Issuing manuals

When you issue manuals it is vital that the examples in it—and there should be a lot of these—are absolutely correct. Thus do not issue the user manual before you have actually run all the examples using your compiler. It is better still if the examples are reproduced directly from computer output, as they are in many books on programming languages, but doing this may mean that the user manual is not ready until some time after the compiler.

Version numbers

If your compiler lasts long it is inevitable that many different versions will be issued. Your users, if they report problems, may be working with a much older one than your current one. It is vital, therefore, that you assign a different version number to each issue of the compiler, and make the compiler print this out at the start of each session. Your documentation should contain a similar system of version numbers. You must keep archives of each version, so that you have a record of exactly what was issued. Moreover you must have the capability of actually running any of the old versions, so that you can investigate error reports from users.

Part 8

SOME ADVANCED AND SPECIALIZED TOPICS

Chapter 8.1

Some Special Compilers

This Part of the book heralds a change of style—a claim which, if true, will doubtless be wholeheartedly welcomed. Previously our discussions have been from a practical standpoint, as if you were implementing the subject matter in your compiler. Now we revert to a more traditional approach, where the reader is assumed to be thirsty for knowledge of topics that do not necessarily apply to him directly. We therefore assume the reader of this book is not only a person of great fortitude in having got this far, but is also an explorer eager to find out about some of the advanced and/or unusual species of compiler that have carved out niches for themselves. We shall describe these in fairly general terms, and try to provide further references for readers who are interested in implementation details.

The topics we shall discuss in this chapter are interpreted compilers, cross-compilers, microprogramming, cascading into an existing language, and, finally, the mixed-code approach.

Interpreted compilers

If a compiler is to run on a very small computer the most important design objective is to make the compiler as concise as possible. Even if the compiler is excellent in all other ways, if it is too big to fit inside the desired computer it is useless.

One good and well-used method of achieving conciseness is as follows. Firstly an ideal machine code is designed for encoding the desired compiler. This machine code contains just the primitive operations the compiler needs. Typical primitives might be 'search for character C in string Y' or, at a rather higher level, 'search for name N in dictionary D'. The representation of the machine code is designed to be as concise as possible, perhaps using similar techniques to those we described in Chapter 3.3 for making Reverse Polish concise.

The compiler is encoded in this ideally concise machine code, thus making it perhaps half the size it would otherwise be. An interpreter is written to make the ideal machine code run on the desired machine. The result is

247

248

that the compiler is interpreted, and runs rather slowly, but the savings in space may make this worthwhile.

As it stands this scheme breaks our earlier requirement that the compiler be written in a high-level language. Instead the compiler is written in a low-level machine language, albeit an ideal one. To remedy this, compilers that use the scheme are often written in a high-level language which maps down into the ideal machine code. This requires a tool, usually a specially written one, to perform the mapping from high-level language to ideal machine code.

The ideal machine-language technique has been used with much software for microcomputers and the smaller minicomputers. See, for example, Allison *et al*. (1976).

Cross-compilers

If a compiler runs on one machine but produces an internal program that is to be run on a different machine, it is called a *cross-compiler*. We call the two machines the *compiling machine* and the *object machine*. If these two machines are coupled together in a smooth network it need not be apparent to the user that two separate machines are involved. Often, however, the coupling is far from smooth and it is a slow and tedious job to transfer the internal program from the compiling machine to the object machine; the end result is a non-interactive compiler and a cross user.

To make users less cross, a simulator of the object machine may be written to run on the compiling machine. Then the user can get his program debugged on the compiling machine, and, when he has a properly working program, he can face up to the rigours of moving it to the object machine.

Unfortunately, such simulators are difficult to write, and it is especially hard to make the simulated environment identical to the real thing. Indeed it is impossible if the behaviour of a program is dependent on the time it takes to perform certain operations; this may apply to interrupt routines—in some environments, if these do not finish within a given time interval, the result is catastrophe.

Because of their disadvantages, cross-compilers are only used when it is impractical to produce a normal compiler. This happens when the object machine is very small, or when it is completely new. The latter case, a 'virgin machine', provides a great challenge to its first conqueror. This is because the very first programs have to be written directly in terms of binary machine instructions. To write a compiler in binary is like sweeping a parade ground with a toothbrush.

The best way of conquering the virgin machine is to build a compiler that will implement a decent software-writing language for that machine. We shall call this language VIRGINL. To avoid having to encode the VIRGINL compiler in binary, we find another machine that already has a decent encoding language, and use this to write a cross-compiler which translates VIRGINL into an internal language consisting of binary instructions that will run on the virgin machine. (If the machine is not a complete virgin, it may be possible to use something better than binary instructions for the internal language.) Once this compiler is working it can be used to encode all the initial software for the virgin machine. The whole task can be simplified if the VIRGINL compiler is itself written in VIRGINL. This is a classic and intellectually pleasing exercise called *bootstrapping*. It was first popularized by NELIAC (Halstead, 1962), and has since been used by many other compilers.

If you want to look at other examples of cross-compilers see Calderbank and Calderbank (1973) or Blazie and Levy (1977).

Microprogramming

When the computer executes a program, this program is executed as a sequence of binary machine instructions. The task of the hardware is to interpret these instructions. In many computers the instructions are interpreted in terms of even lower-level *micro-instructions*, which are directly related to the physical circuits in the computer. Inside the computer there is a *microprogram* to interpret its programs, in a similar manner to the way the run-time system of a compiler interprets an internal program. (Some people confuse the terms 'microprogramming' and 'microprocessor'; there is no relation between the two.)

A few computers allow the microprogram to be varied during a run, with the result that the instruction set of the machine changes. Thus at one stage the machine may have an instruction set geared to manipulating characters, and a little later it may have switched its microprogram and have an instruction set geared to performing complex arithmetic. A well-known machine of this kind is the Burroughs B1700 (Wilner, 1972).

Such machines open up a fascinating possibility for the compiler writer. He can design an ideal internal language, and then microprogram his computer to execute this internal language. The microprogram would be brought into play whenever it was desired to run a user's program. The 'ideal' internal language could be ideal for ease of translation (and perhaps re-creation), ideal for speed of execution, ideal for conciseness, or perhaps some combination of these. Certainly it should be possible to get close to the paradise of a small compiler that runs programs very fast.

The catch comes in the microprogramming; it is an awe-inspiring task to write and debug microprograms. The result is that a lot more people talk about this approach than actually do it. In any case, for some microprogrammable hardware the manufacturer denies the purchaser the capability of writing his own microprograms. This is done partly for commercial reasons and partly from a fear of what a terrible mess the user might make of his microprograms.

For more on the use of microprogramming to help implement compilers, see the August 1974 issue of *SIGPLAN Notices*.

Microprogramming can also be applied to realize the ideal machine code that we discussed under 'Interpreted compilers'. This is likely to be different in detail from our ideal internal language (e.g. the operations needed for *translating* BASIC are quite different from the operations needed for *running* BASIC programs — the ideal internal language is mainly concerned with the latter), but the principles of the microprogramming are similar in the two cases. It would even be possible to combine the two—one microprogram would be used for compiling and another, the internal language microprogram, would be used for running.

Cascading into an existing language

A good way of saving work is to use someone else's compiler to do most of the work of yours. If you wish to implement a source language S, and there already exists a compiler for a language L, then all you need do is to write a translator to map programs in S into equivalent programs in L. The L compiler can then be used to run the L programs. We shall call this technique *cascading* and shall call L the *underlying language*. In most examples of cascading the underlying language offers similar features to the source language, but at a lower level. Many people have used cascading to build languages on the back of some of the popular standard languages such as FORTRAN. One example is the RATFOR language in Kernighan and Plauger (1976). This is an extension of FORTRAN that maps into FORTRAN. An advantage of cascading into a standard language is portability. Because RATFOR programs map into standard FORTRAN, they are as portable as FORTRAN programs.

This brings us back to a remark, made in Chapter 1.4, that extensions to standard languages should be viewed with caution. If the extended language can be made to map into the standard language, then the portability problems are much reduced. (Programs become perfectly portable; the programmers will not be so portable unless the extended language can be implemented on every machine.)

Many true compilers use cascading at a low level by mapping into assembly language rather than binary machine code. However such compilers tend to be a bit slow.

It is a general rule that the more advantages a technique has, the more corresponding disadvantages it has. There seems to be some high-level law that everything should be equal. Thus the technique of cascading has its disadvantages. The following are three of them.

Firstly, there are problems with error messages. Any error messages that emanate from the underlying compiler will be in terms of the underlying language, which may not be familiar to the user. Assume, for example, that a source language S cascades into BASIC and that S contains a CASE statement, which maps into the BASIC ON statement. If the user of S makes a semantic error in his CASE statement the result might be an error message from the underlying BASIC compiler saying 'INDEX IN 'ON' STATEMENT IS TOO BIG'. This might be incomprehensible to the user of S.

Secondly, cascading can be used only for a restricted kind of language. If you select two languages at random it will probably be impossible to map one into the other. Thus it is necessary to choose the underlying language first, and then design the source language in such a way that it can easily be mapped into this underlying language.

Lastly, cascading has mainly been used for batch rather than interactive working. You may, however, regard this as an advantage rather than a disadvantage, as it may give you a chance to enter fields which are unexplored (or from which others have fled). If cascading is applied to interactive languages, there are problems with making sure that interactive capabilities are not lost or reduced; there are particular dangers in error detection and in editing.

The mixed-code approach

We shall now expand on a topic which was mentioned briefly in Chapter 2.7.

Compilers vary over a spectrum between, at one extreme, true compilers, and, at the other extreme, 100% interpreters. The user is not directly interested in where his compiler comes in this spectrum; what interests him is the performance of his program, and he really directs his attention at the compiler only when performance is unacceptable. There are two common problems, as exemplified by the following:

(1) Dr Spend, the nuclear physicist, is angry because his 200 line program takes 10 hours to run.
(2) Mr Conn, the education specialist, is angry because his 25 000 line computer-aided learning program will not fit in the machine. 'I only want to run it for ten minutes', he says.

What Dr Spend wants is a true compiler that will produce super-efficient machine code. What Mr Conn wants is quite different: he needs a compiler with an internal language that will pack his program into the minimum possible space. No single compiler design, therefore, will satisfy both of these eminent gentlemen.

This has led compiler writers to consider adaptable compilers. Such a compiler will first translate the source program into a compact internal language, thus meeting Mr Conn's needs (to the extent they can be met at all). Then, when the program is run, the compiler keeps a record of the number of times each statement is executed. On the basis of this information, heavily executed statements are translated from the original internal language to machine code, whereas lightly executed statements are left in internal language form, and are interpreted. This is called a *mixed-code* approach as the program is encoded in a mixture of internal languages. It satisfies Dr Spend because his heavily executed program is translated into machine code.

The following are some interesting papers on this approach: Dakin and Poole (1973); Dawson (1973); Ng and Cantoni (1976). In some systems the user tells the compiler which parts of his program are likely to be heavily executed, while others rely on automatic feedback. Hansen and Wulf (1976) apply a similar technique to the levels of optimization attempted by a true compiler.

Although interesting and useful, the mixed-code approach has nevertheless not been widely adopted. One reason is doubtless that it is a lot of work for the compiler writer. Another is that, if you do manage to run the programs of Dr Spend and Mr Conn, the former comes back the next day with a program that will run for ten times as long and the latter will produce a program ten times bigger. It is better to stop an unsightly tree before it gets too big.

In the next chapter we discuss an alternative method which attacks the same problem as the mixed-code approach.

Chapter 8.2

Dynamic Compiling

We have described compilers as if translation of the source language into the internal language was a separate activity from running the internal program. We thus placed a strict demarcation between the translator and the run-time system. In this chapter we consider the implications of throwing the distinction away.

Dynamic compiling means translating a program as it runs. One way of doing this is to abolish the translator, and to delay all translation until the user runs his program. When a run starts the program is still in pure source form, exactly as the user typed it. The action is then as follows.

(1) The first statement in the source program is translated to the internal language. We call this the *internal form* of the statement.

(2) The internal form of the first statement is executed.

(3) The next statement to be executed in the program is translated into its internal form. Note that this is the next statement in the run-time flow of the program; thus if the first statement had been a GOTO or a GOSUB, the next statement would *not* be the second statement in the program as written.

(4) The internal form of this next statement is executed.

(5) The above process is repeated. The internal forms of all the executed statements are kept. If a GOTO returns control to a statement that has previously been executed, its internal form is re-used; thus no statement is translated more than once, and if a statement is never executed on a given run it is never translated.

In a typical run, the first few statements are translated, until the program loops back on itself. Then these translated statements are re-run until the program breaks out of its loop into some new statements, at which point some more translation is needed. As the run proceeds the amount of translation tends to decrease as fewer new statements are executed.

This process need not be performed in units of one statement at a time. It could, for example, be done one subroutine at a time in a suitable source language.

As we have described it, dynamic compiling has a crushing disadvantage: since translation is delayed until a program is run, syntax errors will not be detected as the program is typed in. Indeed syntax errors in statements that are not executed during a run will not be detected at all.

253

Running a program as it is typed

A radical alternative is to abolish the run-time system and translate and run a program as it is typed in. Thus the user, instead of typing his program in the usual sequence, types statements in the order they are executed as a result of the test data he has supplied. Thus if he types

$$20 \text{ IF } X > 0 \text{ THEN } 100$$

then, if X is greater than zero, the translator asks for statement 100 to be typed next. An advantage of this approach is immediate detection of certain run-time errors. If the variable X in statement 20 has no value, for example, the user can be told so immediately after having typed statement 20.

This approach could be an interesting and far-reaching topic for research. It involves a completely new attitude on how users should prepare programs and on how programming languages should be designed.

Dynamic compiling of an internal language

To return from flights of fancy to current practicalities, the role in which dynamic compiling has already proved valuable is in providing an alternative to the traditional true compiler. In this use of dynamic compiling, it is not the source language that is dynamically compiled; instead the internal language is dynamically compiled to a lower-level language, usually machine code.

The source language is first translated into an internal language in the normal way. This internal language is designed to be concise and to allow re-creation of the original source. It might, for example, be our internal language based on Reverse Polish notation. The translator reports syntax errors in the usual manner.

When the program is run, as each internal statement is executed for the first time, it is translated into the lower-level language, which we shall assume is machine code. The advantage of this dynamic compiling, when compared with a traditional true compiler, is that the compiler is 'in where the action is'. In particular the dynamic compiler can examine the run-time environment in which the machine code it generates is to run. Because it knows what is happening, it can perform more effective error checking. One example of this is in detecting unassigned variables. The dynamic compiler can check for unassigned variables when it is translating internal language to machine code. Thus the checking is performed once and for all during the translation process, rather than every time the machine code for the statement is executed. This cheaper form of error detection is possible because, once a variable has been assigned a value, it can never subsequently become unassigned, so no further checking is needed. (We assume that if the program is re-run, values of variables remain intact—or at least are not set back to an unassigned value.) A similar principle can be applied to any other error which, if it is to occur at all, will occur the first time a statement is executed. An example is the error of a constant array subscript being out-of-range, e.g. in a reference to the array element $X(16)$, where X has only 10 elements.

A further advantage of dynamic compiling is that the compiler knows much more about the objects it is referencing. Thus when it translates a GOTO instruction it will know where the destination is, and can output a machine-code instruction to jump directly to the correct place.

There is one disadvantage of a dynamic compiler exploiting its extra knowledge about the program and its environment; this is that the assumptions made may become invalid if the program is edited. Thus when a program is edited, all dynamically compiled code must be discarded in case it is wrong (e.g. the destination of a GOTO is in a new position). Hence dynamic compiling is not incremental.

Throw-away compiling

We promised earlier that we would provide a method for resolving the clashing needs of Dr Spend and Mr Conn. An adaptation of dynamic compiling can do this.

The process we have just described, where a dynamic compiler converts internal language to machine code, suits Dr Spend. The system gives a run-time speed similar to that of a true compiler because each statement is translated only once into machine code and then runs as if it had been pre-compiled. In particular all of Dr Spend's loops soon get translated into machine code and these machine code loops are continually run (assuming they are small enough to fit in the store of the machine). Mr Conn, on the other hand, is suited by the compact internal language, and the lack of a need to keep the source program (since this is re-created from the internal program). Thus if his program will fit at all, it will fit in this form. However, when his program is run, more and more machine code is compiled, and eventually storage may run out. (Typically a program in machine code is two to three times as big as an equivalent program in a compact internal language. This shows how much real machines differ from the ideal machine for any particular source language.)

This situation, where storage runs out because of the amount of machine code that has been compiled, reveals another advantage of dynamic compiling. This is that the problem can be solved by 'throwing away' all or part of the machine code that has been compiled, thus releasing more space. If a statement for which the machine code has been thrown away is re-executed, its machine code is dynamically compiled again from the internal program; if such a statement is never re-executed it will not need re-compiling and hence requires no more extra storage.

Given the use of throwing away, a program can be run using a very small amount of storage for the compiled code; it fails only when the storage is so small that the machine-code translation of a single statement is bigger than the storage available. Of course, each act of throwing away tends to lead to more dynamic compiling, so the program will run slower. In the worst case, where there is only room for the machine code of one statement, every statement will need to be dynamically compiled before it is executed because any previous version will have been thrown away.

This technique is called *throw-away compiling*. It provides a system which automatically adapts itself to run as fast as possible in the storage available. If the machine code for the program will fit in the available storage, a throw-away compiler will give a similar performance to a true compiler. As the size of the machine code increases above the available space, its performance gradually deteriorates because of the amount of throwing away. Eventually it becomes as slow as an interpreter for the internal language.

It has a further advantage that only statements that are actually executed on a given run are translated into machine code. This is good news to people like Mr Conn, who have long programs that are sparsely executed.

Note that throw-away compiling only attempts to solve the problem where the machine code of a program is too big for the object machine; it does not help with the problem of the data being too large, such as a 10 000 × 10 000 array on a microcomputer.

For more about throw-away compiling see Brown (1976; 1979) and Hammond (1977); also see Van Dyke (1977) on dynamic compiling.

Summary of the Deadly Sins

The first deadly sin is *to code before you think.*

The second deadly sin is *to assume the user has all the knowledge the compiler writer has.*

The third deadly sin is *not to write proper documentation.*

The fourth deadly sin is *to ignore language standards.*

The fifth deadly sin is *to treat error diagnosis as an afterthought.*

The sixth deadly sin is *to equate the unlikely with the impossible.*

The seventh deadly sin is *to make the encoding of the compiler dependent on its data formats.*

The eighth deadly sin is *to use numbers for objects that are not numbers.*

The ninth deadly sin is *to pretend you are catering for everyone at the same time.*

The tenth deadly sin is *to have no strategy for processing break-ins.*

The eleventh deadly sin is *to rate the beauty of mathematics above the usability of your compiler.*

The twelfth deadly sin is *to let any error go undetected.*

The thirteenth deadly sin is *to leave users to find the errors in your compiler.*

The last deadly sin is *not to read to the end of the book.* But you can't have committed that.

References

Alcock, D. (1977). *Illustrating BASIC*, Cambridge University Press.

Allison, D., happy Lady and friends (1976). 'Design notes for TINY BASIC', *SIG-PLAN Notices*, **11**, 7, 25–33.

Ammann, U. (1978). 'Error recovery in recursive descent parsers', in *State of the Art and future trends in compilation*, IRIA, Paris.

Atkinson, L.V. and J.J. McGregor (1978). 'CONA–a conversational Algol system', *Software—Practice and Experience*, **8**, 6, 699–708.

Atkinson, L.V., J.J. McGregor and S.D. North (1979). *Context sensitive editing as an approach to incremental compilation*, Computing Science Department, Sheffield University.

Barron, D.W. (1971). 'Approaches to conversational FORTRAN', *Computer Journal*, **14**, 2, 123–127.

Bauer, F.L. and J. Eickel (eds) (1974). *Compiler construction*, Springer-Verlag, Berlin.

Bell, J.R. (1973). 'Threaded code', *Comm. ACM* **16**, 6, 370–372.

Blazie, D.B. and L.S. Levy (1977). 'A cross compiler for pocket calculators', *Computer Journal*, **20**, 3, 213–221.

Braden, H.V. and W.A. Wulf (1968). 'The implementation of a BASIC system in a multiprogramming environment', *Comm. ACM*, **11**, 10, 688–692.

Brinch Hansen, P. (1978). 'Reproducible testing of monitors', *Software—Practice and Experience*, **8**, 6, 721–729.

Brooks, F.P. (1975). *The mythical man-month*, Addison-Wesley, Reading, Mass.

Brown, P.J. (1974). *Macro processors and techniques for portable software*, Wiley, Chichester.

Brown, P.J. (1976). 'Throw-away compiling', *Software—Practice and Experience*, **6**, 3, 423–434.

Brown, P.J. (1977). 'More on the re-creation of source code from Reverse Polish', *Software—Practice and Experience*, **7**, 5, 545–551.

Brown, P.J. (1979). 'Software methods for virtual storage of executable code', *Computer Journal*, **22**, 1, 50–52.

Calderbank, M. and V.J. Calderbank (1973). 'A portable language for system development', *Software—Practice and Experience*, **3**, 4, 309–321.

Curnow, H.J. and B.A. Wichmann (1976). 'A synthetic benchmark', *Computer Journal*, **19**, 1, 43–49.

Dakin, R.J. and P.C. Poole (1973). 'A mixed code approach', *Computer Journal*, **16**, 3, 219–222.

Dawson, J.L. (1973). 'Combining interpretive code with machine code', *Computer Journal*, **16**, 3, 216–219.

Denning, P.J. (1970). 'Virtual memory', *Computing Surveys*, **2**, 3, 153–189.

Dewar, R.B.K. (1975). 'Indirect threaded code', *Comm. ACM*, **18**, 6, 330–331.

Dewar, R.B.K. and A.P. McCann (1977). 'MACRO SPITBOL—a SNOBOL4 compiler', *Software—Practice and Experience*, **7**, 1, 95–113.

Feldman, J.A. and D. Gries (1968). 'Translator writing systems', *Comm. ACM*, **11**, 2, 77–113.

Gilman, L. and A.J. Rose (1970). *APL—an interactive approach*, Wiley, New York.

Glass, R.L. (1969). 'An elementary discussion of compiler/interpreter writing', *Computing Surveys*, **1**, 1, 55–77.

Gries, D. (1971). *Compiler construction for digital computers*, Wiley, New York.

Griswold, R.E., J.F. Poage and I.P. Polonsky (1971). *The SNOBOL4 programming language* (2nd ed.), Prentice-Hall, Englewood Cliffs, N.J.

Halstead, M.H. (1962). *Machine—independent computer programming*, Spartan, Washington, D.C.

Halstead, M.H. (1974). *A laboratory manual for compiler and operating system implementation*, Elsevier, New York.

Hamblin, C.L. (1962). 'Translation to and from Polish notation', *Computer Journal*, **5**, 3, 210–213.

Hammond, J. (1977). 'BASIC—an evaluation of processing methods and a study of some programs', *Software—Practice and Experience*, **7**, 6, 697–711.

Hansen, G.J. and W.A. Wulf (1976). 'Adaptive code optimization', in D. Bates (ed.), *Program optimization*, Infotech, Maidenhead, 185–208.

Heher, A.D. (1976). 'Some features of a real-time BASIC executive', *Software—Practice and Experience*, **6**, 3, 387–391.

Hopgood, F.R.A. (1969). *Compiling Techniques*, Macdonald/Elsevier, London.

Iverson, K.E. (1962). *A programming language*, Wiley, New York.

James, J.S. (1978). 'FORTH for microcomputers', *SIGPLAN Notices* **13**, 10, 33–39.

Jensen, K. and N. Wirth (1974). *PASCAL user manual and report*, Springer-Verlag, Berlin.

Kemeny, J.G. and T.E. Kurtz (1971). *Basic programming* (2nd ed.), Wiley, New York.

Kernighan, B.W. and P.J. Plauger (1976). *Software tools*, Addison-Wesley, Reading, Mass.

Kernighan, B.W. and D.M. Ritchie (1978). *The C programming language*, Prentice-Hall, Englewood Cliffs, N.J.

Knuth, D.E. (1971). 'An empirical study of FORTRAN programs', *Software—Practice and Experience*, **1**, 2, 105–133.

Knuth, D.E. (1973). *The art of computer programming* (several volumes), Addison-Wesley, Reading, Mass.

Lang, T. (1974). Book review, *Software—Practice and Experience*, **5**, 1, 110–111.

Lee, J.A.N. (1974). *The anatomy of a compiler* (2nd ed.), Van Nostrand Reinhold, New York.

Lucas Phillips, C.E. (1952). *The small garden*, Pan, London.

Mooers, C.N. (1975). 'Computer software and copyright', *Computing Surveys*, **7**, 1, 45–72.

Moore, C.H. and E.D. Rather (1973). 'The FORTH program for spectral line observing'. *Proc. IEEE*, **61**, 1346–1349.

Naur, P. *et al.* (1960). 'Report on the algorithmic language ALGOL 60', *Comm. ACM*, **3**, 5, 299–314.

Naur, P. (1963). 'The design of the GIER ALGOL compiler: Part I', *BIT*, **3**, 124–140.

Ng, T.S. and A. Cantoni (1976). 'Run time interaction with FORTRAN using mixed code', *Computer Journal*, **19**, 1, 91–92.

Niblett, B. (1977). 'Legal protection of portable software', in Brown, P.J.(ed.), *Software portability*, Cambridge University Press, 164–168.

Ormicki, A. (1977). 'Real-time BASIC for laboratory use', *Software—Practice and Experience*, **7**, 4, 435–443.

Parnas, D.L. (1972). 'On the criteria to be used in decomposing systems into modules', *Comm. ACM*, **15**, 12, 1053–1058.

Pyster, A. and A. Dutta (1978). 'Error-checking compilers and portability', *Software—Practice and Experience*, **8**, 1, 99–108.

Rain, M. (1973). 'Two unusual methods for debugging system software', *Software—Practice and Experience*, **4**, 1, 61–63.

Rees, M.J. and A.W. Oppenheimer (1977). 'SOBS—an incremental BASIC system', *Software—Practice and Experience*, **7**, 5, 631–643.

Richards, M. (1969). 'BCPL: a tool for compiler writing and systems programming', *AFIPS Conference Proceedings*, **34**, 557–566.

Richards, M. (1971). 'The portability of the BCPL compiler', *Software—Practice and Experience* **1**, 2, 135–146.

Rohl, J.S. (1975). *An introduction to compiler writing*, Macdonald/Elsevier, London.

Ryder, B.G. (1974). 'The PFORT verifier', *Software—Practice and Experience*, **4**, 4, 359–378.

Sabin, M.A. (1976). 'Portability—some experiences with FORTRAN', *Software—Practice and Experience*, **6**, 3, 393–396.

Satterthwaite, E. (1972). 'Debugging tools for high level languages', *Software—Practice and Experience*, **2**, 3, 197–218.

Shaw, J.C. (1964). 'JOSS: a designer's view of an experimental on-line system', *AFIPS Conference Proceedings*, **26**, 455–464.

Strunk, W. Jr. (1959). *The elements of style*, revised by E.B. White, Macmillan, New York.

Van Dyke, E.J. (1977). 'A dynamic incremental compiler for an interpretive language', *Hewlett-Packard Journal*, **28**, 11, 17–24.

Waite, W.M. (1975). 'Hints on distributing portable software', *Software—Practice and Experience*, **5**, 3, 295–308.

Wasserman, A.I. (1978). 'PLAIN: programming language design and user software engineering', in E.A. Oxborrow (ed.), *Future Programming*, Vol. 2, Infotech, Maidenhead.

Wichmann, B.A. (1973). *Algol 60 compilation and assessment*, Academic Press, London.

Wilkes, M.V. (1972). *Time-sharing computer systems*, (2nd ed.), Macdonald/Elsevier, London.

Wilner, W.T. (1972). 'Design of the Burroughs B1700', *AFIPS Conference Proceedings*, **41**, 489–497.

Witty, R.W. (1977). 'The switching Reverse Polish algorithm', *SIGPLAN Notices*, **12**, 9, 114–123.

Wulf, W.A. *et al.* (1975). *The design of an optimizing compiler*, American Elsevier, New York.

Index

Multi-line function, 87, 174
Multi-pass translator, 128
Multiple assignment, 172, 173, 180
Mutual recursion, 137

Names, 61–63
N-ary operator, 214
Naur, P., 80, 136
NEGATE operator, 106
NELIAC, 249
Nesting, 31
Newline character, 35, 218
Ng, T. S., 252
Niblett, B., 242
Non-executable statement, 188
North, S. D., 45
Notation, 130
Null case, 233
Numeric overflow, 95, 169, 189, 233

Object machine, 12, 36–37, 248
OLD command, 85, 88
One-pass translator, 128
Open-context form, 102
OPERAND bit, 113
Operand stack, 171–179, 233
Operating system, 37, 77, 86, 226–227
Operator, 106–111
OPERATOR bit, 113
Operator-precedence, 149–152
Oppenheimer, A. W., 210
Optimization, 54, 198, 252
Ormicki, A., 168

Parentheses, 103, 148, 150, 219–220
Parnas, D. L., 130
Parser, 127
Parser generator, 139
PASCAL, 23, 68–69, 129, 154
Performance testing, 240
Peripheral, *see* Input/output device
PIG, 62, 63, 195
PL/I, 168
Planning, 3–25
Plauger, P. J., 16, 250
'Plus' grade compiler, 21
Pointer, 32
Polling break-ins, 90–94
Polymorphic operator, 108, 153, 155, 157
Poole, P. C., 252
Portability, 11, 24, 69, 166, 250
Precedence of operators, 103, 146
Prefix search, 218

Pre-run module, 43, 74, 96, 101, 155, 166, 192, 201–211
Pre-selection of grammatical alternatives, 143, 155
Procedure as compilation unit, 45
Professional, 7
Profile of a program, 57, 170
PROM, 242
Prompt, 85
Pseudo-execution, 205
Puns, 122
Pure interpreter, 39
Pyster, A., 24

Quality assurance, 235

Rain, M., 238
Random-number generator, 176
RATFOR, 250
Rather, E. D., 123
Read-only data, 226
Record, 69
Re-creation table, 215, 218
Re-creator module, 47–49, 131, 212–224
Recursion, 137, 143, 148, 177
Recursive descent, 140–148
Re-entrancy, 226
Rees, M. J., 210
Regular compiler, 17
Research topic, 254
Re-sequencing, 223
Resources, use of, 7
Return address, 174, 178
Returning storage, 183, 184
Reverse Polish notation, 102–121, 214–224
  encoding, 112–121
  execution, 171–194
Richards, M., 23, 24
Ritchie, D. M., 23
Rohl, J. S., 36
Rose, A. J., 5
Row-major order, 186
RUBOUT key, 86
Rule of a grammar, 136
Run-time, 40
Run-time system, 40, 96, 166–193, 253
Ryder, B. G., 24

Sabin, M. A., 24
Satterthwaite, E., 58
SAVE command, 46, 88, 91, 212, 223
Scalar, 63